THE LIMITS OF POSITIVE OBLIGATIONS IN HUMAN RIGHTS LAW

This open access book is a crucial intervention in the debate concerning positive human rights obligations.

There is nowadays no dispute in human rights doctrine over whether rights entail positive duties on the part of the state at the level of principle. But there has been surprisingly little academic commentary devoted to the question of whether there are, or should be, limits placed on how far those obligations extend. Similarly, there has been little scholarly attention paid to the question of how causation can be reasonably attributed in the context of violations of positive obligations. And there are very few sociological explanations provided as to why positive human rights obligations appear to be expanding without principled limits in the first place.

This volume assembles the work of a range of leading scholars in international human rights law to fill these gaps in the literature. Each of its 11 substantive chapters addresses an aspect of positive obligations with a particular focus on issues concerning limits. Taken together, they provide the first serious attempt to grapple critically with the subject of the limits, causality and scope of positive obligations theoretically and doctrinally. This makes the book essential reading for scholars of human rights law.

Hart Studies in Constitutional Theory: Volume 12

Hart Studies in Constitutional Theory

Authors writing for this series cover a wide range of perspectives, methods, and regions, to enhance our understanding of constitutions as central institutions of modern public life. Taken together, the books in this series aim to challenge established wisdom and advance original ideas.

This series is a natural home for books interrogating the concepts and structures of constitutions on the national, the supranational and the international level. Its guiding philosophy is that the task of constitutional theory is not only to delineate the basic structures of government and to protect human rights, but also more broadly to offer methods for grappling with the social, political, and economic problems societies face today.

The series is open to theoretical, normative, analytical, empirical and comparative approaches, stemming from legal studies as well as from political philosophy and political science. In its ambition to become a global forum for debate about constitutional theory, the series editors welcome submissions for monographs as well as edited volumes from all parts of the world.

Recent titles in this series:

Proportionality and Facts in Constitutional Adjudication
Anne Carter

The Methodology of Constitutional Theory
Edited by Dimitrios Kyritsis and Stuart Lakin

A Constitutionalist Approach to the European Convention on Human Rights: The Legitimacy of Evolutive and Static Interpretation
Lisa Sonnleitner

Judicial Avoidance: Balancing Competences in Constitutional Adjudication
Carolina Alves das Chagas

Constitutionally Conforming Interpretation – Comparative Perspectives: Volume 1: National Reports
Edited by Matthias Klatt

Equality Before the Law: Equal Dignity, Wrongful Discrimination, and the Rule of Law
Michael P Foran

Constitutional Courts and Judicial Review: Between Law and Politics
Dieter Grimm

The Limits of Positive Obligations in Human Rights Law

From Protection to Coercion

Edited by
Vladislava Stoyanova
and
David McGrogan

•HART•
OXFORD • LONDON • NEW YORK • NEW DELHI • SYDNEY

HART PUBLISHING

Bloomsbury Publishing Plc

Kemp House, Chawley Park, Cumnor Hill, Oxford, OX2 9PH, UK

1385 Broadway, New York, NY 10018, USA

Bloomsbury Publishing Ireland Limited, 29 Earlsfort Terrace, Dublin 2, D02 AY28, Ireland

HART PUBLISHING, the Hart/Stag logo, BLOOMSBURY and the Diana logo are trademarks of Bloomsbury Publishing Plc

First published in Great Britain 2026

A catalogue record for this book is available from the British Library.

A catalogue record for this book is available from the Library of Congress.

Library of Congress Control Number: 2026934365

ISBN: HB: 978-1-50999-145-7
ePDF: 978-1-50999-148-8
ePub: 978-1-50999-149-5

Typeset by Compuscript Ltd, Shannon

For product safety related questions contact productsafety@bloomsbury.com

To find out more about our authors and books visit www.hartpublishing.co.uk. Here you will find extracts, author information, details of forthcoming events and the option to sign up for our newsletters.

FOREWORD

The concept of positive obligations has become a defining feature of modern human rights law. Yet the expansion of these obligations – requiring states not merely to refrain from interfering with but also to actively secure the conditions under which rights can be enjoyed – raises deep theoretical and constitutional questions. When, and under what conditions, should the state be required to act? And at what point do protection and promotion turn into coercion? These questions are doctrinally complex and politically fraught, touching the core of what it means for a constitutional order to balance liberty, security and responsibility.

In *The Limits of Positive Obligations in Human Rights Law: From Protection to Coercion*, Vladislava Stoyanova and David McGrogan have assembled an outstanding group of scholars to address these questions head-on. The volume explores both the analytical foundations and the normative implications of positive obligations, critically exploring notions such as causation, reasonableness and correlativity. The contributors show how these concepts, while often treated as technicalities, are normatively controversial, shaping the boundaries of state responsibility and the nature of the political community itself.

The contributors are united by a concern that enthusiasm for ever-expanding state duties, however well intentioned, may obscure the coercive dimensions of protection. In exploring this tension between protection and restraint, the book combines conceptual precision with political sensitivity. It illuminates how human rights law, in its modern form, can sometimes blur the line between securing human dignity and constraining human freedom.

Earlier books in the Hart Studies in Constitutional Theory series have examined the evolving roles of courts, legislatures and rights in shaping constitutional orders. This volume extends that inquiry to the normative assumptions underlying those institutions. By clarifying the limits and logic of positive obligations, it deepens our understanding of how constitutional theory attempts to deal with the enduring struggle between liberty and authority.

Maartje De Visser
Charles Barzun
Matthias Klatt
Singapore/Charlottesville/Graz

CONTENTS

CONTRIBUTORS

Tristan Cummings is Lecturer in Law at the Open University, Milton Keynes, UK.

Eric Heinze is Professor of Law and Humanities at Queen Mary University of London, UK. He has authored more than 100 publications on human rights and on legal theory. His most recent books include *Coming Clean: The Rise of Critical Theory and the Future of the Left* (MIT Press, 2025), *The Most Human Right: Why Free Speech is Everything* (MIT Press, 2022) and *Hate Speech and Democratic Citizenship* (Oxford University Press, 2016).

David McGrogan is Associate Professor of Law at Northumbria Law School, UK

Benoit Mayer is Professor of Climate Law at the University of Reading, UK. He is a lead author for the Seventh Assessment Report of the Intergovernmental Panel on Climate Change (IPCC) and a member of the Roster of Experts of the UN Framework Convention on Climate Change.

Ilias Plakokefalos is Assistant Professor of Public International Law at the Department of Political Science and Public Administration, National & Kapodistrian University of Athens, Greece.

Vladislava Stoyanova is Associate Professor in Public International Law at the Faculty of Law, Lund University, Sweden. She is the holder of the Wallenberg Academy Fellowship (2021–26) awarded by the Knut and Alice Wallenberg Foundation and the Royal Swedish Academy of Sciences. She is the author of *Positive Obligations under the European Convention on Human Rights. Within and Beyond Boundaries* (Oxford University Press, 2023) and the co-editor of *The Role of the Causal Inquiry under the European Convention on Human Rights* (Cambridge University Press, forthcoming).

Sophie Treacy is a DPhil in Law Candidate at Mansfield College, University of Oxford, UK.

Johan Vorland Wibye is Associate Professor in Law and Philosophy at the Department of Law and Governance, Norwegian Business School, Norway.

1

Searching for and Identifying the Limits of Positive Obligations and the Boundary between Protection and Coercion

VLADISLAVA STOYANOVA AND DAVID McGROGAN

I. The Importance and Pervasiveness of Positive Obligations in Human Rights Law

The evolution of positive obligations has become a defining feature of the approach of the European Court of Human Rights (ECtHR or 'the Court') to interpreting the European Convention on Human Rights (ECHR). The Court has addressed such obligations in, for example, decisions by social services on whether to place children in care or not,[1] the establishment of paternity,[2] the provision or absence of warning signs by highway authorities,[3] failures to maintain safety in public spaces,[4] waste collection,[5] cases of domestic violence against women or children,[6] police handling of criminal investigations,[7] enforcement of building codes,[8] enforcement of safety regulations,[9] failures by police to apprehend individuals who may pose a threat,[10] harm caused by natural disasters or

[1] *Z. and Others v United Kingdom*, App No 29392/95, 10 May 2001; *TP and KM v United Kingdom*, App No 28945/95, 10 May 2001.

[2] *Moldovan v Ukraine*, App No 62020/14, 14 March 2024.

[3] *Fatih Çakır and Merve Nisa Çakır v Turkey*, App No 54558/11, 5 June 2018; *Smiljanić v Croatia*, App No 35983/14, 25 March 2021, para 67.

[4] *Marius Alexandru and Marinela Ştefan v Romania*, App No 78643/11, 24 March 2020.

[5] *Locascia and Others v Italy*, App No 35648/10, 19 October 2023.

[6] *Kurt v Austria* [GC] App No 62903/15, 15 June 2021.

[7] *X and Others v Bulgaria* [GC] App No 22457/16, 2 February 2021.

[8] *Cevrioğlu v Turkey*, App No 69546/12, 4 October 2016; *Banel v Lithuanis*, App No 14326/11, 18 June 2013.

[9] *Fernández Marínez v Spain* [GC] App No 56030/07, 12 June 2014, para 114.

[10] *Mastromatteo v Italy* [GC] App No 37703/97, 24 October 2002.

industrial activities,[11] shortcomings in the healthcare system's ability to prevent illness or save lives,[12] and inadequate action by the state to lower its greenhouse gas emissions.[13] As a result, positive obligations have become embedded in all provisions of the ECHR, with no predefined limits on the scenarios in which they may emerge. And the mechanisms established, as a consequence, to safeguard the public from harm or mitigate risks are far-reaching. A common thread in most of these scenarios is the assertion that the state should have taken steps to protect individuals from harm or risk. This could involve actions such as issuing a hazard warning, regulating the actions of third (private) parties, removing individuals from dangerous situations, improving the organisation of healthcare or childcare systems, or enhancing police training.

And these developments are of course not limited to the Council of Europe system. Across the United Nations (UN) human rights apparatus, we can see a similar dynamic emerging in which – in the absence of principled limits on the scope or scale of intervention of the state in society – positive obligations appear to be relentlessly expanding, far beyond what was envisaged by the drafters of the relevant treaties.

Considering the state's vast regulatory functions and the wide scope of its activities, virtually any harm could serve as a basis for claiming that the state failed to meet its positive human rights obligations by not preventing or reducing harm or risk. Consequently, there is significant ambiguity regarding the circumstances under which positive obligations might be invoked and the extent of their reach, particularly given the challenge of defining the boundaries of state responsibility in public international law for inaction on the part of the state.[14] This uncertainty is further compounded by the complexities involved in identifying and delineating the state's role in modern society.

A critical question arises in light of all of this: are there any limits regarding when and how these obligations should be developed? Additionally, what principles should guide the establishment of such limits? Another important consideration is identifying the standards relevant in determining whether a state bears responsibility under human rights law for omissions. At the core of this inquiry is the question of whether and how state omissions can be framed as failures to meet positive obligations.[15]

Beyond this technical analytical issue, it is essential to reflect on the broader implications for the political community. How does the process of defining when positive human rights obligations are triggered, as well as their scope and

[11] *Özel and Others v Turkey* App Nos 14350/05, 15245/05 and 16051, 17 November 2015, para 171; *Budayeva and Others v Russia*, App No 15339/02, 20 March 2008.

[12] *Lopes de Sousa Fernandes v Portugal* [GC] App No 56080/13, 19 December 2017.

[13] *Verein Klimaseniorinnen Schweiz and Others v Switzerland* [GC] App No 53600/20, 9 April 2024.

[14] V Stoyanova, 'Framing Positive Obligations under the European Convention on Human Rights Law: Mediating between the Abstract and the Concrete' (2023) 23(3) *Human Rights Law Review* 1.

[15] For philosophical and doctrinal analysis of omissions as basis for responsibility, see S Steel, *Omissions in Tort Law* (Oxford University Press, 2024).

content, shape the political community? A fundamental issue is how the tension between state intrusion and restraint – between protection and freedom from interference – defines the political community and influences the analysis of state responsibility for omissions in various ways. This is because, as many of the authors in this volume make clear, implicitly or explicitly, if the state has positive obligations in any respect, these cannot help but find their way to being imposed upon individuals. In the most indirect way, this comes in the form of an increased tax burden. But it often comes more directly, with further duties being imposed in such a way as to permeate economic, social and family life, and shape the scope of individual conduct within those settings.

The chapters in this volume seek to explore these pressing issues. They have two main objectives: first, achieving better analytical clarity; and, second, exposing the challenge of finding a balance between intrusiveness and restraint.

II. Better Analytical Clarity

The evolution of positive obligations under the ECHR began in the 1970s, and since then, the Court has progressively broadened its interpretation and application, often venturing into uncharted territory.[16] Scholarly works have examined this development in a fragmented manner. Specific topics reflected in the case law, such as domestic violence,[17] climate change[18] and criminal investigation,[19] have been examined.[20] But there is no general volume available which is dedicated to the issue at the level of cross-cutting conceptual issues and standards. These conceptual issues and standards include causation, reasonableness, correlativity, risk prevention and the role of conflicting interests. It is these standards that more generally shape the legal analysis for finding state

[16] See, eg, *Rantsev v Cyprus and Russia*, App No 25965/04, 7 January 2010 (human trafficking); *Verein Klimaseniorinnen Schweiz and Others v Switzerland* [GC] App No 53600/20, 9 April 2024 (climate change); *Ilareva and Others v Bulgaria* App No 24729/17, 9 September 2025 (protection in the digital sphere); *Volodina v Russia (No 2)* App No 40419/19, 14 September 2021 (cyber-domestic violence).

[17] R McQuigg, 'Domestic Violence as a Human Rights Issue: Rumor v Italy' (2016) 26 *European Journal of International Law* 1009.

[18] V Stoyanova, 'In Search for the Content of States' Positive Obligations under the European Convention on Human Rights: *KlimaSeniorinnen* and Climate Change' in C Amado Gomes, H Oliveira, A Roch and M Fermeglia (eds), *Climate Change before International Courts: A Comparative Study* (Routledge, 2025).

[19] K Kamber *Prosecuting Human Rights Offences* (Brill, 2017); K Kamber, 'Substantive and Procedural Criminal Law Protection of Human Rights in the Law of the European Convention on Human Rights' (2020) 20(1) *Human Rights Law Review* 75.

[20] See also P Collins, *Putting Human Rights to Work: Labour Law, the ECHR, and the Employment Relation* (Oxford University Press, 2022); M Salomon, *Global Responsibility for Human Rights: World Poverty and the Development of International Law* (Oxford University Press, 2007); M Jovanovic, *State Responsibility for Modern Slavery in Human Rights Law: A Right Not to Be Trafficked* (Oxford University Press, 2023); R McQuigg, *International Human Rights Law and Domestic Violence: The Effectiveness of International Human Rights Law* (Routledge, 2011).

responsibility for omissions. But while there have been contributions that more generally focus on positive obligations in a more descriptive[21] or analytical way,[22] these standards have been barely addressed in the literature. Causation has more recently gained attention since the Court devoted some analysis of this standard in *Verein Klimaseniorinnen Schweiz and Others v Switzerland*, but only in a piecemeal fashion.[23]

This volume therefore addresses a gap by precisely isolating and examining the distinct analytical components – such as causation, reasonableness, correlativity, and risk prevention and conflicting interests – that underpin state responsibility for failing to meet positive obligations. It emphasises the analytical steps involved in determining state responsibility for omissions. Through this approach, the volume provides a valuable contribution to the broader study of obligations in human rights law.

III. The Challenge of Finding a Balance between Intrusiveness and Restraint

The central challenge in shaping positive obligations lies in striking a balance between protection and freedom from excessive intrusion. Protecting individuals from harm or risk often entails measures by the state that may intrude upon the very person being protected,[24] target other individuals who may pose a threat,[25] intrude upon the interests of certain groups so that other groups can be arguably protected,[26] or impact specific societal groups that might face resource

[21] For descriptive works, see A Mowbray, *The Development of Positive Obligations under the European Convention on Human Rights by the European Court of Human Rights* (Hart Publishing, 2004); J Akandji-Kombe, *Positive Obligations under the European Convention on Human Rights* (Council of Europe Publishing, 2007).

[22] C Dröge, *Positive Verpflichtungen der Staaten in der Europäischen Menschenrechtskonvention* (Springer, 2003); D Xenos, *The Positive Obligations of the State under the European Convention of Human Rights* (Routledge, 2012); L Lavrysen, *Human Rights in a Positive State* (Intersentia, 2016).

[23] On causation, see V Stoyanova, 'Causation between State Omission and Harm within the Framework of Positive Obligations under the ECHR' (2018) 18(2) *Human Rights Law Review* 309; D McGrogan, 'The Problem of Causality in International Human Rights Law' (2016) 65 *ICLQ* 615 (with a focus on UN monitoring system). See also V Stoyanova, '*KlimaSeniorinnen* and the Question(s) of Causation', https://verfassungsblog.de/klimaseniorinnen-and-the-questions-of-causation; V Stoyanova, 'Causation and Breach of Positive Obligations under the ECHR: Correcting the Past, Preventing the Future' in V Stoyanova and M Andenas (eds), *The Role of the Causal Inquiry under the European Convention on Human Rights* (Cambridge University Press, forthcoming).

[24] See, eg, *Hiller v Austria*, App No 1967/14, 22 November 2016 (prevention of suicide).

[25] See, eg, *Kurt v Austria* [GC] App No 62903/15, 15 June 2021 (domestic violence).

[26] See *Vavřička and Others v The Czech Republic* [GC] App No 47621/13, 8 April 2021 (compulsory vaccination). See V Stoyanova, 'Positive Obligations as Coercive "Rights" and Compulsory Vaccination under the European Convention on Human Rights' *International Journal of Constitutional Law* (forthcoming).

deprivation.[27] In many cases, where causal links are uncertain, it can be challenging to identify the individuals or groups within society who bear the cost of such protective actions.

The state must navigate a complex landscape of competing interests, each with varying degrees of importance, specificity and clarity regarding their holders. Amid this complexity, a fundamental tension emerges concerning the role of the state. Expanding the state's role often necessitates greater intrusiveness in the name of mitigating known or potential risks, which may involve curtailing certain liberties to ensure protection. Conversely, inaction by the state, including a failure to impose limitations on rights, can impose significant costs on specific individuals or groups within society.

Against this background, the collected chapters in this volume provide an analysis of the risks associated with positive obligations that are overly broad in scope or excessively intrusive in content. It is worth noting that the existing literature tends to justify positive obligations and to advocate for their expansion.[28] These scholarly works have been instrumental in reshaping human rights law into a framework that extends beyond merely safeguarding individuals from state interference, requiring instead the active engagement of the state to fulfil human rights.

The volume highlights the shortcomings of any account of positive obligations that does not seriously address their limits, potential intrusiveness and coercive power. It begins from the standpoint that, while risk aversion is a key rationale behind positive obligations, it can carry a cost that the political community may find unacceptable due to the coercion and restriction of personal freedoms it entails. A central issue explored in the volume is the challenge of striking a balance between state intervention to prevent risks and protect individuals, and safeguarding the individual's sphere of autonomy and inviolability. It examines the tension between two opposing extremes: intrusive statism, where the state is seen as an omnipresent protector, and unrestrained libertarianism, which views state intervention as inherently unjustified intrusion.

Opening up a debate on this matter is especially pressing in certain contexts. Perhaps currently climate change is one of the most prominent. In addition to a chapter on climate change written by Benoit Mayer, the volume contains a chapter by Tristan Cummings where the tension between protection and intrusiveness arises in the context of state interventions for protecting the parent–child

[27] *Öneryildiz v Turkey* [GC] App No 48939/99, 30 November 2004, para 107: 'It therefore accepts the Government's argument that in this respect an impossible or disproportionate burden must not be imposed on the authorities without consideration being given, in particular, to the operational choices which they must make in terms of priorities and resources.'

[28] S Fredman, *Human Rights Transformed: Positive Rights and Positive Duties* (Oxford University Press, 2008); H Shue, *Basic Rights: Subsistence, Affluence, and U.S. Foreign Policy* (Princeton University Press, 1996).

relationship. In these circumstances, as in many others,[29] concerns are raised that security or protection from harm and risk are over-emphasised. When this is done, the price to be paid for security or protection seems to be ignored. And the related tension between security and freedom from intrusiveness is, as a consequence, downplayed.

This volume incorporates both theoretical and doctrinal perspectives on the question of where the limits on positive obligations should (or does) lie. Stoyanova and McGrogan have previously addressed the matter to some extent, with the emphasis on, respectively, doctrinal and theoretical considerations. Stoyanova has provided a thorough doctrinal analysis of the jurisprudence of the Court with regard to positive obligations.[30] McGrogan's scholarship, meanwhile, roots human rights law's 'positivisation' in a particular conception or idealisation of the state that has to be understood as having emerged in modernity itself and that is coeval with the state's expansion accordingly.[31] This edited collection seeks to build on this earlier scholarship by focusing specifically on the limits of positive obligations.

The volume is organised into two parts. Part I is framed as searching for limits. It includes chapters written by David McGrogan, Eric Heinze, Benoit Mayer and Tristan Cummings, where the main argument formulated is that such a search might be fruitless and this is problematic. Concrete examples pertaining to the regulation of public protest, climate change and child–parent relationships are provided in order to show why it is problematic. Part II is framed as identifying limits. It includes chapters written by Sophie Treacy, Vladislava Stoyanova, Ilias Plakokefalos and Johan Wibye, where the main argument is that despite the unavoidable ambiguities and related limits of positive obligations, there are certain standards. These standards provide a valuable means of identifying the limits of such obligations. They are therefore essential to articulate and uphold, so as to prevent human rights law from drifting away from its protective function and towards an instrument of coercion.

IV. Searching for Limits

The objective of Part I is to engage with the fundamental questions of why the state is expected to have positive obligations and why we find ourselves in a position where we have to ask where the limits on such obligations might lie. Relatedly, we ask: what problems arise from the existence and expansion of positive obligation?

[29] See, eg, P Leisure, 'Contextualizing Causation: Beyond the Negligence Analogy for Understanding States' Positive Obligations to Supervise Schoolchildren' in Stoyanova and Andenas (n 23).

[30] V Stoyanova, *Positive Obligations under the European Convention on Human Rights: Within and Beyond Boundaries* (Oxford University Press, 2023).

[31] D McGrogan, *Critical Theory and Human Rights: From Compassion to Coercion* (Manchester University Press, 2021).

And, in turn, what are their limits, and what standards should be proposed for the identification of such limits?

Part I starts with David McGrogan's '"For Everyone, Everywhere": On Positive Obligations and the Impossibility of Limits'. McGrogan explains that positive obligations justify the existence of a framework of governance. Positive obligations themselves provide justification for the expansion of the role of the state in the society. The expansion of positive obligations appears inevitable as the state constantly needs to justify itself and its role. This is helpful in understanding why there does not seem to be a principled basis on which positive obligations can be limited. McGrogan's contribution also shows that given their justification (ie, the existence of the state and its role), the scope of such obligations will continue to grow. This is a prediction that seems to be accurate in certain areas, the most prominent example being climate change addressed by Benoit Mayer's chapter. Tristan Cumming's chapter also suggests the relevance of the prediction. Yet, Cumming's contribution also illustrates the Court's sensitivity to the state's prerogative to govern and regulate in certain domains – such as the intimate sphere of parent–child relations – and its corresponding restraint in imposing positive obligations.

Eric Heinze's chapter, 'Public Protest in Jeopardy: The Limits of Positive Free Speech Rights', also highlights problematic aspects from the 'ever-greater widening of the scope for positive obligations to be read into human rights' that McGrogan describes. Heinze does this by equating redistribution of costs and wealth with *redistribution of freedoms*. He then argues that it follows from this that positive obligations necessary imply redistribution of freedoms, including limiting the freedoms of some individuals and groups within society. Heinze argues that even if there are no costs involved, positive obligations necessary imply a redistribution of freedoms. This throws into relief the coerciveness that positive obligations might imply, which in turn justifies the endeavour of inquiring into their limits.

Heinze then goes further by showing how once the state alleges that it has no capacity to fulfil its resource-intensive positive obligations, it can avoid findings that it has breached its negative obligations. In this way, positive obligation can serve to shield the state. In particular, Heinze depicts the following conundrum that deserves to be cited in full from his chapter:

> Public protest therefore creates a conundrum. The state maintains a positive obligation to safeguard free speech, but remains silent about how far that obligation extends, indeed precisely as to those protesters who, due to their controversial messages, are likely to stand in greatest need of protection. This ambiguity surrounding the positive component leads in turn to uncertainty about the negative component; yet, uncertainty about whether one may or may not speak lawfully creates risks of chilling expression – we refrain from expression because it *may* be unlawful, even when it is perfectly lawful.

In light of this ambiguity, it is more likely that governments defer to police determinations about risk and deployment of resources, which in the course of possible judicial proceedings would mean that courts would defer to the state. Heinze adds that:

> Once a state alleges its incapacity to fulfil resource-intensive positive obligations, this may well suffice for judges to reject findings that the government or police have breached their negative duties. In such cases, the positive duty will have served to shield the state more than the individual rights holder. The grim reality is that Western democracies' longstanding presumptions in favour of speech will not necessarily equate to government or judicial presumptions in favour of protesters.

Similarly to Heinze, Benoit Mayer's focus lies on the interaction between positive and negative obligations. Mayer's chapter, 'Is Climate Change Mitigation within the Scope of Positive Human Rights Obligations?', does this by highlighting the ambivalence of human rights law towards action on climate change mitigation. Specifically, Mayer explains how states' efforts to mitigate climate change, whether demanded as a matter of positive obligations or not, do *not* 'necessarily or obviously advance the enjoyment of human rights'. Such actions, even if forming part of the content of states' positive obligations (a proportion that Mayer seriously questions), can be in tension, even in conflict, with negative obligations. Mayer's central argument is that even if we were to rigorously apply the limits of positive obligations – such as those embodied in the standards of causation and the correlativity framework, as proposed in Part II of the volume – positive human rights obligations would not be relevant to begin with. In other words, human rights law is inherently unsuited to address the problem.

Although addressing a completely different topic, Tristan Cummings' chapter, 'The Limits of the Positive Obligation to Respect the Parent–Child Relationship', makes a similar argument. Cummings does this by asking the following questions: how could positive human rights obligations, including their coercive aspects, be used to restore intimate connections and intimate relationships? How far can the state go in its efforts, arguably as a matter of positive obligations, to ensure that certain behaviour changes be internalised within each family? Cummings explains that the Court is sensitive to the difficulties in responding to these questions. Yet, as Cummings shows us, a more rigorous appreciation of the standard of causation and the correlativity framework seems to be absent, and this serves to foster the expansion of the positive obligation in question.

V. Identifying Limits

Part II acknowledges the difficulties in finding limits, but also concretely engages with the standards, tests and analytical frameworks that have been developed for delimiting the scope of positive obligations. In Part II, Sophie Treacy and Vladislava Stoyanova address the standard of causation. Illias Plakokefalos focuses on reasonableness. Finally, Johan Wibye addresses correlativity between rights and obligations as a logical framework that could be used for delimiting positive obligations.

The standard of causation has barely been addressed in human rights law.[32] This volume makes an important contribution by offering two chapters that contain a sophisticated analysis as to the role of causation in determining the trigger and scope of positive obligations. Sophie Treacy's chapter, 'Causation, Reasonableness and Positive Obligations', explains how the causal inquiry can be performed with varying degrees of abstraction. The degree chosen can be perceived as a judicial choice that might make the finding of a breach more or less difficult. The choice is political and normative. Treacy further demonstrates the existence of normative choices by showing that causation is not a separate test, as it is in tort law, but rather a relevant consideration that is part of the broader reasonableness inquiry that the ECtHR performs to assess breaches of positive obligations.

Similarly to Treacy's chapter, Vladislava Stoyanova's chapter demonstrates the normative choices at stake that are masked with the invocation of causation in the ECtHR's reasoning. Her main point is that the Court is really inventing positive obligations; however, it masks these inventions by mixing factual and legal causation. Like Treacy, Stoyanova invokes tort law as a comparative lens to formulate an argument that for there to be some level of legal certainty in the adjudication of positive obligation, the Court needs to be more sensitive of the distinction between factual and legal causation.

Treacy and Stoyanova concur that normative considerations are integral to the causation standard. Another manifestation of this normativity is the reliance of the human rights reasoning on the standard of reasonableness. This is further explained in Ilias Plakokefalos' chapter, 'The Standard of (Un)Reasonableness in Human Rights Positive Obligations', which focuses precisely on reasonableness, a standard barely addressed in the existing human rights law scholarship. Plakokefalos argues that courts use the standard of reasonableness as a substitute for extra-legal considerations. In this way, by invoking reasonableness, the ECtHR tries to draw the line between law and non-law.

Drawing this line has become even more difficult, given the absence of engagement and actual application of correlativity as a framework for understanding the relationship between rights and obligations. By emphasising correlativity, Johan Wibye proposes a tool for clearer and more transparent limits on positive obligations. Wibye's chapter, 'Correlativity in Human Rights Law', argues that one must be able to clearly identify duties that correspond to rights rather than simply generating rights without considering what the corresponding duties are. Wibye explains the implications when the correlativity framework is neither consistently employed nor reflected in legal reasoning. In particular, the implication is that there are no limits on the expansion of positive obligations.

[32] Stoyanova, 'Causation between State Omission and Harm' (n 23); McGrogan (n 23); Stoyanova and Andenas (n 23).

Mayer offers a concrete illustration. As mentioned before, he engages with the proposition that states have positive obligations to fight climate change. Yet, these invocations ignore correlation, since there are no actual or potential victims. These invocations also apply a very broad notion of causation, and ignore the economic and human cost of mitigating climate change.

VI. From Protection to Coercion?

As the opening chapter by David McGrogan in this volume explains, human rights law can no longer be imagined without positive obligations and the related assumption that human rights law *demands* the state actively intervene in all life spheres to protect important individual interests. By drawing inspiration from Anthony de Jasay, McGrogan also predicts the inevitability of the tendency in favour of:

> [A]n ever-greater widening of the scope for positive obligations to be read into human rights as a matter of both substantive law and policy, and a consequently increased role for courts, and human rights practitioners, in the formulation of public policy.

The protective character of this ever-expanding scope of positive obligations is often taken for granted. Yet not everything about positive obligations is in fact positive or necessarily protective. This volume seeks to unsettle that assumption by exposing both the coercive dimensions hidden within the language of protection and the analytical looseness that often sustains it. Ultimately, the appeal of desirable outcomes should not blind us to the coercive means by which they may be pursued or to the weak reasoning that may be invoked in their defence.

PART I

Searching for Limits

2

'For Everyone, Everywhere'

On Positive Obligations and the Impossibility of Limits

DAVID McGROGAN

I. Introduction

Human rights theory and doctrine has, after the divisions that characterised the Cold War and the subsequent 'East Asian Challenge', settled on an orthodoxy.[1] This is that all human rights are 'universal, indivisible, and interdependent and [*sic*] interrelated'.[2] According to this orthodoxy, purported distinctions between 'positive' or 'negative' rights, or social and economic versus civil and political ones, reflect an incomplete conceptualisation of the content of either. All human rights are, in fact, composed of both negative and positive elements, and all must be realised in the same way – through obligations imposed on the state to 'respect, protect and fulfil' them.[3] This might be said to have 'positivised' rights both in the doctrinal sense that all are now considered to have positive dimensions to some degree, and in the grander, more theoretical sense that the human rights movement is now broadly considered to require positive state action to realise goals or outcomes.

This is generally described, and accepted, by human rights scholars as being necessary in order to realise an ideal of some kind – a 'richer view of freedom', perhaps, than that provided by mere civil liberties, or else a full expression of the

[1] On the former, see, for example, J Thérien and P Joly, '"All Human Rights for All": The United Nations and Human Rights in the Post-Cold War Era' (2014) 36 *Human Rights Quarterly* 373; on the latter, see, for example, J Bauer and D Bell (eds), *The East Asian Challenge for Human Rights* (Cambridge University Press, 1999).

[2] This formulation is from the World Conference on Human Rights' Vienna Declaration and Programme of Action, 25 June 1993.

[3] I Koch, 'Dichotomies, Trichotomies, or Waves of Duties?' (2005) 5(1) *Human Rights Law Review* 81 provides an excellent overview.

true meaning of 'human dignity'.[4] And the end result is a vision of a circumstance in which 'all human rights are achieved for everyone, everywhere'[5] – an inchoately millenarian end state. But it is not a phenomenon that has been subject to widespread political sociological analysis,[6] with 'the political' here referring to that sphere of reason which concerns the grounding and rationalisation of authority.[7] Scholars who have given sociological accounts of the existence and development of human rights law have tended to associate it with the construction of a specific form of liberalism.[8] They have not tended to inquire how this 'positivisation' of human rights law serves an 'authority-generating function'[9] in the sense of providing a justification and rationale for the existence of a framework of governance per se. This has left a gap in our understanding, because it has caused us to overlook the importance, in the development of human rights law, of incentives that operate at a more foundational level than that of ideas or values.

This chapter provides the outline of such an analysis. In doing so, it draws inspiration from a thought experiment conducted by Anthony de Jasay. De Jasay suggested that it was useful, in understanding the modern state, to treat it as though it were a person, with a single 'point of view' and with motives and desires of its own. Such an exercise would be, undoubtedly and admittedly, reductive. But it would produce a 'simulation' with both explanatory and predictive power.[10] This was because it would display to us the basic logic of political power in modernity: it must have an end of its own. Since every individual not in a state of nature necessarily pursues his own ends within the context of a surrender of sovereignty to the state itself, and since individual ends will necessarily come into conflict with one another (and the aggregate of such ends in the form of the 'public interest'), the state emerges as the means through which such conflicts are resolved.[11] And since in order to resolve conflicts it must attach different weights to different priorities, it must itself choose among those priorities – something it can only do if it has priorities of its own. De Jasay's provocative conclusion was that these priorities would lead to a kind of rationalisation of totalitarianism in the sense that it would drive the state to seek, at the margin, to diminish internal competition and reliance

[4] The phrase 'a richer view of freedom' is from S Fredman, *Human Rights Transformed: Positive Rights and Positive Duties* (Oxford University Press, 2008) 3; on 'human dignity', see, for example, P Gilabert, *Human Dignity and Human Rights* (Oxford University Press, 2018).

[5] UN Office of the High Commissioner for Human Rights (OHCHR), *Management Plan 2024–2027* (United Nations, 2024).

[6] In general, political sociological analyses of the role of human rights are rare. Perhaps the most prominent example is in systems theory; see C Thornhill, 'The Foundations of International Human Rights Law: A Sociological Inquiry' (2016) 4 *Revista Brasileira de Sociologia do Direito*.

[7] C Schmitt, *The Concept of the Political*, G Schwab (trans) (University of Chicago Press, 2007 [1932]).

[8] See J Charvet and E Kaczynska-May, *The Liberal Project and Human Rights: The Theory and Practice of a New World Order* (Oxford University Press, 2008); A Ingram, *A Political Theory of Rights* (Oxford University Press, 1994).

[9] M Louglin, *Political Jurisprudence* (Oxford University Press, 2017) 1.

[10] A de Jasay, *The State* (Liberty Fund, 1998 [1985]), 'Author's Note', xi–xii.

[11] The influence of Hobbes is obvious.

on democratic consent – it would rather be totalitarian to the extent that it could 'get away with it' at any given moment.[12] And this in turn would bias it towards a totalitarian drift, with the state gradually but inexorably expanding in size and ambition across time.

Thinking about the state in this sense helps us to look at human rights, and in particular their gradual 'positivisation', in a fresh light. It first suggests that positive human rights obligations are par excellence a tool through which the state achieves its immediate end of governing, because they provide a mechanism and rationale through which individual ends and the 'public interest' can be reconciled; 'all rights are [to be] achieved for everyone, everywhere', and this requires a perfectly calibrated system of careful adjudication and balancing (and hence of governing). This obviously helps explain why it is that the 'positivisation' phenomenon has taken place at all – quite simply because it provides the 'authority-generating function' to which I alluded earlier. But it also helps explain the deeper drive towards the creeping expansion of the horizons of positive obligations evident to any observer. To repeat, the state is driven at the margins to be as totalitarian as it can 'get away with' at any given moment, and the use of rights language, which has the consequence of depoliticising or constitutionalising whatever phenomenon is under analysis, contributes effectively to the gradual diminishment of competition and reliance on consent in such a way as to ensure that the calculation of what can be 'gotten away with' is always appropriately performed. In this sense, the 'positivisation' of human rights law serves not just to ground a framework of governance, but also to shape it in light of the state's foundational incentives.

All manner of objections can be raised to this analysis, not the least of which being that de Jasay's exposition relies on an (admitted) abstraction that conceals the fact that individual human beings all have motives of their own which are generally sincere. Similarly, in the context of human rights, claimants, activists, scholars, politicians and judges all pursue their own objectives and ideals, and ascribing these as 'totalitarian' would appear at first glance to be too sweeping. Moreover, the implications of analysing human rights in this way leads to an almost diametrically opposite understanding of the role this body of law plays in bolstering democracy, good governance or 'responsive constitutionalism' to the way in which this matter is typically understood.[13]

Nonetheless, in this chapter I conclude that thinking of rights in this way is uncomfortably accurate and helps us to both explain and map out the future trajectory of doctrinal and theoretical developments. First, I argue that the trend towards 'positivisation' will only increase, as it has no natural or reasoned limits. Second, it will raise profound doctrinal uncertainties that will not be resolved, since they stem from the understanding that the role of the state is to reconcile the

[12] De Jasay (n 10) 273.

[13] See, for example, R Bellamy, 'Political Constitutionalism and Populism' (2023) 50 *Journal of Law and Society* 7; A Tomkins, 'The Role of the Courts in the Political Constitution' (2010) 60 *University of Toronto Law Journal* 1; R Dixon, 'The New Responsive Constitutionalism' (2024) 87(4) *MLR* 1468.

conflicts that arise in a society with heterogeneous preferences and therefore serve its need for 'authority-generation'. In this respect, a level of doctrinal uncertainty may be considered beneficial, since it suggests a permanent modulating role for the governing apparatus.

In section II, I describe the phenomenon of 'positivisation', and in section III, I set out some of the conceptual consequences – namely, an inchoate understanding of the state as being the means through which rights conflicts are resolved. In sections IV and V, I then posit de Jasay's analysis of the state, and in section VI, I explain why his analysis is a productive way of conceptualising why the gradual 'positivisation' of rights has occurred. In section VII, I elucidate this further by situating the phenomenon of positivisation within a discussion of the state's overarching ends, and in section VIII, I conclude the argument by describing positivisation as necessarily both limitless and doctrinally uncertain.

II. The Positivisation of Human Rights Law

The question of whether there are meaningful distinctions to be drawn between positive versus negative, or what have been called 'welfare' versus 'liberty' rights,[14] is an old and persistent one in human rights theory.[15] But in respect of practice, this debate has largely been superseded by the emergence of a broad consensus, which is that when it comes at least to implementation, the division of rights into separate camps, 'families' or 'generations' is neither desirable nor useful.[16]

The consequences of the emergence of this consensus have been twofold, First, it has brought about what, in effect, might be called the death of a concept of 'negative' rights in respect of human rights jurisprudence. The converse of that phenomenon, of course, is that rights can be said to have been universally 'positivised': whether or not at one time the matter was understood differently,[17] and whether or not this development is justified with theoretical precision,[18] 'actually existing human rights', as it were, can all now be said to contain a positive dimension within their composition.

The chief theoretical development in this regard has been the elaboration of the idea that human rights all give rise to the same basic triumvirate of

[14] H. Breakey, 'Positive Duties and Human Rights: Challenges, Opportunities and Conceptual Necessity' (2015) 63(5) Political Studies 1198.

[15] M Sepúlveda, *The Nature of the Obligations under the International Covenant on Economic, Social and Cultural Rights* (Hart Publishing, 2003).

[16] See, for example, I Koch, *Human Rights as Indivisible Rights: The Protection of Socio-economic Demands under the European Convention on Human Rights* (Martinus Nijhoff, 2009).

[17] There is no doubt that there has until recently been genuine, strong disagreement between human rights scholars. See, for example, C Gearty, 'Against Judicial Enforcement' in C Gearty and V Mantouvalou (eds) *Debating Social Rights* (Hart Publishing, 2011) 1.

[18] O O'Neill, 'The Dark Side of Human Rights' (2005) 82(2) *International Affairs* 427.

obligations – to 'respect' (ie, to refrain from violating the rights of an individual), to 'protect' (ie, to ensure that individuals or groups do not violate the rights of an individual) and to 'fulfil' (ie, to 'take the measures necessary to ensure for each person within its jurisdiction opportunities to obtain satisfaction of those needs, recognised in human rights instruments, which cannot be secured by personal efforts').[19] While this insistence that rights all give rise to the same pattern of obligations is fairly new – it was only really elaborated doctrinally in 1987[20] – it is now generally presented as though it is simply a necessary feature of human rights themselves that has always been recognised. Hence, the *Training Guide* of the UN Office of the High Commissioner for Human Rights (OHCHR) for representatives of States Parties reporting to the UN treaty bodies simply notes that 'by becoming parties to human rights treaties, States assume obligations and duties under international law which entail the threefold responsibility to respect, protect and fulfil the human rights enshrined in those treaties' as though it were ever thus.[21]

And this formulation has, whether explicitly or not, bled into human rights case law at the domestic, regional and international levels. The stereotypical illustration of this might be the jurisprudence of the European Court of Human Rights (ECtHR) with respect to Article 10 of the European Convention on Human Rights (ECHR). While the right to freedom of expression may have initially been framed as a 'negative' or 'liberty' right, and probably remains so in the public imagination, the modern interpretation of its content in juridical terms includes an extensive range of positive duties imposed on the state both to preserve speech and, to a certain extent, even nurture it. For example, the ECtHR has held variously that the existence of the right imposes on the state obligations to ensure that the public has access to impartial and accurate information reflecting diversity of opinion within the country,[22] that access of broadcasters to the market is made effective so as to guarantee diversity of content,[23] that an appropriate legislative and administrative framework is put in place to guarantee media pluralism,[24] that 'channels' should be put in place for public interest reporting and disclosures (or 'whistleblowing'),[25] and so on. The Court does not itself use the language of 'respect', 'protect' and 'fulfil', but it is not difficult to see the formulation mirrored in its jurisprudence[26] – with, to continue the example, Article 10 being interpreted to require states not

[19] A Eide, 'The Right to Food as a Human Right', UN Doc E/CN.4/Sub.2/1987/23, 7 July 1987, paras 66–69.

[20] ibid. Eide was building on a formulation originally postulated in H Shue, *Basic Rights: Subsistence, Affluence and U.S. Foreign Policy* (Princeton University Press, 1980).

[21] UN OHCHR, *Reporting to the United Nations Human Rights Treaty Bodies: Training Guide – Part 1* (United Nations, 2017) 5.

[22] *Manole and Others v Moldova*, App No 13936/02, 17 September 2009, para 100.

[23] *Centra Europa 7 SR and Di Stefano v Italy* [GC], App No 38433/09, 7 June 2012, para 130.

[24] ibid para 134.

[25] *Gawlick v Lichtenstein*, App No 23922/19, 31 May 2021.

[26] On the tripartite typology and the ECtHR specifically, see, for example, J Wibye, 'Reviving the Distinction between Positive and Negative Human Rights' (2022) 35 *Ratio Juris* 363.

just to respect the right to freedom of expression in the sense of not acting to violate it, but to 'protect' it vis-a-vis 'diversity of content' and whistleblowing, and indeed to 'fulfil' it in respect of 'guarantee[ing] media pluralism'.

The second, as it were grander, consequence of the emergence of this consensus has been a total reconceptualisation of the role or character of a rights-respecting state. While at one time it was possible to imagine that a 'laissez-faire' or minimalist state could be 'rights-respecting' (the Committee on Economic, Social and Cultural Rights (CESCR) indeed stated as much in 1990)[27] simply by refraining from violating rights, it is now the case that – since literally every right is thought to have a wide-ranging and open-ended positive dimension – a 'rights-respecting' state can only be conceptualised as one with a very extensive interventionist stance towards the economy and society. The culmination of this conceptual dynamic can be found in the most recent (at the time of writing) *Management Plan* of the OHCHR.[28] In it, we find laid out a 'Theory of Change', which orients itself towards a 'long-term goal of "all human rights, for everyone, everywhere"'.[29] This theory posits 10 requirements that will, it is 'assumed', ensure that 'every person everywhere will be able to enjoy their human rights'.[30] And these requirements take for granted that human rights are required to be realised *en bloc* not just through legislation or rule making but also through 'policies and programmes'; through institutional support for 'implementation' that is 'adequately resourced'; through the creation of 'protection systems and accountability mechanisms' to 'monitor, investigate and redress' violations; and also, implicitly, through an extensive programme of education so as to make sure that 'public support for human rights' is 'widespread', and through enacting whatever policies are required to ensure that 'individuals and groups [are] able to participate in public processes meaningfully, safely and in an inclusive manner'.[31]

The accumulation of roughly 75 years of theoretical, doctrinal and jurisprudential reasoning with respect to human rights has, then, brought us to a point at which it is possible to say that there is no longer any wide support for the idea that human rights merely constrain, rather than facilitate, state action. In the mainstream view, rights all require the state to engage actively in shaping society towards particular objectives and, taken as a whole, indeed suggest an extensive framework of law and policy through which the state intervenes in, and guides, society in the interests of respecting, protecting and fulfilling rights universally across its jurisdiction. The concept of purely 'negative' rights has disappeared; all human rights are in some respect or other positive rights.

[27] CESCR, General Comment No 3, UN Doc E/1991/23 (1990), para 8.
[28] OHCHR (n 5).
[29] ibid 14.
[30] ibid.
[31] ibid.

III. The Rights-Respecting State

The question then naturally arises as to what a 'rights-respecting state' – that is, a state which aims to realise 'all human rights, for everyone, everywhere' – would look like in practice. Clearly, it is impossible to ensure that all human rights are realised for everyone, everywhere, absolutely, if rights are understood to have any sort of positive dimension whatsoever. This is for the obvious reason that attempting to do so would produce practical and conceptual zero-sum conflicts between rights claims, and therefore requiring trade-offs. This observation is trite, and many readers will be aware of its implications. But it remains the case that it often goes unstated or unacknowledged, in such a way that – as we shall see in the light of what follows – is instructive.

Many such examples of unstated or unacknowledged trade-offs indeed appear within the very *Management Plan* mentioned above, in which the 'all human rights for everyone, everywhere' maxim is deployed. Strictly speaking, much of the *Plan*'s contents concern activities in which the OHCHR intends to engage itself during the period in question. But its underlying assumptions about what the realisation of 'all human rights, for everyone, everywhere' entails are very useful in illuminating the kind of conflicts that a rights-respecting state understood in these terms would encounter.

For instance, as the *Plan* unconsciously makes clear, the positive dimensions of a right (that is, the means through which it is 'protected' and 'fulfilled') can conflict with its negative ones (that is, the means through which it is 'respected'), the most obvious illustration being the right to freedom of expression, with regard to which the *Plan* advocates 'promoting meaningful participation' through facilitating access to information and the construction of 'participatory spaces that are enabling, inclusive, and safe', while at the same time suggesting that 'anti-rights narratives' and 'anti-gender narratives' ought to be 'countered' through 'effective frameworks'.[32] In other words, in order to 'protect' and 'fulfil' the right to freedom of expression (though the *Plan* conceptualises this under the rubric of the 'right to participate'), it is necessary, in the *Plan*'s reasoning, to limit the negative 'respect' accorded to the speech rights of those who are construed as engaging in 'anti-rights' or 'anti-gender' narratives or, as we see elsewhere, 'disinformation' or 'hate speech'.[33]

At the same time, naturally, the positive dimension of one right can also conflict with the negative dimension of another. The *Plan*, for instance, suggests that it is important to 'work with businesses to help them contribute to and improve equality and diversity in line with international law', in connection with the right to non-discrimination.[34] This can obviously be conceptualised as a way to protect

[32] ibid 36.
[33] ibid 35–36.
[34] ibid 40.

and/or fulfil that right. But, while the *Plan* itself does not acknowledge as much, this will tend to produce conflicts with the negative dimension of the rights to freedom of association, and freedom of conscience, of business owners (the trade-off between these competing priorities being of infamous and longstanding concern in discussions about rights).[35] In other words, despite the framing of 'working with businesses', the effort to operationalise equality and diversity through legal requirements necessarily requires a trade-off against business owners' alternate priorities where they exist.

And, at a broader level, of course, any attempt to realise rights across any dimension – positive or negative – always contains within it an implicit and often unconscious value judgement about what is or is not in the public interest, and this will typically tend to conceal trade-offs and conflicts. In the most basic sense, of course, rights are always limited by public interest concerns: even the most extreme example of a classically 'negative' right, the protection of speech in the First Amendment of the US Constitution, is curtailed with respect to speech that incites 'an immediate breach of the peace'.[36] And resource constraints will also necessarily, and naturally, limit the extent to which rights can be protected or fulfilled.

But there is a deeper sense in which the positivisation of rights implicitly raises questions about what it is actually in the public interest to attempt to achieve. For example, the authors of the OHCHR's *Plan* clearly understand equality in the substantive sense to be required by non-discrimination rights: in its positive dimensions the right to non-discrimination requires the 'counter[ing] of socio-economic inequalities', the use of 'budgets, taxation and other socio-economic tools' that 'tackle' inequality and so on.[37] But the authors of the Plan also appear to understand economic and social rights to require economic development in order to achieve realisation.[38] That there might be a zero-sum trade-off to be made between the policy goals of substantive equality and economic development is not entertained; the authors' position is that 'sustainable development' can be achieved through 'highlight[ing] inequality' and 'leveraging data to protect human rights'.[39] More likely, however, is that in practice there is indeed such a trade-off to be made and that, ultimately, decisions must be taken about whether to prioritise substantive equality or economic development in any given circumstance – with those decisions, obviously, being informed by different perspectives on what the 'public interest' requires.

[35] The most prominent recent example of such a trade-off confronting the modern state being the similar 'gay cake' cases of *Lee v Ashers Baking Company Ltd and Others* [2018] UKSC 49 and *Masterpiece Cakeshop v. Colorado Civil Rights Commission*, 584 US 617 (2018).

[36] *Chaplinsky v New Hampshire*, 315 US 568 (1942), para 10, citing JR Zechariah Chafee, *Free Speech in the United States* (Harvard University Press, 1941).

[37] OHCHR (n 5) para 39.

[38] ibid 27.

[39] ibid 46.

All of this is simply to make explicit what is widely recognised implicitly in human rights doctrine (chiefly through assessments of proportionality, which can be understood in most cases simply to indeed mean the making of trade-offs,[40] but also through the provision for resource constraints in applicable treaties)[41] and what is sometimes acknowledged in writing on the subject.[42] This is the fact that any state which attempts to achieve 'all human rights, for everyone, everywhere' will be put in a position of something akin to a management function which coordinates finite resources in respect of what would otherwise be essentially infinite claims, based on decisions about what to prioritise at any particular given moment and in any particular context, and guided by particular interpretations of human rights concerns.

And the managerialisation of the 'rights-respecting state' is indeed a vision which the *Plan* implicitly embraces. The 'Theory of Change' it presents, as we have seen, is predicated on a series of requirements which, if met, it is 'assumed' will ensure that 'every person everywhere will be able to enjoy their human rights'. If the state is aligning its legislation, policies and programmes with 'human rights standards'; if there are adequately resourced state institutions to support implementation; if there are 'protection systems and accountability mechanisms'; if there is widespread public support for human rights; and if 'individuals and groups' are able to 'participate in public processes' – and if this is all supported by the UN human rights system – then the end state of 'all human rights, for everyone, everywhere' will inevitably emerge.

What is notable about this is that it is in essence a procedural – or, to return to the word used above, managerial – vision rather than a substantive one. It is, to repeat, to be understood as a means through which the state coordinates resources and priorities – informed, that is, by the participation of a public which supports human rights, and operationalised through conformity with 'standards'. There is no substantive political vision underlying this – in that sense, the *Plan* is agnostic. There is instead only a means through which priorities are selected and given effect, and which is 'assumed' will result in all human rights being achieved for all.

This immediately calls to mind the description of the modern state as the quintessence of 'government' in the sense of being the means through which a 'relationship of forces' is structured.[43] The state, examining the different priorities of 'individuals and groups' through the lens of human rights, thus determines which of those priorities – or 'forces' – should be supported through public resource and which should not. Will the state 'promot[e] meaningful participation' through 'participatory spaces that are enabling, inclusive, and safe', and thereby suppress

[40] See, for example, K Möller, 'Proportionality: Challenging the Critics' (2012) 10(3) *International Journal of Constitutional Law* 709, 710.

[41] An example being the International Covenant on Economic, Social and Cultural Rights, art 2.

[42] D McGrogan, 'Anti-individual Morality in the International Human Rights System' (2022) 40(2) *Netherlands Quarterly of Human Rights* 137.

[43] N Poulantzas, *State, Power, Socialism* (Verso, 1980) 128–29.

'anti-rights narratives', 'disinformation' and so on? Or will it prioritise a more formal and restricted approach to speech rights? Will it prioritise development or substantive equality? Will it prioritise freedom of conscience, or the imperatives of equality and diversity? The vision of the state which emerges is thus one which acts not exactly as a neutral or objective umpire between competing rights claims, but as an executive which makes decisions about which, amongst many competing priorities, public resources should be directed towards.

The image of human rights that emerges from this analysis is of a conceptual framework within which decisions about priorities are made. And the question therefore naturally arises as to how those priorities are selected. In the mainstream understanding, the selection process derives from a conception of 'the good' in a very broad sense – what would be in the interests of dignity, freedom, equality, justice and so forth. However, a more accurate way of putting it would be that in selecting priorities (and thereby making trade-offs), decision-makers are really choosing between competing ideas about what dignity, freedom, equality, justice and so on entail. To return to an earlier example, in prioritising the protection and fulfilment of participation rights by suppressing 'disinformation', 'hate speech', 'anti-gender narratives' and so on, a decision-maker would be implicitly prioritising one iteration of dignity (concerning those whose public participation would otherwise be, as it were, 'drowned out' by others) over another (concerning those whose public participation is suppressed on the grounds of being in some respect undesirable or objectionable).

This is, in a sense, simply another way of making the old and familiar point that law tends to mask the existence of competing normative visions. And there is, of course, a vast literature concerning that topic.[44] Most of that literature is dedicated to explicating a distinction between a hegemonic liberalism and/or capitalism and a subaltern or suppressed socialism.[45] But there is a thinker, Antony de Jasay, who offers us an entirely different – and, I aim to show, genuinely novel and insightful – way to approach the matter. It is to his work on *The State*, then, to which I now turn.

IV. De Jasay's State

In *The State*, de Jasay aims to provide a new theory of the state by imagining that, rather than being an instrument that might serve some set of interests or other at a particular moment in time, it has its own will, interests and ends. The state is admittedly an immensely complex phenomenon. But, as de Jasay puts it, describing it as

[44] For an illustration, see S Fish, 'The Law Wishes to Have a Formal Existence' in *There's No Such Thing as Free Speech and It's a Good Thing, Too* (Oxford University Press, 1993) 141.

[45] One thinks here of R Unger, *Law in Modern Society* (Free Press, 1976); see also S Marks, 'Human Rights and Root Causes' (2011) 74(1) *MLR* 57.

a person with intentions of its own can produce a 'simulation' or 'schematic history' which is able to explain important features of its development.[46] This is because, simply put, a given state always has to confront the fact that – provided that there is a heterogeneity of interests in society – it has to pick and choose between which interests it should further. Since resources are finite, it cannot satisfy all interests. It must therefore determine which interests to prioritise if it is to do anything at all.[47] And given that this is the case, it must have a non-neutral means of determining how to take sides, and which sides to take – it must therefore have ends, and since it must have ends, it is useful to imagine that it also has intentions and a will.

De Jasay therefore dismisses two typical ways of understanding the state, roughly corresponding to the Marxian and the liberal. In the Marxian perspective, the state is 'subservient to the interests of the ruling class and assur[es] its dominance'.[48] In the liberal perspective, the state is a benign means through which public goods or social welfare are produced in collectively preferred amounts through democratic decision-making.[49] For de Jasay, the former of these claims is 'gratuitous' (and indeed, though he does not make this explicit, tautological).[50] It simply raises the further question as to which class and which set of interests the state chooses to be dominant and why. And the latter of these claims is simply false – since there is no way, even in a 'pure' direct democracy, to take into account literally everybody's expressions of preferences, there is no way to aggregate individual utility functions into a total 'social welfare function' without 'somebody's will deciding how it should be done'.[51] Policy is enacted in uncertainty – there is no way of knowing *ex ante* whether a given policy will maximise utility. And since this is the case, ultimately, willed decisions must be made about which policies to pursue or, at a higher level of abstraction, how calculations or assessments are to be made about policy choices. 'Whoever has authority to choose the "best" judgement or the method for calculating a composite one', de Jasay therefore concludes, 'is in effect implicitly choosing his own.'[52]

What emerges from this is a picture of the state as the means through which conflicts of interest are resolved. But because resolving conflicts necessarily involves attaching different weights to the ends of those involved, this is tantamount to saying that the state must choose which ends are the most important, which in turn is tantamount to saying that it must have its own conception of where 'importance' lies. Clearly, in reality, the state's ends are the product of a 'shifting and uncertain hierarchy of diffuse and sometimes partially conflicting wills, none of which can be said knowingly to make the state's decisions', and those ends are composite ones

[46] De Jasay (n 10) xi–xii.
[47] ibid 267.
[48] ibid 2.
[49] ibid.
[50] ibid 267.
[51] ibid 67.
[52] ibid 99–100.

rather than the choices of any given individual.[53] Yet, de Jasay insists that nonetheless we can make some declarations about what those ends will necessarily consist of, by conceiving them as the product of a single unitary intention.

Undoubtedly the most difficult aspect of de Jasay's thesis is the way in which it marries what is in essence a highly abstract description of the rationale underlying what Foucault once labelled 'political reason'[54] – that is, the justification for Botero's 'founding, conserving and expanding dominion'[55] – with a very concrete metaphor in the form of the individuated and personalised 'state'. This makes it easy to mistake it to be a reduction of the 'chaotic and largely unpredictable witches' cauldron'[56] of motives, interests, preferences, values and decisions that comprise the modern state to a falsely purposive and self-directed mechanism.

The truth, however, is that what de Jasay's argument achieves is to release, from the tangle of the admittedly great complexity of modern political organisation, the – as it were – thematic essence of modern government. His theory is 'is not directly about the State but rather about how we should think about [it]'.[57] It is not that any state, even one under the personal rule of a dictator or absolute monarch, actually has individual motives, goals or desires. Indeed, that it does not – that preferences even within a governing class are never homogeneous – is, as we have seen, the base on which the edifice of de Jasay's argument rests. It is rather that, at the level of metaphor, the act of governing has to be understood as purposive, at least in the sense that selecting 'neutrally' or objectively between preferences or reconciling them in a perfectly 'balanced' way is not possible. Since it is not possible, it must be the case that there are priorities which stem from the nature of governing itself – ie, which can 'impute' to government, whatever form it takes and whatever collection of individuals may be construed to rule, 'some behavioural regularity'.[58]

Irrespective of whatever 'tenant' happens to be in charge, in the sense of the 'real persons'[59] or 'plenipotentiary agents'[60] who actually form the governing 'regime'[61] of a state as such, then, and irrespective of their personal motives or interests, there is an underlying rationale that does not vary. The 'tenants' who form a government at any particular point in time may have all manner of different goals – 'promotion of a supreme value, patronage of the arts, and

[53] ibid 210.

[54] M Foucault, '"*Omnes et Singulatim*": Toward a Critique of Political Reason' in J Faubion (ed), R Hurley (trans), *Power: Essential Works, Vol 3* (New Press, 2001) 298.

[55] G Botero, *The Reason of State* [1589] in R Bireley (ed) *Botero: The Reason of State* (Cambridge University Press, 2017) 4.

[56] A de Jasay, 'The Maximising State' (2010) 15(1) *The Independent Review* 5, 6.

[57] H Kliemt, 'The Defensive State' (2015) 20(1) *The Independent Review* 12.

[58] De Jasay (n 56) 7.

[59] ibid.

[60] ibid.

[61] I use here Harvey Mansfield's definition of a 'regime' simply as the rule of a certain 'some' over the 'many'. H Mansfield, *Machiavelli's Virtue* (Harvard University Press, 1996).

establishment of a firmly based kleptocracy are plausible examples'[62] – but the incentives which they face in doing so do not change. There are, as it were, transcendent or universal ends, which apply to all 'tenants', whether in power or prospectively so, and which filter through into priorities which must be realised whatever other personal goals are at stake. And it is this ineluctable set of ends, deriving from unalterable incentives, which can be understood to be personalised in the form of de Jasay's individuated 'state'.

Thinking about the state in this way helps us to understand something important about every aspect of modern government, including indeed the positivisation of human rights. This is that, whatever immediate goals might be purported to be achieved by a particular policy, law or regulation, there will be supervening ends which derive from the underlying rationale of political reason in the modern state. And human rights, which of course tend to be operationalised in the name of particular goals and objectives (whether at the abstract level of 'human dignity' or 'equality' or 'justice', at the policy level of securing non-discrimination, social housing and so on, or at the instrumental level of the particular litigant in a particular case) are no different. Alongside those goals or objectives, human rights must also be understood as contributing to the state's other, fixed ends. These ends, as we shall see, drive the state in a 'totalitarian' direction. And the reasons for this will be elaborated in the next section.

V. The State's Ends

The first end which the state must always have, de Jasay decides, is to justify and maintain its status. This is for the obvious reason that if its 'tenants' have any other end at all which they seek to achieve, they cannot do so without retaining their position. And this will tend to lead the state in the direction of what Leo Strauss called 'political hedonism' – that is, the identification of the political good with the absence of displeasure, and hence the purchasing of consent through making a promise to maximise utility.[63] Relying on a perception of legitimacy is too uncertain, and relying on violence or suppression does not produce long-term stability. But if the population can by and large see themselves as being better off with the state than without it, or with this particular 'tenant' of the position rather than another one, then they will consent to being ruled, and power can be thereby retained in perpetuity.[64]

The problem with this, however, from the personal perspective of the state is that it has no end point except for the state itself becoming a 'welfare-dispensing

[62] ibid.

[63] De Jasay (n 10) 65, citing L Strauss, *Natural Right and History* (University of Chicago Press, 1971) 169.

[64] ibid 131.

drudge'.[65] In order to purchase the consent of a sufficient proportion of the population to retain its status, the state must inevitably become redistributive – it must 'carve out a majority' and prioritise that majority's interests through transferring assets to it from the minority (typically in the form of taxation of the wealthy to fund a generous welfare state).[66] And once this process has begun, the redistributive function will become subject to 'ceaseless enlargement' by a product of shared incentives on the part of the population and the state itself.[67] In other words, any 'tenant' of the state will become vulnerable to rivals who promise yet more redistribution to a bigger majority. And the population will become increasingly reliant on redistribution and increasingly expectant of it by force of habit, and thereby increasingly demanding in their requirements for the giving of their consent. The result of this will be an increasingly complex and unworkable situation of not so much robbing Peter to pay Paul, but of both Peter and Paul being paid and robbed in a wide variety of ways accompanied by a 'crazy quilt of loopholes and asymmetrical favours' and often without an evident rationale.[68]

This eventually puts the state in the undesirable position of using all of its power up merely on retaining power – its sole activity becomes the management of redistribution and its 'addictive' effects.[69] And this is undesirable for an important reason: it results in the disappearance of the state's 'discretionary power',[70] meaning simply 'power not required for its own reproduction and maintenance'.[71] Since this would interfere with whatever other ends the state's tenants might have (beyond simply remaining in power), it follows that the state must necessarily have a further end – the maximisation of that discretionary or 'surplus' power so as to create the space within which to achieve whatever outcomes it desires beyond mere welfare-dispensing 'drudgery'.[72] In other words, it must attempt to achieve an equilibrium where it can maintain majority support through redistribution while at the same time pursuing whatever other ends it (that is to say, its 'tenants') might have. It must seek to 'improve its environment' such that it has to spend less of its power on, as it were, staying in power, and can therefore use it for other purposes, whatever they might be.[73]

This, de Jasay continues, will lead the state inevitably to seek to do two things. Since it wishes to minimise the amount of power it spends on its own 'reproduction and maintenance' through redistribution, it must attempt to diminish the extent to which it is reliant on consent, while at the same time diminishing the likelihood of other, rival 'tenants' taking power through offering an

[65] ibid 12–13.
[66] ibid 141.
[67] ibid 132.
[68] ibid 11–12.
[69] ibid 228.
[70] ibid 12–13.
[71] De Jasay (n 56) 7.
[72] De Jasay (n 10) 268–69.
[73] ibid 271–72.

ever-greater dispensation of welfare. Importantly, the interaction between these two priorities will not permit any 'tenant' to redistribute *less*, ie, by reducing its welfare-dispensing activities, because to do so would immediately open it up to usurpation by a prospective 'tenant' promising to redistribute *more*.[74] Instead, de Jasay concludes, the state will have to come up with other solutions, falling into two corresponding categories.

The first category of solution is to 'retain bourgeois democracy', but progressively to restrict its scope such that consent becomes less relevant – that is, to ensure that the winning party in an election does not gain an unlimited licence for decision-making, but is restricted in what it can achieve. This then diminishes the extent to which the state is reliant on, so to speak, the popular will.[75] This is by no means an absolute process, because the state must at all times be careful to ensure that it does not destabilise itself through oppression. Rather, it should be understood as a drive to maintain a position of equilibrium where whatever 'plenipotentiary agent' is in power, it simply cannot deploy a more radically redistributive governing model than currently exists.

The second category is to 'regulate entry' such that 'while an elected assembly continues technically to dispose of State power as a whole',[76] it becomes less and less possible to elect people who might usurp the current 'tenant' of the state. This then has the effect of diminishing threats from rivals, and thereby securing the state from competitors. It can then concern itself less with obsessive redistributive 'drudgery' and free up space to achieve whatever other ends its 'tenants' might have.

In summary, then, the incentives facing the state, conceived as a rational actor, produce a situation in which will be as 'totalitarian' as it can 'get away with'.[77] First, the state must have ends as such – it must have priorities, interests, purposes and values, whatever these might be. This is because it is only through possessing its own ends that it will be able to choose between competing priorities. Second, its immediate end must be to retain its own status, and it can only realistically achieve this in the long term through the obtaining of consent – achieved hedonistically by building a majority coalition and redistributing resources from the minority to that majority. But because the effects of redistribution are 'addictive' and tend towards 'ceaseless enlargement' of welfarism, and because the existence of potential rivals will incentivise further and further redistribution, this will result in all of the state's power being eventually used up on fulfilling this end. And this will have the result that any other ends its tenants have might have go unrealised. The third stage, then, is for the state to seek 'environmental improvement' by diminishing its reliance on consent and regulating entry to the extent that the existing tenants' status goes unthreatened.

[74] ibid 132.
[75] ibid 285.
[76] ibid 286.
[77] ibid 273.

The picture that emerges from this is of a managerial state, governed by different agents at different times, but always 'tenanted' by a relatively monolithic political class, and essentially always picking and choosing between competing preferences, values and interests, and seeking to do so in such a way as to diminish reliance on consent and making it more difficult for radical or revolutionary 'tenants' to emerge. And this gives it a totalitarian drift – because, of course, it indicates an end point at which there is no requirement for consent and no possibility of rivals emerging: the point at which 'citizenship and livelihood' are 'integrated' so that 'the subject's whole existence shall be ruled by one and the same command'.[78] De Jasay is at every stage at pains to emphasise that this outcome is by no means inevitable, but it is the trajectory across which the modern state travels given no corrective or barrier, as a product of the incentives which face it.

Painting the state in this way, it will be clear, has certain implications for the way in which we conceive of the role of human rights, with a particular emphasis on how those rights have gradually been 'postivised' over time. We have already described the 'rights-respecting state' as one which has an essentially managerial function, choosing between, as it were, competing preferences, values and interests. And it will be evident that this recalls de Jasay's starting position of the state as being in the position of reconciling conflicts in a society in which preferences are not homogeneous. It now falls for us to consider what he described as being the incentives which flowed from that starting point, and what they mean for human rights in particular, with an emphasis specifically on their 'positivisation'. In section VI, I demonstrate why it is that this helps to explain why the positivisation phenomenon occurs at all; in section VII, I elucidate this further by drawing attention to how that phenomenon aligns with the those incentives.

VI. The State and the Positivisation of Human Rights

The description of the role of the state as a managerial function which places different weights on various competing preferences gives us, in the most immediate sense, a way to understand the sociological function of human rights. Put somewhat simplistically but usefully, it depicts rights holders as possessing claims with respect to an array of different individuated preferences, and the state as being the means through which all of those competing rights claims are sorted out, prioritised and traded-off against one another and the 'public interest'.[79] And, of course, in de Jasay's reading, the state would do this by attaching different weights (implicitly or explicitly) to different priorities and giving them effect by attaching

[78] ibid 277.

[79] The echoes here to the work of JAG Griffith and the so-called 'LSE tradition' will be apparent. See JAG Griffith, 'The Political Constitution' (1979) 42 *MLR* 1; R Rawlings, 'Distinction and Diversity: Law and the LSE' in R Rawlings (ed), *Law, Society and Economy: Centenary Essays for the London School of Economics and Political Science 1895–1995* (Clarendon Press, 1997) 20.

respectively more weight to some rights than others, in differing contexts. Hence, for example, in the stereotypical scenario of the conflict between the right to non-discrimination of an individual of a particular group and the right to freedom of association of an individual who wishes to exclude members of that group from some location or process, generally speaking, the modern state places the weight on the former. In the scenario of a qualified right held against the public interest – for example, the right to respect for private life vis-a-vis the public interest in mandatory vaccination of preschool children[80] – the state may place the weight on the latter. And so on.

In this respect, rights can be conceptualised as one of the means through which the state achieves its governing role – that is, through operationalising, or rationalising, the selection of preferences to prioritise or trade-off against other preferences. And if the analysis were to limit itself to this observation, it might suggest only a variation of Kelsen's description of a 'legal order' which 'brings about such a compromise between opposing interests as to minimise the possible frictions' and thereby secures 'social peace'[81] – or, cast in a more negative light, Engels' description of the state as a power which stands above society to reconcile conflicts and antagonisms, and which would disappear once those conflicts dissipated.[82]

But de Jasay's contribution is not limited to such observations, because of his insistence that, far from achieving mere 'compromise between opposing interests', the state instead picks and chooses between them in accordance with its own priorities. In other words, it does not act as a neutral arbitrator or referee, but rather acts to implement its own ends by weighing different preferences accordingly. This is because – to repeat an earlier point – even the selection of a means through which to weigh preferences is itself to implicitly stipulate priorities. The best that any state can do is therefore in the end to 'further its own composite conception' of opposing interests rather than to reconcile them perfectly objectively.[83] Put more straightforwardly, in order to discern why it is that the modern state would appear to prioritise non-discrimination over freedom of association when it comes to the provision of goods and services, and to prioritise the public interest over freedom of conscience with regard to vaccines, it is necessary to understand its ends.

What this means is that, as critics of human rights have long pointed out,[84] while rights language tends to convey the appearance of objectivity or neutrality by depoliticising whatever issue is at hand through a process of

[80] *Vavřička and Others v The Czech Republic*, App No 47621/13, 8 April 2021.

[81] H Kelsen, *General Theory of Law and the State*, A Wedberg (trans) (Harvard University Press, 1945) 13–14 and 49.

[82] F Engels, *The Origins of the Family, Private Property, and the State* (Penguin, 2010 [1884]).

[83] De Jasay (n 10) 71–72.

[84] For a recent example, see L Pantzerheim, 'On Multiple Objects and Ontic Fixes: Human Rights and the "Forgotten" Politics of the United Nations' Human Rights Based Approach' (2023) 51(2) *Millennium: Journal of International Studies* 519.

constitutionalisation, the truth is anything but. The selection of which human rights to respect, protect and/or fulfil at any given moment is implicitly a selection of some priority or suite of priorities over another. And this is far from an objective or neutral matter; rather, it is one of the state selecting 'whom it had better please' among the range of options available.[85] Should, for example, it please the gender-critical feminist who demands protection for his or her right to freedom of expression? Or should it please the transgender activist who demands fulfilment of their own right to freedom from discrimination through suppression of the 'anti-gender' views of the former? Should it please the parents of preschool children who would prefer their children to avoid the perceived health risks of vaccination? Or should it please the 'public interest' in the form of the rights of those who are at heightened risk from communicable diseases? And so on.

Critiques of rights typically adopt this reasoning and, at this juncture, proceed to describe rights as achieving some unconscious or implicit ideological agenda – the construction, perhaps, of the autonomous self-governing subject of neoliberalism[86] or the instantiation of a 'European colonial project'.[87] But it will be seen that de Jasay's analysis opens up a very different pathway in directing our attention not to ideology, but to the state's ends. In other words, irrespective of the ideology of its 'tenants' and of whatever motives or purposes they might have in mind, the state's 'totalitarian' drive to diminish its reliance on consent does not change.

This initially allows us to hold up for reflection the phenomenon of the positivisation of rights in particular, and thereby to explain why it is that the idea of the purely 'negative' civil right has largely disappeared from rights discourse. For, as de Jasay points out, once the state is understood to possess ends of whatever stripe, it becomes impossible to conceptualise a way in which those ends could be realised through mere respect for negative freedoms. This is for the simple reason that if negative liberty were to be perfectly realised throughout society (de Jasay calls this 'freedom-as-immunity'),[88] this would interfere with the state's capacity to redistribute, which is the means through which, in conditions of political hedonism, it secures consent. In a society of perfect negative liberty, there would be no equality because even if one could somehow equalise financial resources, one could not equalise genetic variability between individuals or sheer luck. In other words, there would still be, so to speak, winners and losers in such a society, and therefore still a means through which a prospective 'tenant' of the state could win consent through creating a majority (the 'losers') and prioritising its material well-being through the redistribution of the resources of the minority (the 'winners'). As such, a system of purely negative freedom would be unstable: it would be vulnerable at

[85] De Jasay (n 10) 103.

[86] See, for example, L Odysseos, 'Human Rights, Liberal Ontogenesis and Freedom: Producing a Subject for Neoliberalism?' (2010) 38(3) *Millennium: Journal of International Studies* 747.

[87] M Mutua, 'The Complexity of Universalism in Human Rights' in A Sajo (ed), *Human Rights with Modesty: The Problem of Universalism* (Springer, 2004) 51.

[88] De Jasay (n 10) 142.

any time to usurpation by a tenant willing to govern through redistribution. And once that happened. freedom-as-immunity would have to disappear, because in restricting the scope of state action, it would 'curtail the State's ability to help' the majority in redistributive terms.[89]

In other words, as soon as it is conceded that the state is necessarily to have its own ends, then a purely 'negative' conceptualisation of rights will disappear. That rights will be 'positivised' necessarily follows. And the twofold benefits to the state in this are equally clear.

First, on the one hand, the positivisation of rights serves as a means through which to operationalise redistribution as a mode of governing per se. Of course, this is most obvious in respect of economic, social and cultural rights. Conceptualising the population as comprising a mass of individual rights holders who all possess ostensibly limitless claims to particular goods (education, housing, food and so on) serves both as a justification for redistribution in the first place – because the state must redirect resources where best suited to realise those claims – and also as the rationale for the existence of the state as the means through which the various preferences and interests represented in those rights claims are reconciled. Since the claims are ostensibly limitless but must necessarily be traded-off against each other, against the scarcity of resources and against the public interest, a mode of managerial governance is constructed. And through this the state is legitimated as such – its existence becomes necessary in order to achieve the optimisation of all of these 'forces' and, crucially, it will be 'tenanted' in such a way as to ensure that it retains majority consensus through heading off any potentially more redistributive rival.

And, naturally, although the dynamic is not so immediately obvious in respect of civil and political rights, precisely the same rationale is evident within that field. The claims in question are not so obviously reconciled through redistribution to the extent that is the case within the field of economic and social rights. But since realising the positive aspects of those rights necessarily requires different emphases in the way in which social resources are deployed and find effect, the consequences of the way in which claims are reconciled in the context of such rights are in their own way as significant in terms of re-allocation.

To return to the example of freedom of expression to illustrate, it will be recalled that the case law of the ECtHR has developed an extensive positive dimension to the scope of that right, encompassing among other things duties to ensure access to impartial and accurate information reflecting a diversity of opinion, to guarantee diversity of content through facilitating access of broadcasters to the market, to put in place an appropriate legislative and administrative framework to guarantee media pluralism, and so on. Fulfilling these duties clearly has resource implications with respect to the public purse. But it also bears broader implications for the allocation of resources in society because it brings with it the need to

[89] ibid 142–43.

make a range of decisions about what is or is not 'impartial and accurate information', 'diversity of opinion', 'diversity of content' and so on. And these decisions will of necessity result in trade-offs having to be made in respect of which views are deemed to require protection so as to achieve the right amount of impartiality, accuracy, diversity and so on.

Such decisions cannot but have consequences in terms of the way in which public goods become distributed. If, for example, it is decided to be the case that scepticism about man-made climate change is not founded in 'accurate information' and is not an opinion which ought to be protected by the umbrella of 'diversity of opinion', then this will cause it to lose prominence in the public square, and this will in turn tend to contribute to particular distributive consequences in terms of the allocation of resources to some ends (connected with preventing climate change) rather than others. In this sense, even the way in which civil and political rights are interpreted with respect to their positive dimensions has the potential to powerfully shape the deployment of resources in a society indirectly – and generally in respect of a particular interpretation of what might be meant by welfare or well-being.

The existence of positive dimensions of human rights therefore has the consequence of operationalising redistribution. In other words, through their vehicle, the immediate and most basic end of the state – that is, sustaining itself through the dispensation of welfare via redistribution and re-allocation of resources – is secured. Because the individual members of the population possess positive rights, it is necessary for the state to reconcile them, and thereby reallocate resources between them. And this in itself allows it to fulfil its immediate requirement to maintain its status by providing it with a means through which to identify and satisfy 'whom it had better please' – ie, to determine whose positive rights to prioritise.

Of course, this in itself provides a ready explanation for why the positivisation of human rights has taken place at all. But it is only in itself half of the story, because although de Jasay emphasised the inevitably redistributive nature of the modern state, he also, as we have seen, was at pains to make clear that matters would not end at that point. The modern state, seeking to maximise its discretionary power, searches for ways to improve its environment by diminishing the requirement for consent and restricting rivalry or competition, since it is those things which threaten its capacity to exercise that discretion. In this respect, the positivisation of human rights proves itself to be even more useful – and it is to this further benefit that we now turn.

VII. The Usefulness of Positive Rights

The state, in de Jasay's 'simulation', seeks to 'emancipate itself'[90] from the status of a mere 'welfare-dispensing drudge' first by acting 'progressively to restrict

[90] ibid 13.

the scope of popular sovereignty'.[91] This is a careful balancing act. The state, relying on an essentially politically hedonistic calculus, must 'maintain majority support at the [point] where it still needs it',[92] so it cannot be seen to openly or nakedly act to narrow the extent to which it is responsive to the demands of the population. Yet being responsive to the demands of the population is something which the state does not want to take too far, lest it find itself in the position, as we have seen, where the 'addictive' effects of welfarism lead to the position of 'drudgery' and the expenditure of all power on the retention of tenure. What the state prefers is instead to calibrate the extent to which it sustains welfarism such that it is able to secure the optimal level of consent while retaining the maximum amount of discretionary power that it can. This means narrowing the requirement to be responsive to the population's demands to within acceptable bounds.

It will be seen straight away that the underlying rationale for the positivisation of rights – 'all human rights for everyone, everywhere' – is a useful mechanism through which to realise that narrowing. If human rights can be thought of as having a neutral instrumental function, then, as we have seen, it is to constitutionalise particular values or norms and thereby place them beyond the scope of democratic decision-making or, crudely, the popular will.[93] Of course, this is to say nothing about the substance of those values or norms, and it is theoretically just as possible for them to enshrine purely 'negative' freedom or 'freedom-as-immunity' as it is possible for them to stake out positive obligations in respect of this or that. But, as we have seen, purely 'negative' freedoms, which restrict the extent to which the state may engage in distributive or allocative decision-making, have the effect of undermining the state's capacity to achieve the optimal level of redistributive welfarism that is necessary to sustain itself. 'Positive' obligations, on the other hand, when put into effect across the gamut of rights under as broad a rubric as 'all human rights for everyone, everywhere', provide an opportunity for it to do precisely that. This is because they are predicated on a fundamentally distributive model – they, as we have seen, operationalise welfarism – while at the same time, crucially, providing a mechanism through which outcomes can be made contingent not on democratic decision-making, but rather on judicial or administrative processes. They extend to individuals the rights to potentially limitless claims or entitlements on various grounds, but at the same time make the realisation of those entitlements contingent on being balanced or traded-off against those either of other specific individuals or the aggregate of other individuals in the form of the public interest (typically on the basis of some assessment of proportionality).

[91] ibid 285.
[92] ibid 273.
[93] Ronald Dworkin provides the most pithy phenomenological description of a right as a 'trump' against the state and hence, of course, the public interest or popular will. See R Dworkin, *Taking Rights Seriously* (Harvard University Press, 1977).

The potential for transforming this into a technical or managerial rather than a democratic exercise is clear. The picture that emerges is not one in which elected decision-makers make policy on the basis that they represent the settled will of the electorate, however reductive or nebulous that connection might be. Rather, it is one in which policy is conducted through assessments being made as to the appropriate or optimal level of balancing of different priorities, perceived through the perspective of whatever duties human rights are construed to impose on the state. To return to the OHCHR's *Plan*, the point is not to facilitate decision-making in the representative sense, but rather to stake out a scope within which decision-making discretion is granted to elected decision-makers, and to stake out the grounds on which that discretion may be restricted or narrowed. 'Legislation, policies and programmes' must 'comply with international human rights standards', there must exist adequately resourced institutions to 'support the implementation of those standards', there must be brought into being 'protection systems and accountability mechanisms' and so on.[94] Elected representatives may come and go, and different political parties may form a government at any one time, but the extent to which they are able to make decisions which 'produce incompatibilities' with the 'planned functioning'[95] of the interaction between all positive rights claims is curtailed. And the result of that, of course, is precisely to make the state's continued existence less contingent on consent – not through diminishing consent to an irrelevance, but by placing its importance within bounds.

This naturally leads us to the second strategy which the state deploys to maximise its discretionary power, which is to 'regulate entry' such that 'while an elected assembly continues technically to dispose of state power', it is made 'difficult … to elect people who dispose of it inappropriately'.[96] Through this strategy, the risk of the possible surfacing of a rival which makes a bid for greater redistribution to a larger majority is reduced, and the requirement on the incumbent or 'tenant' of the state to try to outcompete such rivals likewise diminishes in importance. Again, the effect of this is to reduce the extent to which the state must expend its power on retaining its own status through redistribution, and to thereby expand the extent to which it may exercise its power through its own discretion.

And it is especially noticeable in this regard that UN Human Rights' 'Theory of Change', as set out in the OHCHR's *Plan*, places such an emphasis on careful curation of public participation in decision-making. Although it makes clear that 'individuals and groups must be able to participate in public processes', it immediately caveats this with the proviso that this participation must happen 'meaningfully, safely and in an inclusive manner'.[97] The question therefore naturally arises as to how it is that what is 'meaningful', 'safe' and 'inclusive' is determined, and who it is that makes such decisions while achieving the

[94] OHCHR (n 5) 14.
[95] De Jasay (n 10) 285.
[96] ibid 286.
[97] OHCHR (n 5) 14.

appropriate balance between competing priorities. To return to de Jasay's point, repeatedly made throughout this chapter, it is impossible to 'include' all perspectives in a 'meaningful' and 'safe' way in a society with heterogeneous preferences. This is because some perspectives in such a society will conflict with one another. Decisions must therefore be made about which perspectives are to be 'included' and which are not. And the state must retain a strong grasp on the capacity to make such decisions – because, to repeat, it must always be in a position to 'regulate entry' into the public sphere.

Conceiving of its own task as being to realise the positive rights claims of 'individuals and groups' in society by managing the interactions between those claims is then precisely in line with the incentives which the state faces. And the alternative, to imagine democratic participation as instead being a matter of achieving purely negative 'freedom-as-immunity' vis-a-vis the rights to freedom of expression, association, conscience and so on, would be correspondingly at odds with those incentives because it would imply a lack of control precisely over how 'entry' into the public sphere is achieved. Another way of putting it is that since 'freedom-as-immunity' would curtail the state's ability to present itself as achieving the proper balance between competing rights claims so as to achieve maximum utility, and would interfere with its ability to redistribute and allocate resources in such a way as it sees fit, it must avoid such a scenario emerging at all costs – rather, it must insist that its own governance of the public sphere is necessary in order to realise participation for, as it were, 'everyone, everywhere'.

Hence, to return to an earlier example, the 'right to participation' must be construed not as a means of achieving a laissez-faire approach to matters of expression and association – an issue concerning purely negative 'respect' – but rather a means to actively foster 'meaningful, safe and inclusive' public discourse. This requires, in the first instance, that 'public support' for human rights be made 'widespread'.[98] And this also implies, as we later discover, 'human rights education', improving 'access for persons with disabilities and the marginalization of older persons as a result of technological change', fostering 'innovative forms of participation, such as popular assemblies and citizens' conventions', and so on.[99] It is beside the point to observe that, along the way, de Jasay's case that it is impossible for the state to govern 'neutrally' without priorities of its own is repeatedly, unconsciously made (empowering 'youth and child participation', for instance, is explicitly identified as being important in respect of 'environmental actions', 'anti-gender narratives' are likewise explicitly identified as requiring 'countering' as a means to better achieve inclusivity, and so on).[100] The more important observation is that it is achieving control over how 'entry' is 'regulated' per se that furthers the state's interests, because it is through such a mechanism that it can restrict the extent to which rival forms of public power can intrude.

[98] ibid.
[99] ibid.
[100] ibid.

In summary, then, as we have seen, de Jasay described the state as being endlessly driven to govern in such a way as to be as totalitarian as it could 'get away with' at any given moment. Seeking to maximise its discretionary power, but reliant on using its power to obtain the population's consent, it therefore desires to restrict the scope of popular sovereignty and reduce the likelihood of usurpation by a rival. And seeing things in this way helps us to understand, first, why it is that it would be useful for the state to adopt a positive conceptualisation of human rights in the first place – ie, because a purely negative understanding of 'freedom-as-immunity' will leave the state vulnerable to rivals and leave it unable to win consent. But, second, it also helps us to understand the way in which positive obligations are deployed – that is, as a means through which the state is able to make redistributive or allocative decisions without subjecting those decisions fully to democratic oversight, and to 'regulate entry' into the political arena by facilitating control over, in particular, the way in which the 'positive' aspects of civil and political rights are reconciled between individuals, and between individuals and the public interest.

This is an admittedly abstract and schematic, yet plausible sociological explanation for the phenomenon of positivisation. Describing the matter in this way will, undoubtedly, raise objections, not the least of which being that it would appear to be at odds with the way in which human rights theorists, activists and practitioners typically envisage their role – ie, to shape state conduct in a way that is often diametrically opposed to what individual governments may desire or intend. In other words, adopting de Jasay's lens might be said to cast an unfamiliar light on the activities of human rights advocates by implicating them in the state's very project of government. To the argument made in this chapter, the response will naturally be made that in practice, governments, and individual politicians, typically neglect the importance of positive human rights obligations, particularly with respect to economic, social and cultural rights.[101] Coupled with this response will be an assertion that the human rights movement is, in general, motivated by a more-or-less coherent general idea of justice, and that it is the drive to realise this idea that best explains whatever successes have been made in respect of the positivisation of human rights law after decades of struggle.

However, de Jasay's work allows us to incorporate this conception of the role of positive obligations without damaging the central theme of his analysis, which is that the state ineluctably desires to maximise its discretionary power – the power which remains after it has fulfilled its immediate goal of justifying and sustaining its existence. It will be recalled that this is a value-neutral position in the sense that the reasons why the state seeks to maximise that power are left entirely open. The ends which particular politicians, policy-makers, activists, judges and so forth seek to achieve are not material to what I earlier labelled the universal or transcendent

[101] This is a familiar complaint. See, for example, I Bantekas and L Oette, *International Human Rights Law and Practice*, 4th edn (Cambridge University Press, 2024) 424–31.

ends, which do not vary whatever composition government has at a particular place or time. In this regard, then, it is entirely in keeping with the argument as de Jasay laid it out to suggest that the positivisation of human rights law, whatever *other* ends it might be designed to facilitate, has the fortunate effect of furthering those ends through a mechanism which diminishes the extent to which the state is reliant on consent. That this arises from benevolent motives in respect of this or that individual does not change the underlying logic of the state's rationale, which, to repeat, is to maximise discretionary power *as such* regardless of the particular ends to which that power is directed. That those ends may serve laudatory motives or otherwise is beside the point – which is that, in the end, the state's rationale provides it with a 'totalitarian' bent, as de Jasay described it.

VIII. Conclusion

The argument de Jasay presents in *The State* is *sui generis* and, perhaps because of the 'disturbing'[102] and 'profoundly pessimistic'[103] quality of its conclusions, has generated much admiration but little elucidation or application.[104] Yet its application with respect to the field of human rights law, as I have laid it out here, yields important insights. It reveals the project of human rights to be rooted, alongside whatever motives its advocates and practitioners might have, in the drive of the modern state to maximise its discretionary power through the 'best' form of rule-making.[105] This does not mean that human rights law as such lacks a connection with those motives; rather, it means that those motives – coming under the umbrella of what can be achieved through 'discretionary power' – are brought into alignment with the needs of the state itself. The state must diminish its reliance on democratic consent and 'regulate entry' into the political arena. And it follows that the way in which human rights find effect will be moulded by that necessity.

The implications for the future now fall to be considered. Describing the phenomenon of 'positivisation' as arising from necessity owing to the incentives facing government in modernity not only explains its cause but also maps out its trajectory. We are, then, in the first instance very unlikely to see the process reversed. This is because, for reasons which have now been explained, a 'freedom-as-immunity' conceptualisation of rights obligations is fundamentally unstable under conditions of political hedonism, wherein the winning of consent through claiming to maximise utility is inescapably the state's overarching project. This

[102] Z Stavrinides, 'The State' (1986) 62(4) *International Affairs* 655, 656.

[103] J Buchanan, 'From Redistributive Churning to the Plantation State' (1986) 51 *Public Choice* 241, 243; Buchanan also uses the word 'disturbing' at 241.

[104] Stavrinides (n 102), for example, describes it as 'one of the most remarkable works of political theory to have appeared for a long time'; N Simmonds describes it similarly, in 'The State' (1986) 6 *Legal Studies* 216, 223.

[105] De Jasay (n 56) 12.

means that human rights theory and doctrine will in all likelihood strengthen in its preference for universal positivisation of rights rather than see that preference weaken.

And it follows that we are also unlikely to see the reasoning behind the positivisation of human rights obligations being placed on a principled basis of doctrinal certainty. The hopes that there could be rationalised limits on the scope of positive obligations, or their expansion, will not be realised. This is because – to repeat the point that has been emphasised throughout this chapter – the making of trade-offs between essentially infinite rights claims, and the reconciling of those claims with the 'public interest' through the mechanism of proportionality assessments and 'balancing', is the essence of the governing practice of the modern state. The state, to repeat, can be thought of as the management function which attaches weights to the many differing preferences that inevitably exist in a modern society. And the very positivisation of human rights obligations therefore itself operationalises the state's political reason, in the sense that the phenomenon provides the justification for that weight-setting exercise taking place at all. Since rationalised, principled limits on the expansion of positive obligations would interfere with that exercise by placing its operations within bounds, it follows that such limits are very unlikely to emerge. What is much more likely is that human rights will continue to be deployed to facilitate a 'totalitarian' drift, since ultimately that is the future to which the state's vision is inescapably directed.

The future which beckons, then, is clear. This would appear to be an ever-greater widening of the scope for positive obligations to be read into human rights as a matter of both substantive law and policy, and a consequently increased role for courts, and human rights practitioners, in the formulation of public policy. And the consequences for the state's environment, as laid out in de Jasay's analysis, are equally as evident: a gradual diminishing in the scope of decision-making allocated to the procedures of 'bourgeois democracy', and a gradual elimination of the possibility of rival 'tenants' emerging to chart new political courses. And this is a product not of a particular ideology or set of values, but rather of political conditions which derive from the 'authority generation' which the state necessarily requires.

3

Public Protest in Jeopardy

The Limits of Positive Free Speech Rights

ERIC HEINZE*

I. Introduction

Liberal democracies today widely accept that negative rights entail positive state obligations.[1] For example, assume that a political action group in a Western European nation is planning an open-air demonstration to express an otherwise legal[2] message, and duly provides advance notification to the appropriate local authorities. Under prevailing human rights jurisprudence, the state must respect the negative component of free speech by avoiding undue interference with the event.[3] Yet the state is also generally expected to respect the positive component by taking reasonable steps to accommodate designated gathering and marching sites, for example, through feasible re-routing of traffic, or to safeguard participants, counter-demonstrators and members of the general public.[4] Of course, in the event of disorder, the costs of government investigations or litigation will also generally be paid from the public purse.

We must therefore distinguish between, on the one hand, fully fledged *positive rights* – for example, to minimum levels of nourishment, housing, education or

* This chapter expands on ideas briefly sketched in two op-eds: E Heinze, 'Who Pays for "Free" Speech?', *Merion West* (25 August 2025), www.merionwest.com/who-pays-for-free-speech; and E Heinze, 'Israel-Gaza Protests Have Cost Police at Least £25 Million So Far – But Can You Put a Price on Free Speech?', *The Conversation* (6 March 2024), https://theconversation.com/israel-gaza-protests-have-cost-police-at-least-25-million-so-far-but-can-you-put-a-price-on-free-speech-224710. Many thanks to David McGrogan and Vladislava Stoyanova for their kind invitation to participate in the 2024 Lund seminar on positive obligations, and to the helpful feedback of other participants. All online sources cited herein have been verified as of 29 August 2025

[1] See, eg, L Lavrysen, *Human Rights in a Positive State: Rethinking the Relationship between Positive and Negative Obligations under the European Convention on Human Rights* (Intersentia, 2016) 213–40.

[2] On the heuristic suspension of debates about the content of speech for purposes of examining states' positive obligations, see section II below.

[3] See, eg, *Handyside v United Kingdom* ECtHR, App No 5493/72 (1976) para. 49; *cf* the text accompanying nn 31–32 below.

[4] See, eg, *Plattform 'Ärzte für das Leben' v Austria*, ECtHR, App No 10126/82 (1988).

healthcare[5] – and, on the other hand, the *positive components of negative rights.* For positive rights, resource allocation presents not merely the means to achieve some other end; rather, it becomes an end in itself, such as provision of food, housing and the like. By contrast, for positive components of negative rights, as when the state provides police protection for demonstrators, resource allocation serves as a means to realise some end which is not in itself the allocation of a material resource, such as, in this example, protecting public expression. For fully fledged social and economic rights, then, resource allocation stands as an end in itself – that is, as the very purpose of the right. By contrast, for classically civil rights and liberties, resource allocation stands as a means to respect a right that, in itself, is unrelated to resource allocation.[6]

Due to these differences between ends and means, questions of cost have remained largely distinct from the bulk of free speech jurisprudence. We can read endless court judgments from many countries in which questions of cost are scarcely mentioned, even if the positive component and correlative state expenditures hover unmistakably[7] in the background. To grasp this point, consider the following comparison. A court in an impoverished but otherwise democratic state might legitimately allow authorities to prohibit an otherwise peaceful public demonstration on the grounds that the police would lack resources to protect the public if disruptions were to occur. By contrast, if a court in a prosperous democracy were to find that police unduly obstructed an otherwise peaceful demonstration, then that court might well dispose of the case merely by finding that the negative right was violated, without mentioning positive rights, and yet what is implied is that the state also had a positive duty to place such resources at the police's disposal.[8]

But now assume again a prosperous democracy in which police break up a demonstration that is predominantly peaceful, due only to minor disorder, scuffles or provocations. We can envisage several outcomes. One outcome might run as follows. If the negative right is breached, then the positive right is breached as a matter of sheer logic. For example, if a court legitimately finds that the state breached the negative right, then by definition this means that the police had sufficient means at their disposal to counter any serious dangers without having to obstruct the event. The breach of the positive duty follows by definition from the breach of the negative duty. But here is a second scenario. If the court legitimately

[5] See, eg, International Covenant on Economic, Social and Cultural Rights (ICESCR), 993 UNTS 3, entered into force 3 January 1976.

[6] See, eg, H Shue, *Basic Rights: Subsistence, Affluence & US Foreign Policy*, 2nd edn (Princeton University Press, 1996 [1980]); A Sen, *Development as Freedom* (Oxford University Press, 1999); O O'Neill, *Bounds of Justice* (Cambridge University Press, 2000) 115–42.

[7] See, eg, AT Kenyon and A Scott (eds), *Positive Free Speech: Rationales, Methods and Implications* (Bloomsbury, 2021); AT Kenyon, 'Positive Free Speech: A Democratic Freedom' in A Stone and F Schauer (eds), *The Oxford Handbook of Freedom of Speech* (Oxford University Press, 2021) 231–48.

[8] *cf* J Vorland Wibye, 'Beyond Acts and Omissions: Distinguishing Positive and Negative Duties at the European Court of Human Rights' (2022) 23(4) *Human Rights Review* 479.

finds that the state should have better equipped the police, but failed to do so, thereby compelling the police to impede the free speech, then it is the breach of the positive duty which by definition entails the breach of the negative duty.

A third scenario delivers yet another configuration between the positive and the negative right. If the court legitimately finds that the police were fully equipped but still could not have reliably ensured public safety, then any rationale justifying the positive right serves equally to justify *limiting* the negative right: the positive right was not breached *and therefore* the negative right was not breached. The problem here is that in cases of doubt, even in robust democracies, courts commonly defer to police determinations of risk. Although such democracies can generally claim strong protections for individual expression, public protest therefore ends up in jeopardy, dependent upon opaque determinations about risks to public order.[9]

To examine this conundrum for rights of public expression, I begin in section II by explaining a few preliminary questions about the scope of free speech and about the kind of legal order that such an analysis presupposes. In section III, I recall that the positive component is ordinarily intrinsic even when it is not specifically litigated: in a fully fledged liberal democracy, the right to protest inherently implies some appropriate measure of police protection. Yet, in section IV, using the example of pro-Palestine protests in London in 2025, levels of 'appropriate' protection in this sense are strongly context-dependent, and ambiguities tend to militate against our protest rights.

II. Methodology

Some methodological steps will help to illuminate this problem of positive obligations. First, free speech counts among the most globally recognised rights, having appeared in the 1948 Universal Declaration of Human Rights[10] along with other major international treaties, as well as regional and national laws and instruments.[11] One would be forgiven, then, for expecting that a study of the positive free speech right would have to apply globally if it is to be of any value.

Yet, in this chapter, I will assume only contexts that can be described as longstanding, stable and prosperous democracies. Admittedly, descriptors such as 'longstanding', 'stable', 'prosperous' and indeed 'democracy' are open-ended and subject to dispute.[12] In recent years, influential nations such as the US, India and Brazil have rarely achieved top marks under widely accepted indicators.[13] Only a minority of nations today, perhaps a shrinking minority, still fit this description

[9] See, eg, E Heinze, 'Who Pays for "Free" Speech?', *Merion West* (25 August 2025), www.merionwest.com/who-pays-for-free-speech.
[10] Universal Declaration of Human Rights, GA res 217A (III), UN Doc A/810 at 71 (1948) art 19.
[11] See, eg, E Heinze (ed), *Criminalising Hate Speech* (Asser/Springer, 2025).
[12] E Heinze, *Hate Speech and Democratic Citizenship* (Oxford University Press, 2016) 69–78.
[13] ibid.

today. Nations such as Norway or New Zealand have performed well over many years, even if their democratic institutions and societies too have come under increasing pressure. Nevertheless, this subset of smaller nations suffices to confirm that the model of longstanding, stable and prosperous democracies, whilst setting a high bar, does set an achievable one.[14]

The free speech right does formally extend across the globe, yet for much of the world it remains an 'on paper' right belonging in practice to *lex ferenda* even if it remains nominally *lex lata*. An aspirational study of globally applicable positive rights of expression might well be worth undertaking, but we can only reliably distinguish between respect for negative components of the free speech right versus respect for positive components in sufficiently strong democracies. For example, at the time of writing, if a nation such as Norway or New Zealand were to cancel an LGBTQ+ demonstration, the circumstances would likely be unusual, due to genuine risks posed to participants or to the public and placing unmanageable pressures on the police. Such a decision would likely be reviewable in those countries by a competent and independent judiciary, and, if upheld, would probably confirm that the cancellation did not aim to suppress the pro-LGBTQ+ message per se. Activists would remain free to express that message in other forums, either online or at live events that were easier for the police to protect. In that sense, the denial of the positive component in that instance would leave the negative component essentially unscathed.[15]

Nothing could be less true in, for example, Vladimir Putin's Russia[16] or Xi Jinping's China,[17] where quashing such an event would likely ensue *not* through lack of means to safeguard either the participants or members of the public, even if those were the officially stated grounds, but to silence the message as such in the interest of eliminating voices thought to challenge state authority. For example, in *Lashmankin v Russia* (2017), the European Court of Human Rights aggregated more than a dozen applications from various political groups scattered around the country. The Court found that Russia abused facially neutral notification requirements for the purposes of either cancelling or unduly interfering with rights of peaceful assembly.[18] Such states might even send *agents provocateurs* to incite turbulence, thus seeming to supply public order rationales for bans.[19]

A second point of methodology concerns the substantive scope of the free speech right. If we are to study the positive component of free speech, then our

[14] ibid.

[15] But see the text accompanying n 47 below.

[16] See, eg, UN Human Rights Committee, Concluding observations on the eighth periodic report of the Russian Federation, 1 December 2022, UN Doc CCPR/C/RUS/CO/8, paras 13(d), 28, 29, 32–36.

[17] See, eg, 'Freedom of Expression: China Country Study', *Democracy Web*, Albert Shanker Institute (2024), www.democracyweb.org/study-guide/freedom-of-expression/china.

[18] *Lashmankin v Russia*, App Nos 57818/09 and 14 others, judgment of 7 February 2017.

[19] See, eg, Y Kravtsova, 'Former "Provocateur" Blames Police for Bolotnaya Clashes', *Moscow Times* (21 March 2013), www.themoscowtimes.com/2013/03/21/former-provocateur-blames-police-for-bolotnaya-clashes-a22584.

disagreements about the appropriateness of protecting the negative component must be heuristically suspended. For example, in any given liberal democracy today, legal protections may extend to individuals or groups who seek to express hateful, extremist, terrorist or other such messages[20] that, in some other liberal democracy, would be banned – as in the case of Holocaust denial, which, depending on the form it takes, may be permitted in one democracy, but proscribed in another.[21] Obviously, for the latter type of jurisdiction, no positive state obligation arises, since the ban by definition means that the state has no obligation to protect the negative free speech right. Only with respect to the former type will questions arise about the positive component. However, for the purpose of examining the positive duty, prior questions as to whether Holocaust denial *should* be banned, although pertinent to free speech jurisprudence generally, must be set aside.

A third methodological point is that, in its broadest sense, free speech has always been construed as being linked to several other rights, such as, depending on the context, free association, free assembly, a free press, and freedom of thought and conscience. In this chapter, I refer to free speech as a catch-all, but will assume the relevance of freedoms to engage in activities communicative such as these. Indeed, for my present focus on public protest, rights of speech, association and assembly become largely synonymous.

The fourth methodological point is that a term like 'freedom of expression' is generally more accurate than 'freedom of speech', given that law-makers and courts around the world have construed bans with reference to non-verbal expression, such as silent vigils or displays of symbols or artwork.[22] Again, such examples underscore the considerable inseparability of freedoms of expression, association, assembly and the like. Nevertheless, the term 'free speech' has become widespread, so for the present purposes I will treat these terms as interchangeable. In addition, I will use the term 'speaker' to apply to anyone engaged, or seeking to engage, in verbal or non-verbal communication.

III. Costs of Speech

In October 2014 the far-right Pegida[23] movement began holding weekly street protests in Dresden, a city with a total population of just over 500,000. Six months

[20] E Heinze, 'How We Should – and Shouldn't – Ban Extremist Speech' in R Simcox (ed), *Countering Extremism: Defending Free Speech* (UK Commission for Countering Extremism, 2025).

[21] See, eg, E Fronza, *Memory and Punishment* (Asser, 2018) 3–49.

[22] See, eg, Strafgesetzbuch (StGB) § 86a (Germany) (banning certain public displays of the Nazi swastika).

[23] Pegida stands as an acronym for 'Patriotische Europäer gegen die Islamisierung des Abendlandes' ('Patriotic Europeans against the Islamisation of the West'). See, eg, H Vorländer, M Herold and S Schäller, *Pegida: Entwicklung, Zusammensetzung und Deutung einer Empörungsbewegung* (Springer, 2015).

later, the local authorities reported spending almost €3 million on providing police protection.[24]

In October 2023, the renewed Israel–Gaza conflict led to demonstrations in many countries. A year later, the Metropolitan Police in London, a city of almost nine million inhabitants, recorded that more than £46 million had been spent on safety measures during the intervening five months, suggesting a total at more than £50 million at the time of the present writing.[25]

In June 2025, US Immigration and Customs Enforcement (ICE) waged dozens of surprise raids targeting immigrants in Los Angeles, a city housing around four million residents, sparking demonstrations costing local government more than $20 million,[26] in addition to the subsequent litigation costs.

If we were to dwell on these types of examples, and we could certainly add many more, we would have to conclude that public protests can cost a lot of money.[27] Yet for well over a century, the philosophy, jurisprudence and scholarship of free speech have attended mostly to its negative component, with controversies centred largely on questions of substantive content: what should the state permit or forbid us to say? For example, in the US, an ever-more intricate free speech jurisprudence has emerged for more than a century. Some landmark cases dealing with the speech of political radicals have periodically prompted concerns about public order similar to those still raised today by scenarios such as the three I have just cited here. As late as the 1950s (and contrary to myths about free speech in America dating back to the country's founding), the US Supreme Court upheld crackdowns on activists distributing leaflets,[28] speaking publicly[29] and organising[30] politically. Clearly, insofar as such government restrictions were sustained, no questions arose about the government's positive obligations to protect free speech. The lack of any negative component of the right disposed of any positive component.

[24] '80.000 Arbeitsstunden bei Demos Pegida kostet die Polizei 2,9 Millionen Euro', *NTV* (11 April 2015), www.n-tv.de/politik/Pegida-kostet-die-Polizei-2-9-Millionen-Euro-article14878046.html.

[25] E Heinze, 'Israel-Gaza Protests Have Cost Police at Least £25 Million So Far – But Can You Put a Price on Free Speech?', *The Conversation* (6 March 2024), https://theconversation.com/israel-gaza-protests-have-cost-police-at-least-25-million-so-far-but-can-you-put-a-price-on-free-speech-224710; L Dearden, 'How Gaza Sparked the Biggest UK Protest Movement in Recent History – and a Headache for the Police', *The Guardian* (5 October 2024), www.theguardian.com/world/2024/oct/05/how-gaza-sparked-the-biggest-uk-protest-movement-in-recent-history-and-a-headache-for-the-police.

[26] D Smith, 'L.A. Immigration Protest Costs Reach Nearly $20 Million for Police and City Repairs', *Los Angeles Times* (16 June 2025), www.latimes.com/california/story/2025-06-16/l-a-immigration-protest-costs-hit-nearly-20-million-for-police-repairs.

[27] Heinze (n 9).

[28] See, eg, *Schenck v United States*, 249 US 47 (1919); *Abrams v United States*, 250 US 616 (1919), although see 250 US at 624 (Holmes J, dissenting); *Gitlow v New York*, 268 US 652 (1925), although see 268 US at 673 (Holmes J dissenting, joined by Brandeis J).

[29] See, eg, *Debs v United States*, 249 US 211 (1919); *Feiner v New York*, 340 US 315 (1951), although see 340 US at 327 (Black J dissenting).

[30] See, eg, *Whitney v California*, 274 US 357 (1927), although see 274 US at 375 (Brandeis J concurring, joined by Holmes J); *Dennis v United States*, 341 US at 579 (Black J dissenting) and 341 US at 581 (Douglas J dissenting).

Yet even when the Supreme Court changed course in the 1960s, steadily adopting strong judicial safeguards for the negative component, government authorities placed no great emphasis on the costs of policing public expression, even where police were obviously involved at public expense. In effect, the Court proceeded on a prima facie presumption that government – even at local levels, despite the nation's gaping geographical wealth disparities – could generally be expected to muster the resources required to comply with whatever decisions the Court would hand down. For example, in a 1971 case arising from the Vietnam War era, the Court found that the Constitution protected an individual's right to wear a jacket emblazoned with the words 'Fuck the Draft' in public, contrary to a state government claim that such expression risked a breach of the peace.[31] The implication, although not expressly argued in the case, was that the onus would henceforth have to shift to government to protect even individuals who might be seen as engaging in inflammatory expression. In the US, this obligation is known as a government duty to prevent the 'heckler's veto', meaning that police should not side with members of the public who seek to silence a provocative speaker. Later cases have followed suit, with courts focused on the negative component,[32] although these rulings logically imply positive state duties.

In these cases, it could always be argued that public expression should be as free as is the government's capacity to police it, yet that criterion would only beg the question about how much capacity is to be expected. This deeply political question depends on factors such as how much overall revenue can or should be raised, which in turn involves measures such as taxation, and public debt and borrowing. It is also a question about how much of that revenue should be spent on policing in comparison to other public services, how the funds are spent once distributed and so forth. Rarely can courts intervene in such questions except insofar as cases are brought about the breaches of specific background rules – for example, if a local authority were to fail to disburse funds already legislatively designated for policing.

Recall the aforementioned hypothetical about a cancelled LGBTQ+ demonstration in Norway or New Zealand. Again, heuristically assuming the legality of the message, our ideal model of the longstanding, stable and prosperous democracy would have to maintain a presumption that, in the first instance, such events must be able to proceed and to enjoy police protection commensurate with what local government can reasonably be expected to provide. Yet this is still far from being a self-evident benchmark. Of course, where the message itself is illegal, as are protests by designated extremist groups in many democracies, then those groups' only recourse is either outright disobedience, as in the form of violence, or civil disobedience, whereby they protest peacefully and then face the consequences of arrests, trials and the like.

[31] *Cohen v California*, 403 US 15 (1971).

[32] See, eg, *Bible Believers v Wayne County*, No 13-1635 (6th Cir 2015).

However, for legal messages, instead of restricting speech, the onus must remain on government to police risks of obstruction and danger to protesters or to members of the public. If speakers engage in provocative communications, the police's task is to preserve public order by combating violence and curbing disruption rather than silencing speakers. Action by police forces themselves to cancel or interfere with peaceful protest should be rare and painstakingly justified. In recent decades liberal democracies have adopted these legal presumptions to a considerable extent. One of the first major cases focally concerned with the positive component of free speech was *Plattform 'Ärzte für das Leben' v Austria*, in which the European Court of Human Rights found that Austria had taken serious measures to protect demonstrators marching in opposition to abortion rights, and therefore did not violate the participants' free speech rights for failing to protect some of them from minor scuffles with counter-protesters.[33]

The separation of substantive fulfilment of obligations from questions of available resources is largely absent from the jurisprudence of fully fledged[34] positive rights. Again, available resources arise not merely as concomitant to such rights; rather, they are precisely what these rights lay claim to, so for positive rights, resources play not a supportive, but a central role.[35] Moreover, in any given country, decisions governing revenue and spending tend to be highly political, so monitoring bodies cannot easily reach conclusions about breaches of these rights, and often operate by issuing opinions more in the form of a policy-based recommendation than a forensic adjudication. Except for cases of gross and systemic abuse, or cases brought by individuals that can be adjudicated in case-specific ways, monitors can often do little more than designate areas of need and recommend redress.

As noted earlier, negative rights, by contrast, prompt questions about resource allocation primarily insofar as the positive component is expressly raised. The more obvious the violation of the negative substantive right, the more likely that the finding of breach will moot any further question about a breach of any concomitant positive obligation. Before we return to free speech, some analogies to other rights will help make the point. For example, in a case of severe torture practiced by state officers, claims that the state lacked resources to avoid the abuse would be so far-fetched that no serious government would dare put it to a court. Yet even in harder cases, a violation of the negative right will often dispose of questions about positive obligations. Accordingly, a dispute may arise as to the point at which, say, prison overcrowding amounts to cruel, inhuman, or degrading treatment. In such a case, the state may more plausibly cite financial constraints, even if European courts will impose a high bar.[36] Yet here too, the more convincing the evidence

[33] *Plattform 'Ärzte für das Leben' v Austria*, ECHR App No 10126/82 (1988).
[34] See the text accompanying n 5 above.
[35] See the text accompanying n 6 above.
[36] *cf Torreggiani and Others v Italy*, App No 43517/09, 8 January 2013.

of violation of the substantive negative right, the more likely that this finding will dispose of any question about a breach of the positive obligation. Conversely, the more convincingly state actors can argue that they acted conscientiously in view of the resources available to them, the more likely the logic will be to reverse, such that a breach of the negative component will depend on a breach of the positive one, non-breach of the positive component entailing non-breach of the negative component.

Similarly, in employment contexts, the negative component of protection from discrimination requires that an otherwise qualified candidate not be rejected solely on the grounds of the employer's aversion to disabled persons; by contrast, the positive component of reasonable accommodation depends on available resources. In some disputes about negative rights, the resolution of the negative claim will conclusively dispose of any positive one, as when a particular disability requires little or no expense for the purposes of accommodation, particularly where the employer is of a larger size and capacity. But here too, for a small employer facing a more costly accommodation, the jurisprudential calculation will reverse, such that non-violation of the positive component will logically imply non-violation of the negative component.

In the aforementioned *Lashmankin* case, any positive obligation on Russia to facilitate the protesters would, at most, amount to the police protection ordinarily due for any peaceful assembly, given the lack of evidence of any risk to public order or safety in those cases. The breach of the positive liberty followed from the breach of the negative one, albeit in little more than a tautological sense. Accordingly, the Russian state did not even attempt to suggest that it lacked adequate resources to ensure public safety, and several other cases have reached identical conclusions.[37]

IV. From Controversy to Ambiguity: The Example of Pro-Palestine Protests

Campaigns against Israeli state conduct and policy have taken place for many years. During the first quarter of the twenty-first century, this has counted among the most protested foreign policy issues, perhaps even the single most protested issue, in major Western nations.[38] Given the fierce emotions involved on all sides, these battles shed light on the broader dilemmas surrounding positive free speech rights. At times of Israel–Palestine flare-ups, these protests have

[37] See, eg, *Primov and Others v Russia*, ECHR App No 17391/06 (2014); *Barankevich v Russia* ECHR App No 10519/03 (2007).

[38] However, on difficulties of measurement and comparison, see, eg, M Biggs, 'Size Matters: Quantifying Protest by Counting Participants' (2016) 47(3) *Sociological Methods & Research* 351; F Vassallo, 'The Evolution of Protest Research: Measures and Approaches' (2018) 51(1) *PS: Political Science & Politics* 67.

attracted large crowds.[39] Indeed, after the Hamas attacks of 7 October 2023, worldwide protests against Israel increased in frequency, becoming regular events and involving thousands of protesters.[40] For present purposes, my aim is not to take sides on the situation in the Middle East or on the protesters' substantive opinions, but only to examine a state's positive free speech duties under highly conflicted circumstances.

In January 2025, pro-Palestine protesters notified London's Metropolitan Police ('the Met') of a planned demonstration outside BBC's Broadcasting House headquarters to picket what in their view had been the network's defective coverage of the war. However, given the proximity of a nearby synagogue to the gathering point, and the scheduling of the march on a Saturday, which is the Jewish Sabbath, the Met declined to approve the march, citing risks of public disturbance. The Met referred to concerns voiced by Jews that they had felt unsafe by such protests held in central locations.[41] In earlier months, reports had surfaced about synagogues targeted by such marches in various countries,[42] although one organiser claimed that Saturdays were the only feasible days for the events and that their previous protests had not targeted synagogues.[43]

If we were to assume no spending limit, one solution would be to offer extensive police protection at the synagogue as a means of authorising the protest. However, any such suggestion illustrates how vagueness surrounding the positive free speech component entails vagueness of the negative component. Clearly, a situation lacking any spending limit can rarely if ever be assumed, so questions obviously arise as to appropriate limits; however, such a figure would then depend in turn on prior estimations of risk, which would amount to little

[39] See, eg, R Blundy, 'Thousands Line London's Streets for Pro-Palestine Protest during 12-Hour Gaza Ceasefire', *The Standard* (26 July 2014), www.standard.co.uk/news/london/thousands-line-the-streets-in-london-for-propalestine-protest-as-12hour-ceasefire-is-held-in-gaza-9630516.html; N Slawson, 'Thousands Gather in London for Palestine Solidarity March', *The Guardian* (22 May 2021), www.theguardian.com/uk-news/2021/may/22/thousands-gather-in-london-for-palestine-solidarity-march; I Pappe, 'The BDS Movement in the United Kingdom: Back to Where it All Started' in R Bocco and I Saïd (eds), *De/Colonising Palestine* (Graduate Institute Publications, 2025) 593–609.

[40] See, eg, E Chenoweth, S Hammam, J Pressman and J Ulfelder, 'Protests in the United States on Palestine and Israel, 2023–2024' (2024). *Social Movement Studies* 1, https://doi.org/10.1080/14742837.2024.2415674.

[41] D Boffey, 'Met Police Accused of Stopping Pro-Palestine Marches outside BBC HQ', *The Guardian* (8 January 2025), www.theguardian.com/uk-news/2025/jan/08/met-police-accused-of-stopping-pro-palestine-marches-outside-bbc-hq; N Badshah et al, 'Met Bans Pro-Palestine March from Gathering outside BBC Headquarters', *The Guardian* (9 January 2025), www.theguardian.com/uk-news/2025/jan/09/met-bans-pro-palestine-march-from-gathering-outside-broadcasting-house; H Siddique, 'Pressure Grows on Met over "Heavy-Handed" Policing of Pro-Gaza Protest', *The Guardian* (31 January 2025), www.theguardian.com/uk-news/2025/jan/31/pro-gaza-protest-london-met-police-tactics-trade-unions-complaint.

[42] See, eg, C von Quednow and E Levenson, 'Pro-Palestinian Protest outside LA Synagogue Criticized as "Antisemitic" after Street Fights with Pro-Israel Protesters', *CNN* (24 June 2024), https://edition.cnn.com/2024/06/24/us/los-angeles-synagogue-palestinian-israeli-protest-violence; A Vilches Arguello, 'Anti-Israel Protesters Target European Synagogues amid Escalating Antisemitism Crisis', *The Algemeiner* (26 May 2025); www.algemeiner.com/2025/05/26/anti-israel-protesters-target-european-synagogues-amid-escalating-antisemitism-crisis.

[43] Boffey (n 41).

more than guesswork, given the volume of protesters and the heated nature of the controversy.

Again, unless specific legal rules were at issue, few courts would possess the authority or competence to issue precise determinations about resource allocation. Moreover, even if such a massive deployment were possible, questions would arise as to whether Jews would feel able to conduct Sabbath services under such conflictual circumstances. That point shows how questions about resources involve not only cost and availability but also strategy, equally beyond the scope of judicial determination. In such instances, independent expert testimony can be solicited, although often it is only 'battles of the experts' that result. Insofar as judges cannot easily challenge the state on these minutiae, they will generally be left with no choice but to defer to government and police assessments.[44]

One familiar proposal in such circumstances is for police to authorise an alternative marching route, but if the original one has been selected as thematically or symbolically relevant to the protest's theme, as was BBC Broadcasting House on this occasion, then the route itself becomes part of the message, meaning that the state modifies the message as a condition both for the demonstrators to express it and for the police to fulfil its positive obligation.[45] As the organisers argued: 'The BBC is a major institution – it is a publicly funded state broadcaster and is rightly accountable to the public … It is unacceptable for the police to misuse public order powers to shield the BBC from democratic scrutiny.'[46]

Admittedly, at an alternative event, the demonstrators would be free to speak to the gathered crowd about the re-routing and to openly condemn it, which for some onlookers might serve more to amplify than to mute their message. Yet this too is an essentially strategic concern. Ultimately, an adjudicator must either accept or reject state claims about its capacity to fulfil its positive obligations; but it would be illegitimate (and indeed bizarre) for a government, aiming to deprive protesters of a public forum, to adduce nothing more than the strategic grounds that an alternative event would prove more effective for expressing their views. This would still amount to interference, however benign the intention or outcome might be, since the manner of communicating a message, however well or poorly conceived, cannot be separated from the message itself. To interfere with the manner is to interfere with the message.[47]

In view of the ban on marching on the BBC, the Met initially proposed Russell Square as an alternative London site, but the Palestinian Forum in Britain said they 'categorically rejected' this suggestion,[48] presumably on the grounds that this

[44] *cf*, eg, A Lvovsky, 'The Judicial Presumption of Police Expertise' (2017) 130 *Harvard Law Review* 1995; A Lvovsky, 'Rethinking Police Expertise' (2021–22) 131 *Yale Law Journal* 475.

[45] *cf* E Heinze, 'Taking Legitimacy Seriously: A Return to Deontology' (2017) 32(3) *Constitutional Commentary* 631.

[46] Boffey (n 41).

[47] See, eg, Heinze (n 45).

[48] G Abdul and N Badshah, 'More Than 70 Arrested at London Protest against Israel's War in Gaza', *The Guardian* (18 January 2025), www.theguardian.com/world/2025/jan/18/london-protest-israel-gaza-war-arrests.

site, although central, does not abut structures associated either with government or with mainstream media in the way in which the protesters would have deemed germane to their message. According to the protest organisers, only after 'immense public pressure' was the protest then authorised at Whitehall,[49] in the centre of UK government operations and one of the customary sites for high-profile demonstrations in Britain. As the marchers advanced towards London's landmark Trafalgar Square, more than 70 were arrested for breaking through the police barrier.

Consider now how opposing claims about these arrests further illustrate the ambiguities that arise between negative and positive components of the free speech right. BBC Broadcasting House stands at a distance of just over one kilometre from Trafalgar Square. Presumably a large crowd continuing from Whitehall to Trafalgar Square could be halted well before reaching that structure. The Muslim Association of Britain indeed criticised the Met's decision to block the march, calling it 'an outrageous assault on democracy, freedom of assembly, and freedom of expression'.[50] The Met's statements in turn suggested that their concern was not with the entire crowd, but with participants who might then proceed to a spin-off action in the proscribed areas. In Slonecki's words:

> We could not have been clearer about the conditions in place … Protesters were to remain in Whitehall with no march towards the BBC. I am quite confident this was a coordinated breach with the intention being to reach the BBC at Portland Place in defiance of the conditions. There is video footage of one of the organisers clearly inciting the crowd to join a march and one of the organisations involved has released a statement this evening confirming as much. At the same time as the group was attempting to force its way past police lines, camera crews were seen arriving in Portland Place. It is unlikely that the timing was simply a coincidence.[51]

Factors that might at first appear to be neutrally and objectively ascertainable, such as crowd numbers, or distance between authorised and unauthorised protest sites, turn out to depend on disputed factors such as protesters' intentions and police capacity. Contradicting Slonecki's claim that the Met had made its marching conditions clear, the Green Party deputy leader Zack Polanski accused the Met of arresting protesters 'without warning for inadvertently being outside the ill-defined permitted area'.[52] Protesters also claimed that 'the Met falsely accused protesters carrying flowers – including the former Labour leader Jeremy Corbyn and his shadow chancellor, John McDonnell – of forcing their way through police lines when video footage shows they were initially waved through by officers'.[53]

[49] ibid.
[50] ibid.
[51] ibid.
[52] Siddique (n 41).
[53] ibid. Protesters sometimes hold flowers to signal their non-violent intentions. See, eg, T Reale, 'How Flowers Help to Shape Social Movements', *Charleston City Paper* (12 April 2025), https://charlestoncitypaper.com/2025/04/12/reale-how-flowers-help-to-shape-social-movements/#:~:text=In%20the%201960s%2C%20the%20term,yet%20powerful%20expressions%20of%20resistance.

However, the cited footage, which was posted only on the social media site X, actually displays the police voicing a crowd filtering command, leaving it unclear whether this indicated individual permissions to allow people to pass out of the designated protest area or a more general permission for marchers to proceed to Trafalgar Square, only then to arrest them.[54]

To further complicate matters, at the time of writing, a group called 'Palestine Action' has been added to a list of more than eighty organisations[55] currently outlawed under the Terrorism Act (2000). It became the first organisation to be banned solely on the grounds of having caused 'serious damage to property' without physical harm to individuals. One estimation of the material damage caused by Palestine Action in several hundred acts of sabotage from 2020 through to 2025, often to British military infrastructure or equipment, reached £55 million,[56] hence a taxpayer cost of over £100 million when combined with policing expenditures.[57]

The controversies surrounding this classification further dramatise the indeterminacy shrouding the positive component of free speech. A democratic government cannot set the total damage amount to property too low, as many groups engage only in symbolic or trivial forms of disruption. To draw a comparison, in 2022 animal rights protesters in Manchester poured out cartons of milk onto the floor of a major UK supermarket during daytime shopping hours.[58] They also placed placards over joints of beef with the aim of drawing attention to plant-based alternatives. Animal rights groups have also engaged in acts of trespass or minor damage to call attention to animal suffering,[59] often running risks of criminal charges or fines. To date, however, no such organisation has been listed in the UK as terrorist. Yet nor can a government set the total cost excessively high, which would become an official and open invitation for groups to tread near the line whilst always falling just shy of it; indeed, for that same reason, the government cannot state any pounds-and-pence threshold at all.

Public protest therefore creates a conundrum. The state maintains a positive obligation to safeguard free speech, but remains silent about how far that

[54] Palestine Solidarity Campaign (@PSCupdates), https://x.com/PSCupdates/status/1881015173277966519, post of 19 January 2025, 4:25 pm.

[55] 'Proscribed Terrorist Groups or Organisations', *Gov.uk*, updated 11 July 2025, www.gov.uk/government/publications/proscribed-terror-groups-or-organisations--2/proscribed-terrorist-groups-or-organisations-accessible-version.

[56] 'Cost of Damage by Palestine Action Could Hit £55m', *The Times* (21 June 2025), www.thetimes.com/uk/crime/article/palestine-action-vandalism-xrcnlpdgh?utm_source=chatgpt.com.

[57] See the text accompanying n 25 above.

[58] P Britton, '"Animal Rebellion" Protesters Pour Milk out onto Floor inside Manchester Marks and Spencer', *Manchester Evening News* (16 October 2022), www.manchestereveningnews.co.uk/news/greater-manchester-news/animal-rebellion-protesters-pour-milk-25272333.

[59] J Roberts, 'Shocking Reality of Free Range Egg Farm That Supplies Tesco and Sainsbury's', *Metro* (28 January 2020), https://metro.co.uk/2020/01/28/secret-camera-films-chickens-laying-eggs-surrounded-by-rotting-birds-12131921; 'A Portrait of King Charles III was Defaced in the Latest Act of Activist Vandalism', *Associated Press* (12 June 2024), https://apnews.com/article/britain-king-charles-iii-portrait-wallace-gromit-7b58e557321e09752f6029e817212fbb.

obligation extends, indeed precisely as to those protesters who, due to their controversial messages, are likely to stand in greatest need of protection. This ambiguity surrounding the positive component leads in turn to uncertainty about the negative component; yet, uncertainty about whether one may or may not speak lawfully creates risks of chilling expression – we refrain from expression because it *may* be unlawful, even when it is perfectly lawful. To be sure, it is not 'serious damage' per se under the Terrorism Act 2000 that has provoked criticism. Nonetheless, according to one report: 'UN experts, civil liberties groups, cultural figures and hundreds of lawyers have condemned the ban [on Palestine Action] as draconian and said it sets a dangerous precedent by conflating protest with terrorism',[60] suggesting it is instead the lack of precision as to what counts as serious damage that leaves the extent of protest rights in the UK unclarified.

Notwithstanding the controversies surrounding the Gaza war and protests, one reason why the demonstrations could remain peaceful was that they were met with relatively small numbers of counter-demonstrators, sparking low-level hostilities at worst. By contrast, when patently violent confrontations between opposing groups do occur, the positive obligation becomes even murkier. For example, in 2011, German neo-Nazi groups announced demonstrations commemorating the Allied bombing of Dresden in 1945. Calls for banning the events failed, given insufficient evidence of lawless conduct or the likelihood thereof. Nevertheless, any number of individual marchers had previous criminal records and certainly came prepared to engage in acts of violence; meanwhile, some far-left counter-demonstrators also had official records of having proceeded violently against neo-Nazis and even against police for authorising the demonstrations.[61]

To limit breaches of the peace, the city deployed a force of 4,500 officers,[62] resulting in costs of several million euros and injuries inflicted on participants as well as police officers, along with extensive property damage.[63] Yet not even the wealthiest city can sustain such incidents in any ongoing way. Our sad lesson is that the more controversial the issues and actors concerned, and hence the more in need of public confrontation and debate, the less likely it is that protesters will be able to rely upon their events going forward. Indeed, for years, Germany, like Britain, has engaged in ongoing and fraught debates about what counts as extremist speech, and whether and when it can or should be banned.[64] Clearly, the more

[60] H Siddique, 'Ban on Palestine Action to Take Effect after Legal Challenge Fails', *The Guardian* (4 July 2025), www.theguardian.com/politics/2025/jul/04/ban-on-palestine-action-to-take-effect-after-legal-challenge-fails.

[61] 'Gewalt und Chaos in Dresdens Straßen', *Stern* (19 February 2011), www.stern.de/panorama/verbrechen/nazi-aufmarsch-blockiert-gewalt-und-chaos-in-dresdens-strassen-3667250.html.

[62] 'Seifenblasen und Pflastersteine', *Taz* (20 February 2011), https://taz.de/Nazi-Blockaden-in-Dresden/!5126271.

[63] 'Mindestens 82 Polizisten verletzt', *FAZ* (20 February 2011), www.faz.net/aktuell/politik/krawalle-in-dresden-mindestens-82-polizisten-verletzt-1591597.html.

[64] See, eg, Heinze (n 20).

ambiguous the claim to a positive obligation of protecting free speech, the less likely it is that the negative component will be deemed to be breached by annulation or by state failures to take adequate measures to protect speakers.

V. Conclusion

For the most part, today's democracies have developed strong free speech rights. These protections clearly extend to the negative component of the free speech right, ensuring that even inflammatory expression will enjoy a strong presumption of legality. In principle, they also extend to the positive component, requiring states to provide proactive safeguards for speakers. However, upper and lower spending limits, and concomitant levels of protection, remain overwhelmingly political questions. The more intricate a fact pattern, the more governments will defer to police determinations about risk and deployment of resources, meaning in turn that, in practice, courts will generally defer to the state. Once a state alleges its incapacity to fulfil resource-intensive positive obligations, this may well suffice for judges to reject findings that the government or police have breached their negative duties. In such cases, the positive duty will have served to shield the state more than the individual rights holder. The grim reality is that Western democracies' longstanding presumptions in favour of speech will not necessarily equate to government or judicial presumptions in favour of protesters.

4

Is Climate Change Mitigation within the Scope of Positive Human Rights Obligations?

BENOIT MAYER

I. Introduction

Climate change has increasingly been presented as a human rights issue. For instance, Mary Robinson has asserted that 'climate change is the greatest threat to human rights in the 21st century',[1] whereas Amnesty International has argued that a government's failure to phase out fossil-fuel emissions 'is a violation of some of our most fundamental human rights'.[2] Building on this notion, national courts[3] and international human rights institutions have repeatedly accepted the notion that a state's failure to act on climate change could constitute a breach of its obligation to protect human rights.[4] Similar arguments have occasionally been extended to corporations.[5]

Two types of arguments need to be distinguished at the outset: one relating to adaptation to climate change and the other to climate change mitigation. Adaptation to climate change consists in efforts aimed at reducing the impacts of climate change on society and ecosystems. These efforts are often implemented

[1] M Robinson, 'Why Climate Change is a Threat to Human Rights', *Ted Talk* (May 2015), www.ted.com/talks/mary_robinson_why_climate_change_is_a_threat_to_human_rights.

[2] Amnesty International, 'Climate Change', www.amnesty.org/en/what-we-do/climate-change.

[3] See *Urgenda v The Netherlands*, ECLI:NL:RBDHA:2015:7145 (District Court of The Hague, 24 June 2015), ILDC 2456 (NL 2015); *Klimaatzaak v Belgium* (Court of Appeal of Brussels, 30 November 2023); *Neubauer v Germany*, ECLI:DE:BVerfG:2021:rs20210324.1bvr265618; *Do-Hyun Kim v South Korea*, 2020Hun-Ma389 (29 August 2024); *Held v State of Montana* (Montana District Court, 14 August 2023) CDV-2020-307, 2023 WL 5229257.

[4] See, eg, CEDAW et al, 'Joint Statement on "Human Rights and Climate Change"' (16 September 2019), https://perma.cc/6VXT-LAD4; CESCR, Concluding Observations, Sixth Periodic Report of Norway, UN Doc E/C.12/NOR/CO/6 (2 April 2020), paras 10–11; ECtHR, *Verein KlimaSeniorinnen v Switzerland*, App No 53600/20 (9 April 2024) https://hudoc.echr.coe.int/?i=001-233206.

[5] *Milieudefensie v Royal Dutch Shell* (Court of Appeal of The Hague, 12 November 2024) ECLI:NL:GHDHA:2024:2100.

at the national or local level – for instance, through disaster-risk reduction or freshwater management policies. In contrast, climate change mitigation refers to action aimed at addressing the roots of the problem – the increased atmospheric concentration of greenhouse gas (GHG) – by reducing sources of such emissions or enhancing sinks and reservoirs. While a state's adaptation policy can achieve tangible outcomes on a relatively short timescale, climate change mitigation requires global efforts over a long period of time before it can make a significant difference on atmospheric GHG concentrations.

As far as climate change adaptation is concerned, the application of human rights law as the source of an obligation to act on climate change is relatively straightforward and uncontroversial.[6] States have an obligation to protect individuals from adverse physical events.[7] This obligation applies regardless of whether these events are caused (or exacerbated) by climate change. As such, the attribution of an adverse event to climate change is irrelevant to the application of human rights law as the source of an obligation of the state to protect the individuals under its jurisdiction in the face of this adverse event. Similarly, whether a state has an obligation under human rights law not to expel an individual to a country where she would face dire living conditions depends on how doing so would affect the right of that individual, not on whether the situation in the country of origin is causally related to climate change (eg, sea-level rise).[8] There may be legal arguments about the responsibility of states or corporations *qua* emitters to promote adaptation to climate change, but those arguments would need to rely on primary rules from fields other than human rights law.

This chapter focuses on another question, namely the question as to whether human rights law can also be applied as requiring a state to take measures aimed at mitigating climate change. The prevailing argument in scholarship and judicial decisions points out that climate change impacts the enjoyment of a wide range of human rights. For instance, the exacerbation of extreme weather events as a result of climate change may threaten the enjoyment of the right to life. As states have an obligation to take appropriate measures to protect human rights, so the argument goes, they must take measures to prevent harm from climate change, not only via adaptation, but also, and more preventively still, via climate change mitigation measures. Yet, as this chapter shows, the question is far more complex than often admitted in the academic literature or in judicial decisions, and there are stronger objections to the application of human rights law as the source of an obligation to mitigate climate change than is typically acknowledged. In short, human rights

[6] See *Leghari v Pakistan*, PLD 2018 Lahore 364 (25 January 2018), para 21; CESCR, Concluding Observations, Sixth Periodic Report of Canada, UN Doc E/C.12/CAN/CO/6 (4 March 2016), paras 53–54; CESCR, Concluding Observations, Sixth Periodic Report of Finland, UN Doc E/C.12/FIN/CO/6 (28 November 2014), para 9; *Daniel Billy v Australia*, UN Doc CCPR/C/135/D/3624/2019 (18 September 2022).

[7] See, eg, ECtHR, *Budayeva v Russia*, App No 15339/02 (20 March 2008).

[8] A Betts, *Survival Migration: Failed Governance and the Crisis of Displacement* (Cornell University Press, 2013) 16–17.

may not be the most natural place to look for legal grounds to justify ambitious action on climate change mitigation. While courts have applied human rights as the source of an obligation to mitigate climate change, their decisions are criticised as incoherent,[9] arguably because of their shaky foundations.

Two main objections to the prevailing argument can be briefly outlined at this point. The first objection is that a state's failure to mitigate climate change does not directly affect any individual victims. The harm that a state causes by failing to mitigate climate change is diffuse and protracted in nature. It needs to be emphasised that the point here is not about an epistemological difficulty with the identification of victims (as would be the case for a surveillance regime infringing individuals' data privacy without their knowledge, where there *are* victims, although the applicant and the judge do not know who they are), but a more fundamental, ontological issue: there simply *are* no victims, in any meaningful sense of the word, of a state's failure to take appropriate action on climate change mitigation. The absence of victims is at least a major procedural issue, as the status of victim is often a condition for an individual to have standing before a human rights institution.[10] Yet it may also be a substantive issue: it is far from obvious that human rights law applies against policies that only have remote and diffuse effects on the enjoyment of human rights.

The second objection is that human rights law is, at best, ambivalent towards measures and policies aimed at mitigating climate change. Efforts to reduce GHG emissions come generally at an economic, social and environmental cost.[11] The (strong and persuasive) political argument in favour of ambitious action on climate change mitigation relies on the understanding that these costs are justified in the light of the significant benefit of avoiding more interference with the climate system. Rebuilding our energy system, for instance, is unlikely to be cheap, but is worth doing if this avoids further irremediable harm to society and ecosystems through additional global warming. The underlying comparison of costs and benefits (economic and otherwise) typically follows a broad utilitarian perspective: it considers the costs and the benefits for society as a whole, at a global scale and over the long term. In contrast, human rights lenses tend to emphasise observable effects on individuals living today, especially those within the state's own territory. As such, human rights law, properly interpreted, puts more weight on the cost of climate action – its immediate effect, for

[9] On the ECtHR's decision in *Verein KlimaSeniorinnen*, see, eg, J Sumption, 'ECHR's Climate Change Ruling is its Boldest Intrusion Yet' *The Times* (14 April 2024); V Stoyanova, 'KlimaSeniorinnen and the Question(s) of Causation' (*Verfassungsblog*, 7 May 2024), https://verfassungsblog.de/klimaseniorinnen-and-the-questions-of-causation; G Letsas, 'The European Court's Legitimacy after *Klimaseniorinnen*' (2024) 5 *European Convention on Human Rights Law Review* 444; OW Pedersen, 'Disruption, Special Climate Considerations, and Striking the Balance' (2025) 119 *American Journal of International Law* 129.

[10] See, eg, European Convention for the Protection of Human Rights and Fundamental Freedoms (adopted 4 November 1950, entered into force 3 September 1953) (hereinafter ECHR), consolidated, art 34.

[11] Without accounting for these costs, it is difficult to understand why states, corporations and individuals do not readily stop all GHG emissions.

instance, on individuals losing their job – than on the more remote benefit of mitigating climate change for society generally, or for populations abroad, future generations and other species. While the scope of human rights law may evolve to put more emphasis on collective interests, extraterritoriality and future harm, nothing short of a complete metamorphosis would alter the fact that human rights law puts more emphasis on the cost of mitigating climate change than on its benefits.

Beyond the debate on climate change and human rights, this chapter can be read as a case study illustrating certain issues with positive human rights obligations. There is no limit to the range of measures that any government could take. Many, perhaps all of these measures would have some sort of positive effect on the enjoyment of some human rights by some people, among other consequences. Beyond climate change mitigation, a state's action on road safety, public health or military spending, for instance, could also be justified as action aimed at protecting the enjoyment of human rights. There is at least a theoretical risk that positive human rights obligations could be invoked to justify a never-ending expansion of the scope of human rights law and the competence of courts and other institutions tasked with applying it, prompting these courts and institutions to balance the costs and benefits of various policy options, thus essentially taking over democratic governments. Such judicial over-reach needs to be avoided (if one accepts the value of democracy), most likely by limiting the application of human rights law to situations where there is a victim losing the enjoyment of a right as a consequence of the state's action or inaction. In other words, the application of positive human rights obligations should be limited to circumstances where significant individual harm would be a proximate consequence of the failure to act.

The next section presents the prevailing argument in favour of applying human rights law as the source of an obligation to mitigate climate change. Sections III and IV present more systematically the two objections highlighted above, namely the absence of victim of a state's failure to mitigate climate change and the ambivalence of human rights law towards action on climate change mitigation. Section V concludes.

II. A Human Rights Obligation to Mitigate Climate Change?

A. Climate Law

Scientists have long understood that anthropogenic emissions of GHGs are causing unprecedented changes in our climate system,[12] and that this results in

[12] JT Houghton et al, *Climate Change: The IPCC Scientific Assessment. Report Prepared for Intergovernmental Panel on Climate Change by Working Group I* (Cambridge University Press, 1990) xi; PA Arias et al, 'Technical Summary' in V Masson-Delmotte et al (eds), *Climate Change 2021: The Physical Science Basis. Contribution of the Working Group I to the Sixth Assessment Report of the Intergovernmental Panel on Climate Change* (Cambridge University Press, 2021) 35, 41.

widespread and irreversible ecological and social harm on a planetary scale.[13] In particular, the Intergovernmental Panel on Climate Change (IPCC) has 'high confidence' that '[c]limate change has caused substantial damages, and increasingly irreversible losses, in [many] ecosystems', 'has reduced food security and affected water security', has caused 'increases in extreme heat events [that] have resulted in human mortality and morbidity' and 'has caused adverse impacts on human health, livelihood and key infrastructure'.[14] Scientists have established that additional GHG emissions exacerbate climate change and its adverse impacts on a near-linear basis.[15]

Scientists have thus laid the ground for compelling ethical and policy arguments for reducing global GHG emissions. States have long acknowledged 'change in the Earth's climate and its adverse effects' as 'a common concern of humankind'.[16] They have engaged in three decades of intense negotiations and have adopted and widely ratified three main treaties.[17] Yet, states have also acknowledged that their individual efforts fall short of their collective ambition.[18] In particular, the 'nationally determined contributions' that states have communicated under the Paris Agreement are insufficient to ensure the achievement of the Paris Agreement's objective of holding global warming 'well below' 2°C, or even close to 1.5°C, above pre-industrial levels.[19] Continuing negotiations have struggled to address this ambition gap.

The existence of climate treaties does not preclude the application of relevant norms from other sources. Thus, it has been argued that customary international law, which builds on the concept of sovereign equality, cannot allow a state's unfettered freedom to cause harm to all other states through GHG emissions.[20] As such, states certainly have an obligation to exercise due diligence with the view not to cause harm to the global environment.[21] Some multilateral environmental

[13] WJ McG Tegart et al, *Climate Change: The IPCC Scientific Assessment. Report Prepared for Intergovernmental Panel on Climate Change by Working Group II* (Australian Government Publishing Service, 1990) ch 5 at 10; HO Pörtner et al, 'Technical Summary' in HO Pörtner et al (eds), *Climate Change 2022: Impacts, Adaptation and Vulnerability. Working Group II Contribution to the Sixth Assessment Report of the Intergovernmental Panel on Climate Change* (Cambridge University Press, 2022) 52.

[14] Core Writing Team et al (eds), *Climate Change 2023: Synthesis Report. Contribution of Working Groups I, II and III to the Sixth Assessment Report of the Intergovernmental Panel on Climate Change* (IPCC, 2023) 1, 5–6.

[15] RP Allan et al, 'Summary for Policymakers' in Masson-Delmotte et al (n 12) 28.

[16] United Nations Framework Convention on Climate Change (adopted 9 May 1992, entered into force 21 March 1994) 1771 UNTS 107 (hereinafter UNFCCC), preamble para 2.

[17] ibid; Kyoto Protocol to the United Nations Framework Convention on Climate Change (adopted 11 December 1997, entered into force 16 February 2005) 2303 UNTS 162; Paris Agreement (adopted 12 December 2015, entered into force 4 November 2016) 3156 UNTS 79.

[18] See, eg, Decision 1/ CMA.5, 'Outcome of the First Global Stocktake', FCCC/PA/CMA/2023/16/Add.1 (15 March 2024) 2, para 21.

[19] Paris Agreement (n 17) art 2(1)(a). See also UNEP, *Emissions Gap Report 2024* (24 October 2024).

[20] B Mayer, 'The Relevance of the No-Harm Principle to Climate Change Law and Politics' (2016) 19 *Asia Pacific Journal of Environmental Law* 79; C Voigt, 'State Responsibility for Climate Change Damages' (2008) 77 *Nordic Journal of International Law* 1.

[21] B Mayer, 'Climate Change Mitigation as an Obligation under Customary International Law' (2023) 48 *Yale Journal of International Law* 105; B Mayer, *International Law Obligations on Climate Change Mitigation* (Oxford University Press, 2022).

agreements imply a similar obligation to mitigate climate change, as a way to protect particular environmental resources. For instance, the International Tribunal for the Law of the Sea has interpreted Part XII of the UN Convention on the Law of the Sea, on the protection of the marine environment, as the source of a 'stringent' due diligence obligation of states to mitigate climate change.[22] Advocates for climate action may find it particularly attractive to make similar arguments based on human rights law, as this could facilitate access to national courts and regional human rights courts, or to international quasi-judicial bodies, or even pave the road to state-to-state litigation, potentially leading to judicial or quasi-judicial decisions that might prompt states to enhance their action on climate change mitigation.

B. Links with Human Rights Law

For a long time, climate change was not generally viewed as a human rights issue.[23] Rather, it was approached almost systematically in a broad utilitarian language: as a threat, for instance, to 'natural and managed ecosystems', 'socio-economic systems' and 'human health and welfare'.[24] When states agreed to mitigate climate change, they aimed primarily 'to allow ecosystems to adapt naturally to climate change, to ensure that food production is not threatened and to enable economic development to proceed in a sustainable manner'.[25] Climate change mitigation was thus presented as an objective of public interest, and not specifically as a way to protect individuals' human rights. The Paris Agreement called for strengthening the global response to 'the threat of climate change',[26] that is, the threat 'to human societies and the planet'[27] – in particular to food production[28] – rather than distinctively a threat to the enjoyment of human rights.

From the late 2000s, however, advocates have advocated for the inclusion of a human rights language in international climate negotiations, in two very distinct ways.[29] One argument they have made is that '[g]overnments do not check their

[22] ITLOS, Request for an advisory opinion submitted by the Commission of Small Island States on Climate Change and International Law (COSIS) (21 May 2024), www.itlos.org/fileadmin/itlos/documents/cases/31/Advisory_Opinion/C31_Adv_Op_21.05.2024_corr.pdf, para 400.

[23] Thus, human rights were barely mentioned in the first four IPCC assessment reports, except as a constraint on climate action.

[24] UNFCCC (n 16) art 1(1).

[25] ibid art 2.

[26] Paris Agreement (n 17) art 2(1).

[27] Decision 1/CP.21, 'Adoption of the Paris Agreement', FCCC/ CP/2015/10/Add.1 (29 January 2016) 2, preamble para 6.

[28] Paris Agreement (n 17) preamble para 10, art 2(1)(b).

[29] See B Mayer, 'Human Rights in the Paris Agreement' (2016) 6 *Climate Law* 109, 110–12.

human rights obligations at the door when they respond to climate change':[30] the purpose of addressing climate change does not systematically justify means that infringe human rights. This argument has largely been successful, as the Conference of the Parties to the UN Framework Convention on Climate Change (COP) has recognised that climate action must comply with human rights law,[31] including in a recital of the Paris Agreement.[32] Another, more problematic argument is that the protection of human rights is at least one justification, perhaps even the main rationale, for the mitigation of climate change.[33] This argument has only had a limited effect on international climate negotiations. In particular, in the negotiations leading to the adoption of the Paris Agreement, no consensus has been reached on proposals aimed at framing climate action as itself a way to advance the enjoyment of human rights.[34]

In contrast, some courts and quasi-jurisdictional bodies have been receptive to the idea that climate change could be considered as a threat to the enjoyment of human rights since the second half of the 2010s. In 2019, five UN human rights treaty bodies have asserted that '[i]n order for States to comply with their human rights obligations … they must adopt and implement policies aimed at reducing [GHG] emissions'.[35] Consistently, these human rights institutions have repeatedly considered states' climate action as part of the periodic review on their implementation of human rights treaties.[36] In *Urgenda*, the Supreme Court of the Netherlands interpreted the European Convention on Human Rights (ECHR) as requiring the national government to reduce national GHG emissions by 25 per cent by 2020, compared with 1990.[37] In *Verein KlimaSeniorinnen*, the Grand Chamber of the European Court of Human Rights (ECtHR) found that

[30] See, eg, UN 'Statement by John H. Knox, Independent Expert on Human Rights and the Environment at "The Development of Environmental Human Rights"' (6 November 2014), www.ohchr.org/en/statements/2014/11/statement-john-h-knox-independent-expert-human-rights-and-environment ('Governments do not check their human rights obligations at the door when they respond to climate change').

[31] Decision 1/CP.16, 'The Cancun Agreements: Outcome of the Work of the Ad Hoc Working Group on Long-Term Cooperative Action under the Convention' UN Doc FCCC/CP/2010/7/Add.1 (15 March 2011) 2, para 8.

[32] Paris Agreement (n 17) preamble para 8.

[33] See, eg, J Knox, 'The Paris Agreement as a Human Rights Treaty' in D Akande et al (eds), *Human Rights and 21st Century Challenges: Poverty, Conflict, and the Environment* (Oxford University Press, 2020); M Wewerinke-Singh, *State Responsibility, Climate Change and Human Rights under International Law* (Hart Publishing, 2019).

[34] See Mayer (n 29) 112.

[35] CEDAW et al (n 4), section on 'States' Human Rights Obligations', para 2. See also CESCR, Statement: Climate Change and the International Covenant on Economic, Social and Cultural Rights, UN Doc E/C.12/2018/1 (31 October 2018), para 6; Committee on the Elimination of Discrimination Against Women (CEDAW), General Recommendation No 37 on the Gender-Related Dimensions of Disaster Risk Reduction in the Context of Climate Change, UN Doc CEDAW/C/GC/37 (13 March 2018), para 14.

[36] See, eg, references cited in B Mayer, 'Climate Change Mitigation as an Obligation under Human Rights Treaties?' (2021) 115 *American Journal of International Law* 409, 410–11 (fn 15).

[37] *Urgenda* (n 3). See also other references cited above at n 3.

Switzerland's climate policy lacked ambition and internal consistency, and that this constituted a violation of Article 8 ECHR on the right to respect for private and family life.[38] Meanwhile, the UN General Assembly adopted by consensus a resolution requesting the International Court of Justice to deliver an advisory opinion interpreting states' obligations to mitigate climate change arising from, among other sources, human rights treaties.[39]

C. The Argument that Action on Climate Change Mitigation is a Human Rights Obligation

The argument for the application of human rights law as the source of an obligation to mitigate climate change boils down to a simple legal syllogism. The normative premise is that a state has a positive obligation to take appropriate measures to prevent or mitigate threats to the enjoyment of human rights.[40] The factual premise is that climate change is a threat to the enjoyment of human rights.[41] The conclusion is that the state has an obligation to prevent climate change, if at all possible, or at least to mitigate it.

In a general and abstract sense, the two premises are incontrovertible. Positive human rights obligations have clear textual bases in human rights treaties,[42] and they have long been recognised by states, courts and other authorities.[43] The UN Human Rights Committee, for instance, affirmed that states have an obligation 'to take appropriate measures or to exercise due diligence to prevent' harm caused by third parties.[44] Likewise, there is no serious doubt that anthropogenic GHG emissions exacerbate climate change and its impacts, with adverse consequences for society. For instance, climate change makes some extreme weather events such as heatwaves more likely.[45] All other things being equal, this can be expected to affect the enjoyment of a large range of rights, such as the right to life, to private and

[38] *Verein KlimaSeniorinnen* (n 4) para 657(7).

[39] UN General Assembly Resolution 77/276, Request for an advisory opinion of the International Court of Justice on the obligations of States in respect of climate change (29 March 2023) (referring specifically to the International Covenant on Civil and Political Rights and the International Covenant on Economic, Social and Cultural Rights). See also Chile and Colombia, Request for an advisory opinion of the Inter-American Court of Human Rights on climate change (9 January 2023), www.corteidh.or.cr/docs/opiniones/soc_1_2023_en.pdf.

[40] See, eg, CEDAW et al (n 4) introductory section, para 7 (finding that states must 'dedicate the maximum available resources to the adoption of measures aimed at mitigating climate change').

[41] ibid para 3 ('climate change poses significant risks to the enjoyment of human rights').

[42] See, eg, International Covenant on Civil and Political Rights (adopted 16 December 1966, entered into force 23 March 1976) 999 UNTS 171, art 2(1).

[43] See, eg, Human Rights Committee, General Comment No 31, 'The Nature of the General Legal Obligation Imposed on States Parties to the Covenant', CCPR/C/21/Rev.1/Add.13 (26 May 2004), para 6. See generally V Stoyanova, *Positive Obligations under the European Convention on Human Rights* (Oxford University Press, 2023) 1.

[44] Human Rights Committee, General Comment No 31, 'The Nature of the General Legal Obligation Imposed on States Parties to the Covenant', CCPR/C/21/Rev.1/Add. 13 (26 May 2004) para 8.

[45] Pörtner et al, 'Technical Summary' (n 13) 47.

family home, to health and to property, or more specific rights such as the right to a clean environment.[46]

One caveat to this argument is that a state, on its own, can certainly not prevent climate change. This is because even the most diligent state will not be able to remove all anthropogenic GHGs already emitted, to prevent GHG emissions originating from other countries or even to stop its own emissions all at once. The only thing that a state could reasonably be expected to do would be to take some 'appropriate' measures targeting those GHG emissions that are under its control (in particular, those occurring within its own territory), with the view of limiting and, then, reducing them incrementally, year after year, until that state reaches net zero (or perhaps some level of negative) GHG emissions. But this caveat does not alter the fact that any state can play a part, albeit incremental, in global efforts on climate change mitigation, given that avoiding GHG emissions reduces the harm caused by climate change in a quasi-linear fashion.[47]

More importantly, there are two major objections to the argument, according to which states have positive human rights obligations to mitigate climate change. These two objections are presented in the following sections. In essence, the first objection suggests that the normative premise should be defined more narrowly: human rights law only requires a state to take measures that could have a relatively proximate effect on the right of specific individuals (ie, victims). As no such victim can be identified in relation to the climate impact of a state's failure to mitigate climate change, the objection suggests that human rights law cannot be applied to justify efforts to mitigate climate change. The second objection shows that a state's efforts to mitigate climate change would not necessarily or obviously advance the enjoyment of the human rights that the state has an obligation to protect. A state's action on climate change mitigation is justifiable from a broad utilitarian perspective, but not through the narrower (eg, anthropocentric, individualistic, territorial and short-termist) perspective offered by human rights law. This narrower perspective attaches more importance to the unintended economic and social costs of national action to mitigate climate change than to its intended benefits.

III. Victimless Human Rights 'Violations'?

A. The Problem

An allegation that a state has violated human rights typically relies on the identification of a victim of that violation, that is, an individual whose rights have been infringed as a consequence of the state's conduct. The conduct at issue could consist of an action attributable to the state (breaching a negative obligation), but also of

[46] See UN General Assembly Resolution 76/300, 'The Human Right to a Clean, Healthy and Sustainable Environment' (28 July 2022) A/RES/76/300.

[47] See the text and reference at n 15.

an omission (breaching a positive obligation). For instance, in *Budayeva v Russia*, the ECtHR found that Russia had failed to take disaster-risk reduction measures that could have reduced the risk of landslides, leading among other things to the death of Vladimir Budayev.[48] Similarly, pre-emptive claims that a state must take appropriate measures to comply with human rights law presuppose that failure to take such measures would lead to the rights of some individuals being infringed.

In this context, an objection to the application of human rights as the source of an obligation to mitigate climate change relates to the absence of victims of the failure of a state to take action to mitigate climate change. The problem here needs to be distinguished from situations where individuals who are not actual victims are at risk of becoming victims, for instance, in cases when the removal of an alien resident had been ordered but not yet enforced.[49] It is also different from situations where victims do not know that they are victims, for instance, in cases of covert surveillance programmes,[50] or when future victims are not yet identifiable, but would become if the risk was to realize.[51] In these situations, the identity of the victims could be known at a point in the future, at least to an omniscient observer.

In contrast, climate cases raise more fundamental – ontological rather than epistemological – issues because there simply *is* no victim of a state's failure to take appropriate measures. As will be shown below, a state's failure to mitigate climate change does not directly affect any individual's right in a meaningful way. While there certainly is some causal relation between a state's climate action and an individual's enjoyment of her right, the causal chain is just too long and tenuous for it to be possible, even in retrospect and with a perfect knowledge of all facts, to present, in a meaningful sense of the word, a given individual as a 'victim' of a state's failure to take appropriate measures to mitigate climate change.

B. Tenuous Causal Links

The causal chain between a state's failure to take appropriate measures to mitigate climate change and an individual's loss of enjoyment of her human rights consists of three consecutive links:

(1) a state's failure to take appropriate measures to mitigate climate change exacerbates climate change;
(2) climate change increases the risk or severity of specific physical events; and
(3) physical events have adverse implications for the enjoyment of human rights.

[48] *Budayeva v Russia* (n 7) para 158.
[49] *Soering v United Kingdom*, App No 14038/88 (7 July 1989) para 90.
[50] *Roman Zakharov v Russia*, App No 47143/06 (4 December 2015).
[51] See TR Hickman, 'Tort Law, Public Authorities, and the Human Rights Act 1998' in D Fairgrieve, M Andenas and J Bell (eds), *Tort Liability of Public Authorities in Comparative Perspective* (BIICL, 2002) 41 (considering the wrongful failure of authorities to detain an individual planning to 'kill the first bald-headed man I meet').

Taken individually, these causal links tend to be relatively weak, in the sense that the cause only has a small effect on the consequence, as detailed below. As a whole, a state's failure to take appropriate measures to mitigate climate change has only a vanishingly small effect on the enjoyment of a right by an individual. This causal pathway is far longer and far more tenuous than in other human rights cases, including traditional environmental cases (eg, local air pollution),[52] in relation to which a state is generally able to take effective measures that will make a relatively meaningful difference for specific individuals within the short to medium term. In rights-based climate litigation, by contrast, the remedy sought by the applicants 'would not … alleviate … their harm' in a meaningful way.[53] Further, the argument here is not to deny that each state has an obligation to cooperate in mitigating climate change; the point here is solely that this obligation cannot be inferred from the consequence of a state's failure to take such action on an individual's enjoyment of her human rights.

The first causal link identified above is between a state's failure to take appropriate measures to mitigate climate change and climate change. This causal link is tenuous: a state's omission, which increases national GHG emissions, produces only a small increase in total global emissions and, a fortiori, has only a tenuous effect on the GHG concentrations in the atmosphere and thus on the climate system as a whole. Courts have sometimes ignored this first causal link altogether when identifying victims in rights-based climate litigation: they have sought to identify individuals affected by climate change rather than, more specifically, by a state's failure to take measures to mitigate climate change.[54]

This point can be illustrated with a quick thought experiment. The GHG emissions of Sweden in 2023 were estimated to be equivalent to 49 million tonnes of carbon dioxide equivalent, which represented slightly less than 0.1 per cent of global GHG emissions that year.[55] Let us assume that if Sweden had taken additional measures to mitigate climate change in the previous years, it would have been able to avoid 5 per cent of these emissions that year (ie, 2.5 million tonnes of carbon dioxide equivalent). These additional measures would have reduced global GHG emissions by about 0.005 per cent.[56] Yet this would have produced

[52] See eg *Moreno Gómez v Spain*, App No 4143/02 (16 November 2004), https://hudoc.echr.coe.int/eng?i=001-67478 (cumulative impact of licensing multiple bars); Coroner report on the death of Ella Kissi-Debrah, Ref 2021-0113 (20 April 2021), www.judiciary.uk/prevention-of-future-death-reports/ella-kissi-debrah (listing 'exposure to excessive air pollution' as a cause of death).

[53] J Reich, '*KlimaSeniorinnen* and the Choice between Imperfect Options' (*Verfassungsblog*, 18 April 2024), https://verfassungsblog.de/klimaseniorinnen-and-the-choice-between-imperfect-options. See also Stoyanova (n 9) (noting that the ECtHR does not explain how measures that Switzerland could take could fulfil the Court's own test of having a 'real prospect of altering the outcome or mitigating the harm').

[54] See, eg, *Verein KlimaSeniorinnen* (n 4) paras 487(a), 499, 502; *Neubauer* (n 3) para 108; Committee on the Rights of the Child, Sacchi/Argentina, views (22 September 2021) UN Doc CRC/C/88/D/104/2019, paras 10.13–10.14.

[55] Emissions Database for Global Atmospheric Research (EDGAR), *GHG Emissions of All World Countries* (EU Commission, 2024).

[56] See ibid.

a much smaller effect on climate change, which is caused by the 'stock' of GHGs in the atmosphere rather than by the 'flow' (ie, emission) of GHGs in a particular year. Sweden's avoidable emissions would have caused an increase by about one in a millionth in the stock of carbon dioxide (2.4 trillion tonnes)[57] that human societies have emitted since the Industrial Revolution.[58] Sweden's hypothetically wrongful emissions would have caused an increase in the global average temperature by roughly one millionth of a degree celsius.[59] Even if Sweden persisted in causing such wrongful emissions over many years, or if one was to apply a similar thought experiment to a larger country, the effect on climate change would remain extremely small.

The second causal link is between this exacerbation of climate change (for example, in our thought experiment, the increase in the global average temperature by roughly one millionth of a degree) and any adverse physical impact. Climate is an abstract concept that scientists often define as the average weather over 30 years.[60] Its tangible impacts consist of an exacerbation of extreme weather events (such as heavy precipitations) and slow-onset changes (such as sea-level rise).[61]

Attributing slow-onset events to climate change is relatively straightforward, although this does not address the issues relating to first or third causal links. In fact, attributing an individual's harm to a slow-onset event (ie, the third causal link) is often more difficult than for extreme weather events. This is because the effects of slow-onset events on society are more predictable and thus effects on the enjoyment of human rights may be more manageable, as will be discussed below.

In contrast, the attribution of extreme weather events to climate change is highly problematic. Climate change does not create a distinct type of events, but it makes some existing events more likely or (depending on how one decides to look at this) more intense. A number of studies in recent years have sought to attribute extreme weather events to climate change.[62] However, questions have been raised about both the methodology of these studies and their policy and legal relevance.[63]

[57] Core Writing Team et al (n 14) 44.

[58] A similar argument can be made, mutatis mutandis, with regard to other GHGs. Admittedly, these GHGs have shorter atmospheric lifetimes, which means that the relevant 'stock' of gases causing climate change is that emitted over a period of a few decades (for methane and nitrous oxides) or even a few years (for some F-gases) rather than total emissions since the start of the Industrial Revolution. However, given that carbon dioxide represents the main cause of anthropogenic climate change and given the other points made above, this nuance is not of such a nature as to fundamentally change the argument presented here about the tenuous causal link between climate change and a state's failure to take appropriate measures to mitigate climate change.

[59] Based on Allan et al (n 15) 28 ('Each 1000 GtCO2 of cumulative CO2 emissions is assessed to likely cause a 0.27°C to 0.63°C increase in global surface temperature with a best estimate of 0.45°C').

[60] JB Robin Matthews et al, 'Glossary' in Masson-Delmotte et al (n 12) 2215, 2222.

[61] See, eg, H-O Pörtner et al, 'Summary for Policymakers' in Pörtner et al (eds) (n 13) 3, 11.

[62] See review in R Hope et al, 'Cross-Working Group Box Attribution' in Pörtner et al (eds) (n 13) 149, 150.

[63] See M Hulme, 'Attributing Weather Extremes to "Climate Change": A Review' (2014) 38 *Progress in Physical Geography: Earth and Environment* 499; G Lusk, 'The Social Utility of Event Attribution: Liability, Adaptation, and Justice-Based Loss and Damage' (2017) 143 *Climatic Change* 201.

For instance, it is not clear whether the attribution of a hurricane to climate change should be based on its increased frequency (eg, a category five hurricane became twice more likely) or on its increased severity (eg, an average hurricane caused 25 per cent more rainfall), or whether attribution rather should be based on the sea surface temperature (eg, 400–800 times more likely) that fuelled the hurricane.[64]

A more fundamental issue is that relying on weather attribution studies to attribute responsibility runs the risk of a selection bias to the extent that these studies almost always focus on adverse events. There is no question that, as a whole, the impact of climate change is adverse to human society. Yet it seems extraordinarily unlikely that *every single* consequence of climate change would always be unequivocally adverse to the enjoyment of human rights by anyone. Indeed, the IPCC finds it 'virtually certain' that while climate change increases the risk of heatwaves, it also decreases the risk of cold spells,[65] another type of weather event that is dangerous to human life and livelihood and to the economy.[66] Yet there is little if any social and political demand for studies that attribute the non-occurrence of adverse events to climate change, perhaps because events that do not occur tend not to attract the same level of public attention.[67]

This point can be illustrated here again with a brief thought experiment. Consider that a state's wrongful act has the consequence that every future extreme weather event will occur one year earlier than in a scenario without this

[64] O Milman and J Watts, 'Global Heating Makes Hurricanes Like Helene Twice as Likely, Data Shows', *The Guardian* (9 October 2024), www.theguardian.com/environment/2024/oct/08/hurricane-helene-milton-global-heating-study.

[65] See D Dodman et al, 'Cities, Settlements and Key Infrastructure' in Pörtner et al (eds) (n 13) 905, 927 ('frequencies and intensities of cold spells/cold waves are *virtually certain* to have decreased globally, and are projected to consistently decrease for most warming levels').

[66] Studies tend to agree that climate change will reduce the number of deaths related to cold waves compared to a scenario without climate change, although they disagree on the extent and significance of this effect. See generally ibid at 927. See also PL Kinney et al, 'Winter Season Mortality: Will Climate Warming Bring Benefits?' (2015) 10 *Environmental Research Letters* #064016, 1 (finding that 'variability in daily mortality within cities was not strongly influenced by winter temperature'); E de Schrijver et al, 'Nationwide Projections of Heat- and Cold-Related Mortality Impacts under Various Climate Change and Population Development Scenarios in Switzerland' (2023) 18 *Environmental Research Letters* #094010, 1 ('Population development [in Switzerland] will lead to an increase in cold-related mortality despite the decrease in cold temperature under warmer scenarios'). But see M Smid et al, 'Ranking European Capitals by Exposure to Heat Waves and Cold Waves' (2019) 27 *Urban Climate* 388, 399 (finding that the impact of cold waves 'may be softened by … climate warming', although 'the increasing negative impacts of extreme heat will by far outweigh the[se] positive consequences'); and Y Wang et al, 'Estimating and Projecting the Effect of Cold Waves on Mortality in 209 US Cities' (2016) 94 *Environment International* 141, 141 (finding that 'projected mortality related to cold waves would decrease from 1960 to 2050', although this decrease 'is small and may not be able to offset the potential increase in heat-related deaths if the adaptation to heat is not adequate'); S Vardoulakis et al, 'Comparative Assessment of the Effects of Climate Change on Heat- and Cold-Related Mortality in the United Kingdom and Australia' (2014) 122 *Environmental Health Perspectives* 1285, 1285 ('Projected changes in climate are likely to lead to an increase in heat-related mortality in the United Kingdom and Australia over this century, but also to a decrease in cold-related death').

[67] As an illustration, the index of the latest IPCC reports on climate impacts contains three locators on the effects of 'cold', but 39 locators under 'heatwaves'. See IPCC, 'Index' in Pörtner et al (eds) (n 13) 3005, 3018, 3032.

wrongful act. This consequence is harmful, as one would prefer to postpone the occurrence of harmful events. Yet attributing responsibility to the state for every future extreme weather event on the ground that it would not have happened (at that time) *but for* the state's wrongful act would put a burden on the state out of proportion to the wrongfulness of its conduct. Although the impacts of climate change are far more complex than this putative scenario, climate change likely involves a similar 'reshuffling of the cards' to the extent that it not only causes some adverse events to happen, but also prevents some other adverse events from happening. Anyone who claims to be affected by a climate impact might also have benefited from the non-occurrence of other adverse impacts as a consequence of climate change.

These issues with extreme weather attribution are not questions that can be solved with more empirical research or through methodological refinements. Rather, they illustrate the limitations of causal reasoning. The weather system is a chaotic one: it is characterised by a 'high sensitivity to initial conditions',[68] so that 'a small alteration … will cause subsequent states [of the system] to differ greatly from the states that would have followed without the alteration'.[69] As Edward Lorenz put it, this means that 'the flap of a butterfly's wings in Brazil [could] set off a tornado in Texas'.[70] In this context, any physical event – adverse or otherwise – could potentially be attributed to a state's prior failure to mitigate climate change, but also to its success in mitigating climate change, or to a hand wave of the man on the Clapham omnibus. In this sense, virtually any subsequent atmospheric event could be causally attributed to any action on the atmosphere, provided that sufficient time separates the two events. This would make attribute rather meaningless. An omniscient person could show that she would not have lost the enjoyment of a right had a state taken appropriate measures to mitigate climate change, but only in the sense that the wrongful omission – like the butterfly's wings – has forever changed the evolution of global atmospheric systems.

The third causal link that would need to be demonstrated to identify a victim of a state's failure to mitigate climate change is the link between a physical event and the enjoyment of a human right by an individual. Physical events do not cause adverse social consequences in a vacuum;[71] A mantra in disaster risk studies is that there is no such thing as a natural disaster.[72] A fortiori, there is no such

[68] E Ghys, 'The Lorenz Attractor, a Paradigm for Chaos' in B Duplantier, S Nonnenmacher and V Rivasseau (eds), *Chaos: Poincaré Seminar 2010* (Springer, 2013) 1, 2–3.

[69] EN Lorenz, *The Essence of Chaos* (University of Washington Press, 1993) 206.

[70] ibid 181.

[71] See, eg, C Nicholson, 'Conceptualising "Climate Migration"' in C Nicholson and B Mayer (eds), *Climate Migration: Critical Perspectives for Law, Policy and Research* (Hart Publishing, 2023) 13, 35 (denouncing the frequent assumption of an analogy between the effect of climate change on mitigation and the way Newton's three Laws of Motion operate).

[72] See, eg, C Hartman and S Squires (eds), *There is No Such Thing as a Natural Disaster: Race, Class, and Hurricane Katrina* (Routledge, 2006); A Oliver-Smith, 'Peru's Five-Hundred Year Earthquake: Vulnerability in Historical Context' in A Oliver-Smith and S Hoffman (eds), *The Angry Earth: Disaster in Anthropological Perspective*, 2nd edn (Routledge, 2020) 83.

thing as a climate disaster.[73] Whether a physical event – including one related to climate change – becomes a disaster depends in part on social conditions, including vulnerability, exposure and resilience.[74] A state can decisively alter these conditions, including by taking action aimed at promoting adaptation to climate change.[75]

It is telling that in spite of increasingly severe weather events in recent decades, the number of deaths associated with weather-related disasters has steadily decreased, both in proportion of the world's population and in absolute terms.[76] This observation suggests that economic development, rather than the physical effects of climate change, has so far been the dominant factor on the evolution of the enjoyment of, at least, the human rights to life. And, as briefly noted above, social factors are particularly relevant in relation to slow-onset events, such as sea-level rise, as states have more time to take pre-emptive measures aimed at protecting human rights. A state cannot prevent sea-level rise through adaptation action, but it can often take measures that will reduce the impact of sea-level rise on the enjoyment of the rights of its population. While sea-level rise inevitably causes harm, whether and how this harm affects human rights (eg, whether individuals drown and whether a group loses its cultural identity through relocation) largely depends on social, economic, political, demographic and cultural factors.

The assumption that climate change in general, or certain climate impacts in particular, would create a distinct category of victims is not new. In 1990, the IPCC's first assessment report claimed that '[e]ven a modest rise in global sea-levels could produce tens of millions of [environmental] refugees'.[77] Legal scholars have discussed treaties or other governance approaches to protecting such people facing climate-induced displacement.[78] Yet migration scholars have insisted – and most scholars have progressively come to accept – that while climate change may certainly affect migration in various ways, it is only one of a cluster of causes, so that no individual migrant can be meaningfully attributed to climate change in abstraction from other factors.[79] The IPCC itself has long shifted to a far more

[73] E Raju, E Boyd and F Otto, 'Stop Blaming the Climate for Disasters' (2022) 3 *Communications Earth & Environment* 1.

[74] K Hagon, 'Protecting People in the Context of Climate Change and Disasters: Setting the Scene' (2021) 115 *Proceedings of the ASIL Annual Meeting* 156, 157.

[75] See text at note 6.

[76] H Ritchie, P Rosado and M Roser, 'Natural Disasters' (Our World in Data, 2014), perma.cc/J96P-6AVU. This observation holds true for any subcategories of weather-related disasters considered separately, such as droughts, floods, storms, landslides, wildfires and extreme temperatures.

[77] Tegart et al (n 13) 10.

[78] See, eg, F Biermann and I Boas, 'Climate Change and Human Migration: Towards a Global Governance System to Protect Climate Refugees' in J Scheffran et al (eds), *Climate Change, Human Security and Violent Conflict: Challenges for Societal Stability* (Springer, 2012); S Behrman and A Kent (eds), *Climate Refugees: Beyond the Legal Impasse* (Routledge, 2018).

[79] See, eg, S Castles, 'Environmental Change and Forced Migration: Making Sense of the Debate' (UNHCR Working Paper on New Issues in Refugee Research No 70, 2002); I Boas et al, 'Climate Migration Myths' (2019) 9 *Nature Climate Change* 901; G Jónsson, '"Climate Migration"? Empirical Insights and Conceptual Cautions from Political Ecology and Migration Studies' in Nicholson and Mayer (n 65) 63; R Black et al, *Migration and Global Environmental Change: Final Project Report* (Foresight, 2011) 9.

nuanced narrative about 'climate-related migration',[80] thus acknowledging the difficulty of attributing individual migrants to climate change.

C. Implications

As a whole, these observations show that the causal relation between a state's failure to take appropriate measures to mitigate climate change and an individual's enjoyment of her human right is far too remote to characterise anyone as an actual or potential 'victim' of the state's failure to mitigate climate change in any meaningful sense of the term.[81] Perhaps unsurprisingly, the practice of courts and quasi-jurisdictional bodies shows that they have been unable to address this difficulty in any convincing way.

Thus, in *Sacchi*, the UN Committee on the Rights of the Child has held on a prima facie basis that the authors of communications against Argentina, Brazil, France, Germany and Turkey had standing as victims.[82] Yet, this conclusion was only based on the observation that the authors of the communication were children, a group 'particularly affected by climate change',[83] and that they had 'personally experienced real and significant harm'.[84] The Committee did not show any particularly reason to believe that the harm actually suffered by the authors of the communications could be attributed to climate change, let alone to the failure of any of the states individually to take appropriate measures to mitigate climate change.

In contrast, the ECtHR has not found any individual applicant able to justify his or her standing as victim in a climate case.[85] In *KlimaSeniorinnen*, in particular, the Court was not convinced that the individual applicants 'were exposed to the adverse effects of climate change, or were at risk of being exposed at any relevant point in the future, with a degree of intensity giving rise to a pressing need to ensure their individual protection'.[86] In a bizarre turn, however, the

[80] G Cissé et al, 'Health, Wellbeing and the Changing Structure of Communities' in Pörtner et al (eds) (n 13) 1041, 1079–84.

[81] See Report of the Office of the United Nations High Commissioner for Human Rights on the relationship between climate change and human rights, A/HRC/10/61 (15 January 2009) para 70 ('While climate change has obvious implications for the enjoyment of human rights, it is less obvious whether, and to what extent, such effects can be qualified as human rights violations in a strict legal sense').

[82] Sacchi/Argentina (n 54) para 10.14.

[83] ibid para 10.13.

[84] ibid para 10.14.

[85] *Verein KlimaSeniorinnen* (n 4) para 535; ECtHR, *Careme v France*, App No 7189/21 (9 April 2024).

[86] *Verein KlimaSeniorinnen* (n 4) para 533. It is noteworthy that the ECtHR confused two questions: whether the individual applicants were victims of climate change and whether they were victims of the state's failure to mitigate climate change. The Court did not find that the applicants were victims of climate change, but even if it had found otherwise, the Court would then have to show that these individuals were (or could become) victims, more specifically, of Switzerland's failure to take appropriate measures on the mitigation of climate change. Being a victim of climate change would not suffice to fulfil the condition in article 34 ECHR, namely, of being a 'victim *of a violation by one of the High Contracting Parties*'.

Court has held that associations could have standing 'as representatives of the individuals whose rights are or will allegedly be affected'[87] (ie, victims). Critics have noted that this represented a significant departure from the Court's own case law, and possibly also from the text of the ECHR.[88] But another issue is that the Court did not justify its assumption that such victims existed at the first place. The ECtHR's assumption that victims exist, in spite of the inability of the applicant association to bring any such victims to file an individual application, requires a leap of faith.

If one accepts that a state's failure to take appropriate measures on climate change mitigation does not victimise anyone in any meaningful sense of the term, the next question is whether human rights law can be applied in the absence of victims. One aspect of the question is procedural: standing before human rights institutions often requires individual applicants to show that they are victims of human rights violations.[89] Yet, this obstacle is not absolute, as standing to invoke human rights law could be justified on other grounds. For instance, human rights law can be applied in inter-state adjudication, whether before a regional human rights court[90] or another international court or tribunal.[91] International advisory proceedings are another option bypassing this procedural obstacle. And some national legal systems recognise the right of individuals or associations to engage in public interest litigation. Several prominent cases of rights-based climate litigation cases have relied on such procedural avenues.[92]

A more difficult question regards the substantive (rather than procedural) implications of the absence of victim. Human rights law has generally been applied in cases where victims could potentially be identified, even if these victims were not among the applicants.[93] When no victim can be identified, human rights law no longer acts as a 'trump' to protect individuals against the pursuance of objectives of general interest.[94] Rather, what is then framed as human rights protection

[87] ibid para 498.

[88] See, eg, K Dzehtsiarou, '"KlimaSeniorinnen Revolution": The New Approach to Standing' (2024) 5 *European Convention on Human Rights Law Review* 423.

[89] See, eg, ECHR (n 10) consolidated, art 34; Optional Protocol to the International Covenant on Civil and Political Rights (adopted 16 December 1966, entered into force 23 March 1976) 999 UNTS 171, art 1.

[90] See, eg, ECHR (n 10) consolidated, art 33.

[91] See, eg, *Legal Consequences of the Construction of a Wall in the Occupied Palestinian Territory*, Advisory Opinion, ICJ Reports 2004, 136.

[92] See, eg, *Urgenda* (n 3); *Klimaatzaak* (n 3); *Do-Hyun Kim* (n 3). See generally J Setzer and LC Vanhala, 'Climate Change Litigation: A Review of Research on Courts and Litigants in Climate Governance' (2019) 10 *WIREs Climate Change* e580; C Schall, 'Public Interest Litigation Concerning Environmental Matters before Human Rights Courts: A Promising Future Concept?' (2008) 20 *Journal of Environmental Law* 417.

[93] See VP Tzevelekos, 'Standing: European Court of Human Rights (ECtHR)' in *Max Planck Encyclopedia of International Procedural Law* (Oxford University Press, 2019) para 11 (mentioning *Denmark v Greece*, App No 3321/67, as the only example of an inter-state case brought in the public interest; yet the rights violations invoked in this case certainly involved victims, albeit without connection to the applicant).

[94] R Dworkin, *Taking Rights Seriously* (Harvard University Press, 1977) 6.

is, in fact, more readily characterised as objectives of general interest[95] – the type of goals that are typically used by governments to justify limitations to the scope of human rights. In these circumstances, human rights law no longer advances deontological ethics, but instead drifts into utilitarian arguments, involving value-based judgements, competing conceptions of the common interest and complex arbitrages between conflicting policy priorities. The rationale for allowing courts to ensure that democratic government respects and protects the rights of individuals does not necessarily justify a role of courts in controlling how democratic governments define and pursue the general interest.

Like climate change mitigation, most, perhaps all, policy goals could be framed as a way to protect the enjoyment of human rights, albeit in a diffuse and abstract fashion. For instance, a justification for investment in the military could be presented as a means to ensure the protection of human rights by deterring foreign invasions. The UK's decision to leave the EU, which many predicted would have a widespread economic impact, could be viewed as limiting the ability of the British government to take resource-intensive measures to protect human rights.[96] Some would go as far as arguing that securing international borders is essential to protecting the right to work of people already within the state's jurisdiction. The expertise and technical capacity of judges to weigh on various aspects of these policy questions and their legitimacy in making these decisions are highly questionable, especially in societies where such policy judgements are typically made by democratic institutions.

IV. Human Rights Law's Ambivalence Towards Climate Change Mitigation

A. The Adverse Human Rights Effects of Climate Action

Assuming that the applicability of human rights to climate change mitigation can be justified in spite of the absence of climate victim, questions remain about what climate action is required by human rights law. The standard argument for a human rights-based obligation to mitigate climate change, as described in section II, relies on the fact that climate change has an adverse impact on the enjoyment of human rights.[97] A state must take appropriate measures to mitigate climate change, so the argument goes, as a way to protect the enjoyment of human rights. While this is true, this is only one side of the story.[98]

[95] Protecting human rights is certainly an objective of general interest, but not every objective of general interest can readily be framed as a matter of rights protection. See generally R Alexy, 'Individual Rights and Collective Goods', in CS Nino (ed), *Rights* (Dartmouth, 1992) 163.
[96] Letsas (n 9).
[97] See the text at n 40.
[98] See Sumption (n 9).

The other side to the story, as the following discussion shows, is that a state's efforts to mitigate climate change may just as well have an adverse effect on the enjoyment of human rights because these efforts impose a burden on individuals and society. Further, as these adverse effects tend to unfold in the short term, within the state's territory and often in relatively direct and concrete ways, they fall more readily within the scope of human rights law. In contrast, the benefits of such national action on climate change mitigation unfold on a global scale, on a relatively long scale (mostly over millennia) and in a diffuse way, and thus largely beyond the scope of human rights obligations. As a whole, human rights law appears more as a hindrance than an incentive to action aimed at mitigating climate change.

A state's measures and policies on climate change mitigation affect human rights in several ways. First, climate action can involve human rights violations[99] – for instance, when populations are forcibly displaced to give way to a hydroelectric project[100] or when traditional farmers are dispossessed of their land by companies seeking to produce biofuel.[101] Second, the recognition of a 'climate emergency'[102] might provide a justification for exceptional measures that states would present as a justification for derogating from their human rights obligations.[103] Third, action on climate change mitigation will have an adverse effect on the enjoyment of human rights, particularly for some of the most vulnerable individuals and communities[104] – closing coal mines, for instance, means that coal miners will lose their jobs. Admittedly, many of these violations and derogations could be avoided. Likewise, the adverse impact on vulnerable populations could partly be reduced through efforts to promote a 'just transition'.[105] Yet there is also a more fundamental tension between the goal of mitigating climate change and the goal

[99] See also OW Pedersen, 'The Janus-Head of Human Rights and Climate Change: Adaptation and Mitigation' (2011) 80 *Nordic Journal of International Law* 403 (noting that 'human rights restrictions will sometimes have the potential to run counter to the adoption of effective climate change responses').

[100] PM Fearnside, 'Belo Monte: Actors and Arguments in the Struggle over Brazil's Most Controversial Amazonian Dam' (2017) 148 *Die Erde* 14.

[101] UNEP, *Climate Change and Human Rights* (2015) viii.

[102] See, eg, Parliament Resolution on the Climate and Environment Emergency, 2019/2930(RSP) (28 November 2019) (EU); House of Commons, Journals, 42-1, No 435, Vote No 1366 (17 June 2019) (Canada); Hansard (Debates) (2 December 2020) 749 NZPD 233-250 (New Zealand); 659 Parl Deb HC (6th ser), cols 225–318 (2019) (UK).

[103] S Humphreys, 'Introduction: Human Rights and Climate Change' in *Human Rights and Climate Change* (Cambridge University Press, 2010) 6. By analogy, see A Devis, 'Change of Paradigm in EU Environmental Law: Does the Climate Crisis Now "Override" the Biodiversity Crisis?', *European Law Blog* (21 November 2024), www.europeanlawblog.eu/pub/l74pacq5/release/4 (showing a similar collision course between climate law and environmental law).

[104] Vulnerability in political and academic discourses on climate change is often presented as vulnerability to the impacts of climate change. Yet, vulnerable populations are also vulnerable to the unintended economic and social impacts of climate policies. The poorer segments of the population, for instance, will be the first impacted by the costs of a green transition. A recognition of the multidimensionality of vulnerability is essential to making sense of the fact that support for climate action remains concentrated among the less vulnerable populations on both the international and domestic planes. See, eg, European Commission, 'Special Eurobarometer 538: Climate Change' (2023) 22.

[105] See, eg, *Statnett SF v Sør-Fosen sijte* (Supreme Court of Norway, 11 October 2021) HR-2021-1975-S.

of protecting the enjoyment of human rights. Mitigating climate change requires a complete overhaul of many economic and social systems – changes to the ways in which society produces electricity, transports goods and people, processes raw materials, produces food, manages land and treats waste, among other things. Although some measures aimed at reducing GHG emissions may occasionally achieve immediate economic and social benefits, most of them come at a net cost, at least in the short term.[106]

States have long acknowledged the tension between climate change mitigation and human development.[107] This tension exists most conspicuously in developing countries, but certainly also in developed ones.[108] As Stephen Humphreys has observed: 'Human rights fulfilment in any given state depends upon a basic level of economic wherewithal and stable access to resources.'[109] Accordingly, extensive efforts to mitigate climate change will unavoidably 'curtail the development policy options available to governments everywhere', which 'in turn will tend to set limits on the capacity of countries to fulfil basic human rights'.[110]

To illustrate this argument, one may consider several ways in which a government may seek to mitigate climate change. For instance, the imposition a carbon tax in the electricity sector that was passed on to households would risk impoverishing the population, in particular its more vulnerable members, thus reducing the ability of many individuals to access rights-enabling goods and services (eg, food and water, a decent home, an adequate standard of medical care, and education). Alternatively, the state may seek to pay the cover the cost itself – for instance, by subsidising renewable energy from the general budget. However, this would force the government to reduce public spending in other sectors, to increase taxes or to incur new debt.[111] Either way, the policy would result in additional constrain on public or private spending, at present or in the near future, including on rights-enabling goods and services. There may be ways to reduce the adverse social impact of climate action, for instance by funding climate policies through progressive taxation that focuses on the wealthy, but there are also political limitations to what can realistically be achieved. There are also circumstances where reducing GHG emissions may achieve economic and social 'co-benefits', but only to a limited extent: the reluctance of states, corporations and individuals to reduce their GHG emissions reflects their assessment that reducing GHG emissions generally comes at a cost. One way or the other,

[106] Economists have long recognised the cost of climate change mitigation when comparing it to the benefits of such action in order to determine the 'optimal' level of ambition. See, eg, M Grubb et al, 'Introduction and Framing' in PR Shukla et al (eds), *Climate Change 2022: Mitigation of Climate Change: Working Group III Contribution to the Sixth Assessment Report of the Intergovernmental Panel on Climate Change* (Cambridge University Press, 2022) 180.

[107] UNFCCC (n 16) arts 3(2), 4(7).

[108] ibid arts 3(4)–(5), 4(2)(a); Paris Agreement (n 17) arts 3, 4(3).

[109] Humphreys (n 103) 22.

[110] ibid.

[111] A government could also print currency, thus devaluating existing currency, which would in effect be similar to a tax.

prioritising a green transition will inevitably mean de-prioritising other, more direct and effective ways of advancing human rights.

Thus, the economic and social cost of mitigating climate change has an impact on the enjoyment of human rights. At times, this impact directly affects specific individuals: coal miners, for instance, may lose their job as a direct consequence of a state's policy of closing coal mines in order to mitigate climate change. More frequently, however, the impact is diffuse, and no victim can be identified. Of course, if one accepts the argument presented in section III, human rights law would not apply as a hindrance to action on climate change mitigation based solely on this diffuse effect, but nor would human rights law justify such action. *A contrario*, if one assumes that human rights law can apply in spite of the absence of victims, human rights law would inevitably give more weight to the *relatively* proximate costs of climate action on the enjoyment of human rights than to its more remote and diffuse benefits.

B. The Narrow Focus of Human Rights Lenses

Ambitious action on climate change mitigation has major benefits for society. Economists who have sought to compare the costs and benefits of climate action have generally supported extensive action to mitigate climate change.[112] These studies considered all the costs and all the benefits (economic or otherwise) of climate action from a broad utilitarian perspective.

Yet the picture would be dramatically different if such cost-benefit analysis was limited to the costs and benefits of climate action that can be framed in terms of individuals' enjoyment of their human rights. Admittedly, the scope of a state's human rights obligations differs from instrument to instrument, as well as between human rights treaties and domestic law, and it is open to different interpretations, which may evolve over time. Nonetheless, it remains the case that human rights law cannot embody every possible political justice argument. For the following three reasons, human rights law as it exists today puts more emphasis on the adverse effects of action on climate change mitigation, and less on its benefits, than the broad utilitarian perspectives used to justify climate action.

First, human rights obligations tend to focus on situations where individual harm is the proximate consequence of a state's action or omission. The ECtHR has not defined a clear and consistent standard of causation, but it has generally limited its findings of a breach of a positive obligation to situations where there was a 'strong enough link' between the state's conduct and the harm caused[113] or otherwise some

[112] See K Riahi et al, 'Mitigation Pathways Compatible with Long-Term Goals' in Shukla et al (n 106). But see W Nordhaus, 'Climate Change: The Ultimate Challenge for Economics' (2019) 109 *American Economic Review* 1991, 2003 for a more nuanced argument.

[113] ECtHR, *Dubetska v Ukraine*, App No 30499/03 (10 February 2011).

'significant influence' of the state on the harm caused[114] or some 'real prospect' that the state could have avoided or reduced the harm.[115] It is not difficult to imagine how measures aimed at mitigating climate change can directly cause harm to an individual (eg, a coal miner losing his job due to the phasing out of coal) or have a diffuse but relatively localised and immediate effect on particularly vulnerable segments of society (eg, coal-mining regions and the poor suffering more directly from an increase in the price of electricity). By contrast, as the previous section has shown, it is virtually impossible to establish any meaningful influence of a state's action on climate change mitigation on an individual's right.

Second, human rights obligations – and positive obligations in particular – are primarily territorial in nature.[116] Even in some of the most expansive interpretations of human rights law, extraterritorial human rights obligations remain limited to 'exceptional situations'.[117] It is relatively straightforward to apply negative human rights obligations extraterritorially:[118] a state can reasonably be expected to refrain from killing individuals in foreign countries.[119] By contrast, the extraterritorial application of positive human rights obligations is less likely, except in circumstances (eg, locations) in which the state exercises some degree of control.[120] No state punishes crimes and runs schools and hospitals overseas in the same way as it does within its own territory. At most, a state's extraterritorial positive human rights obligation is one of providing financial and technical assistance.[121] This territorial focus of human rights obligations puts more emphasis on the adverse effects of action on climate change mitigation (which are mainly territorial) than on its benefits (with are mainly extraterritorial).[122]

Third, human rights law has generally been concerned with the protection of the human rights of individuals living today against threats, especially those that would unfold within a relatively short timeframe. Here again, most impacts of climate action readily fall within this timeframe: a decision to shut down coal plants, for instance, would immediately affect coal miners' right to livelihood. Likewise, a decision to subsidise renewable energy would have a short-term effect

[114] ECtHR, *E v United Kingdom*, App No 33218/96 (26 November 2002) para 100.

[115] ECtHR, *O'Keeffe v Ireland*, App No 35810/09 (28 January 2014) para 149. See Stoyanova (n 43) 47–48.

[116] See Stoyanova (n 43) 221.

[117] Environment and Human Rights, Advisory Opinion OC-23/17 (15 November 2017) IACtHR Series A No 2, para 104(d).

[118] See M Milanović, *Extraterritorial Application of Human Rights Treaties* (Oxford University Press, 2011).

[119] ECtHR, *Al-Skeini v United Kingdom*, App No 55721/07, 2011-IV ECHR 99.

[120] See, eg, Milanovic (n 118) 209–12; T Altwicker, 'Transnationalizing Rights: International Human Rights Law in Cross-Border Contexts' (2018) 29 *European Journal of International Law* 581, 590.

[121] See, eg, International Covenant on Economic, Social and Cultural Rights (adopted 16 December 1966, entered into force 3 January 1976) 993 UNTS 3, art 2(1).

[122] See I Jelić and E Fritz, 'The "Living Instrument" at the Service of Climate Action: The ECtHR Long-Standing Doctrine Confronted to the Climate Emergency' (2024) 36 *Journal of Environmental Law* 141, 152 (noting that 'the most direct victims of climate change … live outside Europe hence outside the territorial jurisdiction of the Contracting parties').

on the ability of individuals to enjoy various human rights. In contrast, the mitigation of climate change is in large part aimed at advancing – as states put it – 'the benefit of … future generations of humankind'[123] and, more generally, 'intergenerational equity'.[124] The adverse impact of a state's failure to mitigate climate change would unfold slowly over centuries or millennia, a timeframe that does not readily fall within the ambit of human rights law, since most courts do not recognise human rights to future generations. Here again, the short-sightedness of human rights lenses would result in more emphasis on the short-term adverse effects of climate action than on its long-term benefits.

It is not possible for this chapter to do justice to all the arguments that have been made (or could be made) to justify an extension of human rights law to climate change beyond what the three previous paragraphs have outlined. First, human rights courts could conceivably adopt laxer approaches to causation by imposing an obligation on states to protect human rights against diffuse and abstract threats. Second, a state's obligation to protect human rights within its territory might be interpreted as implying an obligation to cooperate with other states on the mitigation of climate change.[125] Third, there may be moral, perhaps even legal arguments in favour of recognising human rights to future generations. I do not exclude the idea that there may be some merit to some of these arguments. Yet, as a whole, these arguments outline a completely different legal field. This new field would no longer focus on what George Letsas presents as 'individual justice'; rather, it would encompass – and allow judges to impose their vision of – virtually 'the whole realm of political justice'.[126] Whether this metamorphosis of human rights law is desirable is far from obvious, especially in a democratic society, since it would constitute an obvious shift towards government by judges.

V. Making Sense of the Debate

Action on climate change mitigation has increasingly been framed as a human rights obligation, not only by advocates and scholars, but also increasingly by judges. Climate change is a threat to the enjoyment of human rights and as states have a human rights obligation to address such threats, so the argument goes, they also have an obligation to mitigate climate change. Yet the argument faces two major objections, which this chapter has exposed. The first objection relates to the absence of any actual or potential victim of a state's failure to mitigate climate change. Applying positive human rights obligations in situations where nobody is or could be the victim of the state's omission would radically expand human rights

[123] UNFCCC (n 16) art 3(1).
[124] Paris Agreement (n 17) preamble para 8.
[125] See JH Knox, 'Climate Change and Human Rights Law' (2009) 50 *Virginia Journal of International Law* 163, 198; Mayer (n 36) 433–36.
[126] Letsas (n 9) 446.

law, potentially to any policy matter. The second objection is concerned with the ambivalence of human rights law towards climate action. Anything states do to mitigate climate change also has some adverse effects on the enjoyment of human rights. While a broad utilitarian argument rightly justifies climate action in light of its long-term global and diffuse benefits, human rights lenses put more emphasis on the adverse effects of state action on climate change mitigation, inasmuch as those adverse effects are more likely to unfold in the short term within the state's territory and to affect individuals in concrete ways.

These two objections are closely related: it is largely because of the absence of victims that the application of human rights law as the source of an obligation to mitigate climate change requires judges to engage in a delicate cost-benefit analysis. If judges look beyond the proximate effect of a state's conduct on the enjoyment of human rights, they are likely to face similar questions of comparing the multiple remote effects of the conduct. Experience with climate litigation so far suggests that judges are ill-equipped to engage in such broad policy-making exercises: their decisions have been counterproductive,[127] inconsistent[128] or, at the very least, confused.[129]

These objections are not new; some might even find them somewhat obvious. This begs the question as to why these objections are often eluded. At times, fuzzy thinking may play a role, for instance, in the frequent parallel between traditional environmental cases or adaptation cases, which may have a relatively proximate adverse effect on the human rights of individuals, and climate change mitigation cases, which are far more problematic. Further, a human rights court might also find it important to 'have its say' in relation to climate change 'in order to remain relevant'.[130] Overall, scholarly and judicial activism might play a role.[131] For climate action advocates, framing climate action as a human rights obligation can be viewed as a strategic goal, as this facilitates access to adjudication mechanism, both domestically and internationally. There have been pledges, signed by scholars and even former judges, to collaborate in advancing this goal, including by seeking to 'adopt climate-friendly interpretation of legal norms and instruments'.[132] Notwithstanding its laudable intentions, the selection of legal theories based on factors other than their apparent validity erodes the credibility of expert institutions on which democracy relies, running the risk of making governance – including effective climate action – increasingly difficult.

[127] See B Mayer, 'The Contribution of *Urgenda* to the Mitigation of Climate Change' (2022) 35 *Journal of Environmental Law* 167.

[128] See B Mayer, 'The Duty of Care of Fossil-Fuel Producers for Climate Change Mitigation: *Milieudefensie v. Royal Dutch Shell* District Court of The Hague (The Netherlands)' (2022) 11 *Transnational Environmental Law* 407.

[129] C Hilson and O Geden, 'Climate or Carbon Neutrality? Which One Must States Aim for under Article 8 ECHR?', *EJIL:Talk!* (29 April 2024), www.ejiltalk.org/climate-or-carbon-neutrality-which-one-must-states-aim-for-under-article-8-echr.

[130] Dzehtsiarou (n 88) 426.

[131] Letsas (n 9) 447.

[132] See, eg, 'The Full Pledge', World Lawyers' Pledge on Climate Action (2024), https://lawyersclimatepledge.org/full-text.

5

The Limits of the Positive Obligation to Respect the Parent–Child Relationship

TRISTAN CUMMINGS

I. Introduction

When families fall apart, the state comes under a positive obligation to maintain and restore a vital connection: the parent–child relationship.[1] The ECHR makes little reference to 'children', yet it is certain that children possess human rights and that parents have rights in relation to their children, too.[2] The primary right which concerns the parent–child relationship is Article 8: the right to private and family life. Article 8 entails a right enjoyed by both parents and children to the 'mutual enjoyment' of one another's company and the state has a duty to respect that right and to support enforcement action to secure contact or restore custody when this relationship is disrupted.[3] As with many rights under the Convention, the state has a range of positive duties and different options for fulfilling these obligations.[4] This chapter examines these positive duties and the limits imposed on the state's duty to enforce the rights relating to the parent–child relationship, including the state's coercive obligations to respect and protect[5] this

[1] *Johansen v Norway* App No 17383/90 (1997) 23 EHRR 33 at [52].

[2] Children are referred to in art 6, providing for the privacy of judicial proceedings where their interests require it. Article 5(1)(d) introduces an exception for the 'purposes of educational supervision' of 'minors'. Children are also specifically referred to in Protocol 7, art 5, upholding the equality of spouses within marriage and upon its dissolution. Article 3 does not mention children, but has had a significant impact in relation to child protection and has also imposed positive duties on the state to prevent mistreatment. See C O'Mahoney, 'Child Protection and the ECHR: Making Sense of Positive and Procedural Obligations' (2019) 27(4) *International Journal of Children's Rights* 660.

[3] *Hokkanen v Finland* (A/299-A) (1993) 16 EHRR CD47 at [62].

[4] S Fredman, *Human Rights Transformed* (Oxford University Press, 2008) 69–71.

[5] The ECtHR refers to its duty to 'respect' the parent–child relationship. However, it is also clear that it must 'protect' this relationship, for example, from the negative consequences that follow from the lapse of time between judgment and enforcement of contact or custody rights: *Ignaccolo-Zenide v Romania* (31679/96) (2001) 31 EHRR 7 at [102].

right.[6] It focuses on cases in which one parent (or carer) obstructs the access of another parent in developing or maintaining their family ties with a child. Two examples are used as case studies where individual cooperation and compliance are central to realising rights: the domestic enforcement of custody and access arrangements and parental child abduction.[7] As an analytical lens, this chapter employs a systems theoretical analysis of the case law to elicit the limitations and contingency of state power as it relates to family life.

The ECtHR employs a distinct family law framework, cognisant of the principled and pragmatic limits to enforcing parent–child relationships. The state has three main positive duties: procedural, facilitative and enforcement. The state must ensure that parents can put forward arguments in support of their rights of custody and access, and receive relevant documentation;[8] the state must *facilitate* the restoration of contact by taking 'measures' intended to make effective the contact between parent and child.[9] The preparatory measures are primarily tasked with preventing harm to the *relationship* between parent and child.[10] Moreover, to act without taking preparatory measures would be a violation of Article 8.[11] Here, the logic of prevention is often inverted because of the positive duty, on the one hand, to respect family ties, but, on the other hand, to be mindful of exposing the child (and the other parent) to harm resulting from contact or involvement of another parent.[12] Ultimately, it is the latter, determined by the child's welfare, that takes precedence. The state must also ensure that there is an effective enforcement mechanism and implementation of those steps expeditiously, which includes, in certain instances, a duty to punish the non-compliance of a private individual.[13]

With these basic components in mind, the duty to respect parental and child rights of custody and access by way of positive duties under Article 8 exposes a complex picture because of the ways in which the state's duties relate to the *systems*

[6] *Maumousseau and Washington v France* App No 39388/05 (2007) 51 EHRR 35 at [83]; *Amănălăch ioai v Romania* App No 4023/04, unreported (26 May 2009) (ECHR) at [94].

[7] These examples form a continuum rather than entirely distinct circumstances because the family ties between one parent and their child are disrupted. However, in the case of international child abduction, core international law obligations interact with the Convention: namely, the Hague Convention and Brussels II. The ECtHR interprets art 8 in light of these international laws and expects states to utilise the powers available: *Iglesias Gil and AUI v Spain* App No 56673/00 (2005) 40 EHRR 3 at [51] and [56]–[57]. This chapter mostly focuses on the domestic enforcement of contact and custody rights.

[8] The ECtHR has consistently highlighted the importance of procedural obligations on the part of the state and that a failure to involve a parent in the process sufficiently may amount to a violation: *Hoppe v Germany* App No 28422/95 (2004) 38 EHRR 15 at [52]; *Kosmopoulou v Greece* App No 60457/00 [2004] 1 FLR 800 at [49]; *N.TS v Georgia* App No 71776/12 [2017] 1 FLR 898 at [72]. However, this chapter will focus on the substantive duties to facilitate contact and enforce non-compliance.

[9] *Hokkanen v Finland* (n 3) at [55]; and *Ignaccolo-Zenide v Romania* (n 5) at [94].

[10] *cf Osman v United Kingdom* App No 23452/94 (2000) 29 EHRR 245 at [115]. However, harm to the relationship amounts to harm to the individual because the personal identity is partially constituted by our relationships with others.

[11] *N.TS v Georgia* (n 8) at [71].

[12] Birchall and Choudhry (2018); Hunter (2020).

[13] *Maumousseau* (n 6) at [83] (concerning child abduction under the Hague Convention)]; *Amănălăchioai* (n 6) at [94] (concerning failure of grandparents to return a child to his father).

of family life. These positive duties expose the *contingency* of state coercive power as it relates to private action, the welfare of the child and psychological connections. Moreover, this chapter will contend that these conclusions reflect a basic truth about the relations between different systems of social life.[14] These arguments are illustrated through analysis of the European Court of Human Rights' (ECtHR) concept of 'preparatory measures' and 'exceptional diligence', the importance of cooperation, the inversion of responsibility onto individuals and away from the state, and the primary importance of the welfare of the child in the balance. All of these features exemplify how the state cannot make good on its primary duty to respect 'normal family life' and the 'mutual enjoyment' of parent–child relationships without the cooperation of the parties involved, and that the enforcement of contact or access rights may not be possible (and might actively be harmful) without prior, expeditious[15] and (partially) non-coercive steps being taken by the state *and* by individuals, who must take an active role in enforcing their own rights. Ultimately, this suggests there must be scope for more indirect means of inducing compliance, such as by facilitating negotiation and mediation.

II. Context and Analytic Framework

Although many examples and jurisdictions are utilised throughout this chapter, it is helpful to illustrate some of the ways in which the state's coercive powers are used in the family context and why these situations occur. This section also introduces the basic outline of a systems theoretical framework as a lens to analyse these examples.

A. Context

When families break down, both parents may wish to have access to their children and have them spend time with them. In many cases, the custody and access questions will be achieved by private agreement, with little involvement of the state, although in some jurisdictions, decisions about custody and access form part of divorce proceedings.[16] In other instances, the parties may not be under any obligation to resolve contact and custody judicially, but may decide to seek a court

[14] In this respect, 'systems' takes on a specialised meaning derived from systems theory: see, N Luhmann, *Social Systems* (Stanford University Press, 1995).

[15] *Pisica v Moldova* App No 23641/17, unreported, ECHR (29 October 2019) at [66]–[73].

[16] TMC Asser Instituut, 'Comparative Study on Enforcement Procedures of Family Rights' JLS/C4/2005/06 (The Hague, 19 December 2007) 9. See also, J Mair and E Örücü, 'Juxtaposing Legal Systems and the Principles of European Family Law on Parental Responsibilities (Intersentia, 2010). For more recent country summaries, see Commission on European Family Law, 'Country Summaries', https://ceflonline.net/country-reports-by-jurisdiction.

order to determine or formalise these arrangements anyway. So, the ways in which contact and custody arrangements are regulated varies across Europe, but certain commonalties do exist.[17] Overarching these jurisdictions is the ECtHR's jurisprudence, reflecting the need for preparatory measures prior to enforcing family rights, but recognising that, ultimately, some element of sanction might be necessary. These duties extend beyond direct public authority involvement: the state is still implicated in situations where the dispute is between private individuals, for example, where one party obtains a court order mandating a certain contact arrangement.[18] In *Glaser v UK*, the ECtHR explained that one aspect of the state's duty is to establish an adequate 'framework of adjudicatory and enforcement machinery'.[19] Indeed, although the use of coercive means are, in many cases, not justified under the Convention because they might undermine the child's welfare, it is also necessary that the enforcement machinery is 'adequate' for respecting family ties, which may require appropriate sanctions for non-compliance.

The variety of approaches is evident upon examination of some examples. In England, the Children Act 1989 includes a range of measures intended to enforce compliance with child arrangement orders: these include 'activity directions', which may include classes and counselling,[20] with compliance monitored by the state.[21] The state can also monitor whether contact is being carried out and issue warnings where there is a failure to comply with a child arrangement order and enforcement action.[22] The state can enforce an order through imposing unpaid work, issuing fines and, at the most extreme end, imposing criminal liability for contempt. These sanctions, however, have not been well utilised.[23] English law is, in some ways, similar to the sorts of provisions that exist across Europe. As another example, in France, Article 373-2 of the Civil Code imposes a duty to 'maintain' the relationship between each parent and their child following parental separation, with the 'exceptional' application of coercive measures to enforce a decision of a family court.[24] At the point of enforcement, although the court's bailiff may seek a compromise, ultimately the matter may be enforced by the police. More often, the court may issue a civil fine following the report of the bailiff to the effect that the parent concerned is refusing to respect the rights of the other parent to contact.[25]

The area of principal interest to this chapter concerns coercive measures and the measures preceding enforcement action. Whether the state has coercive powers of enforcement depends on a number of factors: for example, whether a

[17] TMC Asser Instituut (n 16) 7-55.
[18] *Hokkanen v Finland* (n 3) at [55].
[19] *Glaser v United Kingdom* App No 32346/96 (2001) 33 EHRR 1 at [63].
[20] Children Act 1989, s 11A.
[21] ibid s 11G.
[22] ibid ss11–HJ.
[23] L Trinder et al, *Enforcing Contact Orders: Problem-Solving or Punishment?* (Nuffield Foundation, 2013).
[24] French Civil Code, art 373-2, as modified by Law No 2024-233 of 18 March 2024, art 6.
[25] F Ferrand, 'National Report: France' in CEFL (n 16) at sections 57–58, https://ceflonline.net/wp-content/uploads/France-Parental-Responsibilities.pdf.

court has made an order concerning contact, non-compliance of which would typically amount to contempt; the preference for mediation and other settlements prior to enforcement proceedings; and whether coercive measures can be brought against the parent or carer or the child.[26] Some jurisdictions, such as Belgium, Denmark and Finland prioritise mediation prior to effecting coercive measures against the parent with care of the child.[27] Even in England, as explained above, less coercive means are preferred to resolve contact and custody disputes. It is not surprising that a shift in focus away from sanctions and towards mediation and parenting programmes have taken place precisely because coercive measures have the potential to cause harm to children.[28] It is also clear that English law, by introducing non-criminal sanctions, also attempted to broaden the range of measures available for enforcement.

B. Analytic Framework

This article utilises a modified systems theoretical conception of society as a lens by which the ECtHR approach to positive obligations can be evaluated.[29] The basic premise of systems theory is to conceptualise society as being functionally differentiated between non-hierarchical, semi-autonomous systems and sub-systems.[30] These systems are constituted by their *communications*, and these communications mediate the boundaries of the system. Moreover, systems are geared at particular functions of social life, including the family and the legal system. Family systems are differentiated by *intimate* communications. The unique function of the family as a social system is that it allows individuals to be fully themselves and to make themselves vulnerable and open to others.[31] The family as a functional system encounters the individual 'in their wholeness'.[32] Hence, the function of the family as a system means to include 'participants in communication as a whole person'.[33] The function of the legal system is encoded, amongst other things, in differentiating between the legal and illegal. As society becomes more complex, our systems

[26] TMC Asser Instituut (n 16) 11–13.

[27] S Harvie-Clark, 'Resolving Parenting Disputes: Scotland Compared to Other Countries' (20 November 2019) https://digitalpublications.parliament.scot/ResearchBriefings/Report/2019/11/20/Resolving-parenting-disputes--Scotland-compared-to-other-countries-1, 25–26.

[28] ibid 26.

[29] T Cummings, 'Utilizing Systems Theory Insights and Reflexive Law to Negotiate the "Collision between … Un-connecting Worlds" in Family Law' (2021) 9 *Journal of Law, Religion and State* 212.

[30] N Luhmann, 'Operational Closure and Structural Coupling' (1991–92) 13 *Cardozo Law Review* 1419; G Teubner, 'Substantive and Reflexive Elements in Modern Law' (1983) 17 *Law & Society Review* 239.

[31] C Baraldi, G Corsi and E Esposito, *Unlocking Luhmann*, K Walker (trans) (Bielefeld University Press, 2021).

[32] For further discussion of systems theory in the context of the family, see T Cummings, 'Compensation: Rejuvenated? A Critical Re-appraisal of the Principle of Compensation in the Award of Financial Remedies upon Divorce' (2024) *Child and Family Law Quarterly* 133, Section 3.

[33] Baraldi et al (n 31).

of social life also become more complex and systems become more specialised at performing their functions. Consequently, as the language of these communications become more functionally specialised, this also leads to some degree of communicative closure.[34]

The consequence of this functional differentiation is that systems employ their own language, specialised to their function, which makes it difficult for one system to directly communicate and cause changes in another. Crucially, this calls on us to reconfigure our understanding of the state and the effectiveness of state laws at directly influencing systems of family life. The argument of this chapter is that systems theory allows for a powerful explanatory framework: the reason why the enforcement of legal orders is so complex is partially down to the communicative closure between law and the family. Therefore, the effective enforcement of positive duties means overcoming these communicative closures.[35] The risk of a direct, coercive mode of intervention is described by Teubner as a threefold challenge: interventions may be ineffective, the target system may be unresponsive, or the effect of the intervention is destructive.[36] The idea that legal interventions regulating family life may harm the relationships which the state is duty-bound to protect is reflective of Teubner's contention that 'command and control' regulations perform badly when attempting to impose positive, substantive constraints on other systems.[37] The following sections examine the positive duties the state comes under in the context of respecting the parent–child relationship through this lens, deconstructing the case law so as to sketch out the limitations of state power.

III. Positive Dimensions: A Systems Theoretical Analysis

The right to family life goes beyond the state's obligations not to interfere in the private life of individuals, although this is said to be its 'essential object'.[38] It also has *positive* dimensions.[39] As Ursula Kilkelly argues, the positive dimension of Article 8 has particularly great importance to children as they represent a group that is especially vulnerable, with their rights and interests often dependent on the care of others and the adequacy of the state's protective framework.[40] However,

[34] N Luhmann, *Social Systems* (Stanford University Press, 1995).

[35] Fredman (n 4) ch 6.

[36] G Teubner, 'Social Regulation through Reflexive Law' in *Law as an Autopoietic System* (Blackwell, 1990) 21–22, 27.

[37] G Teubner, 'Juridification: Concepts, Aspects, Limits, Solutions' in *Juridification of Social Spheres* (Walter de Gruyter, 1989).

[38] *Hokkanen v Finland* (n 3) at [55].

[39] See an outline of these duties in section I above. See also U Kilkelly, 'Protecting Children's Rights under the ECHR: The Role of Positive Obligations' (2010) 61(3) *Northern Ireland Legal Quarterly* 245.

[40] *A v United Kingdom* App No 25599/94 (1998) at [22]; Kilkelly at 256–57. See also O'Mahoney (n 2) 3–4.

many of the cases are framed around the rights of parents to have contact with their children, even if the balance is struck in light of the child's welfare. The ECtHR grounds these positive dimensions in the requirement that the state 'respect' the family ties between parent and child by rendering these rights 'effective'.[41] The idea of real and effective protection of rights is a lynchpin of the positive dimension of rights within the Convention.[42] However, the ways in which the right to the enjoyment of the parent–child relationship is rendered 'effective' raises interesting questions.

In *Hokkanen v Finland*, the ECtHR derived the principles concerning private interferences with family rights from the cases on compulsory care proceedings, where the state is obligated to promote the reunion of the child with their parents, if this is compatible with the child's welfare.[43] The same principle as concerns *public* interference in family life was extended by the Court, without detailed justification, to the provisional transfer of care in *private* arrangements. From this point, the Court recognised that parental obstruction of custody and access rights in the context of private disputes might give rise to positive obligations on the state. In *Hokkanen*, the applicant father argued that the Finnish authorities failed to promote the reunion with his daughter, Sini, by allowing her grandparents to keep her in their care. The grandparents obstructed the father's contact with the child. These actions were in violation of relevant court decisions and the provisions of Finnish law. The father complained that the authorities had transferred Sini's custody to the grandparents.[44] At the time, Finland had a comprehensive scheme for enforcing contact orders, pursuant to which a 'conciliator' might be appointed to mediate between the parties. The aim of this mediation is not to re-examine the court's decision, but to promote voluntary compliance with the order. However, the law at the time also provided that mediation might not be justified where there are 'strong reasons' for immediate enforcement.[45] Fines and criminal sanction were permissible under this scheme, although the child's own wishes are determinative in cases where the child is over the age of 12 or 'sufficiently mature'.[46] The nature of these measures depends on the facts of each case and, crucially, requires the cooperation of 'all concerned', including the children.[47]

The ECtHR, in order to locate state responsibility in what had essentially become a private dispute, focuses on this legal framework and the practical steps taken pursuant to domestic law to enforce the father's rights of contact. However,

[41] *Marckx v Belgium* (1979–80) 3 EHRR 230 at [31].

[42] V Stoyanova, *Positive Obligations under the European Convention on Human Rights* (Oxford University Press, 2023) 11. See, as it relates to the parent–child relationship, *Hokkanen v Finland* (n 3) at [55].

[43] These principles were first established in a line of cases concerning public authority interventions in private and family life, where the state is obligated to promote family reunion where compatible with the child's welfare: see *Eriksson v Sweden* (1989) 12 EHRR 183 at [71].

[44] *Hokkanen v Finland* (n 3) at [8]–[9].

[45] ibid [45]–[48].

[46] ibid [47].

[47] ibid [62].

it is worth pausing to consider the differences between cases in which the state removes a child from the care of his or her parents and where parents or other family members obstruct access to a child. The Court examined one important factual distinction: in some cases, a care arrangement will arise 'de facto' from the conduct of the parties over time. In other instances, the parties will have sought a judicial basis for childcare arrangements, regulating access and custody, usually in cases where the parents cannot agree privately on these matters.[48] Indeed, Finland argued that the cause of the interference was the 'non-compliance' of private individuals, for which the state is 'not directly responsible'.[49] In the latter case, the state is clearly implicated: it is the defiance of a court order securing custody or access rights which is the cause of the complaint or the ineffectiveness of the remedies or measures taken to enforce that order. In other instances, the state might become implicated where it *legitimises* the de facto care arrangement or where the parent seeks enforcement of his or her rights as a parent with custody to the child, with the other party obstructing those rights.[50] In this case, the state's machinery is engaged because of the election of a private individual for protection of his rights. Indeed, this is how the interference is framed in *Hokkanen* and all subsequent cases: it is not, per se, the obstruction of private individuals with the realisation of family rights, but the *adequacy* of the regulatory framework and its enforcement mechanisms, the *decisions* of courts and public bodies and the *procedures* pursuant to these decisions following the obstructive behaviour of a parent or carer, insofar as these decisions prevent a parent from enjoying their Article 8 rights in relation to their child.[51]

However, the analytic distinction between positive and negative duties is not considered important by the ECtHR in the context of respect for the parent–child relationship, as is also true in other contexts under the Convention.[52] The Court has held that the distinction between positive and negative duties 'do not lend themselves to precise definition'.[53] Although these positive duties might suppose a distinct analytic approach, the ECtHR has asserted consistently that 'both contexts' require a fair balance to be struck between the various interests of the parties involved.[54] In other words, the 'applicable principles are similar' as between cases where the state arbitrarily interferes in private and family life and in relation to the positive duties placed on the state to protect and promote the family rights.[55] The ECtHR declined to determine the arguments concerning 'forcible' measures

[48] ibid [56].

[49] ibid [57].

[50] For example, by granting rights to the parent or carer who is acting contrary to the established rights of the custodial parent.

[51] *Amănălăchioai v Romania* (n 6) at [74]: 'Les *décisions* et l'ensemble des *procédures* dénoncées à la suite du refus des grands-parents de restituer l'enfant constituent une ingérence' (emphasis added).

[52] JV Wibye, 'Beyond Acts and Omissions: Distinguishing Positive and Negative Duties at the European Court of Human Rights' (2022) 23 *Human Rights Review* 479.

[53] *Hokkanen v Finland* (n 3) at [55].

[54] ibid; *Ignaccolo-Zenide v Romania* (n 5) at [94].

[55] *Hokkanen v Finland* (n 3) at [55].

of ensuring compliance, but did find violations on account of the state's failure to enforce the father's rights of access.[56] For example, the imposition of 'administrative fines' against the grandparents was insufficient, given their persistent refusal to comply.[57] The authorities failed to arrange meetings between the parties to conciliate. Although difficulties did arise from 'animosity' between the parties, the state was 'inactive' in the face of obstructive behaviour and did not take all 'reasonable efforts' to facilitate reunion.[58] Ultimately, however, once Sini had sufficient maturity to come to her own view, she refused to have contact with her father and from that point onwards, the Court held that it was justified not to pursue further enforcement measures.[59] The state failed to enforce the father's custody rights pending a determination of child custody, but the decision to give custody to the grandparents – after five years of caring for the child – was not disproportionate to protecting Sini's welfare.[60] Ultimately, therefore, the Court established the principles that form the basis of the positive obligations to respect and protect the parent–child relationship. The following sections analyse these in light of the subsequent case law and the systemic framework outlined above.

A. Relational and Systemic

Two initial arguments emerge from the foregoing analysis of the nature of Article 8 and its development by the ECtHR in the context of respecting family ties. First, it is the *relationship* which justifies the imposition of the duty and forms the object of its protection. When the focus is placed on the relational dimension of Article 8, the vulnerability of the right to state coercive overreach becomes apparent. So too, this relational aspect to the duty exposes the contingency of the state's power to respect family ties by way of employing coercive measures. Second, the systems theoretical account demonstrates that because the family is defined by its own systems of meaning, the boundaries of family life are defined according to the criteria which matter to the individuals, not the state. This means that the state's ability to directly regulate family life through law is inherently limited.

In *Iglesias Gil and AUI v Spain*, the Court examined the different aspects of the state's positive duties, including the need to adopt 'measures' designed to 'secure respect' in the 'sphere of relations between individuals'.[61] The state must also establish an adequate regulatory framework and enforcement machinery to protect individual rights and to enforce those rights through the making of 'specific steps'.[62] In *Iglesias Gil*, the applicant complained of a violation of her

[56] ibid [58] and [62].
[57] ibid [60].
[58] ibid [60]–[61].
[59] ibid [61]–[62].
[60] ibid [64].
[61] *Glaser* (n 19) at [63].
[62] Ibid; see also *Kosmopoulou v Greece* (n 8) at [43].

rights where the child's father abducted his son to the US from Spain.[63] The mother sought judicial permission that the father's calls be intercepted and that his family members be interviewed as part of the criminal complaint against the father for child abduction.[64] The judge initially refused these requests as well as refusing to issue an international search and arrest warrant against the father or to take further steps in relation to the father's refusal to comply with judgments of the family courts.[65] Meanwhile, a different judge of the family court revoked the father's parental responsibility and awarded full parental responsibility to the mother.[66] The ECtHR recognised in *Iglesias Gil* that the positive duty to 'facilitate reunion' is not absolute and the 'understanding and cooperation of all concerned is always an important ingredient'.[67] The question was whether the state took all measures that could 'reasonably be demanded' to facilitate the applicant's custody and responsibility for her child.[68] Spain's removing of the father's parental responsibility and awarding the mother sole custody were justified. In this case, the abduction of the child abroad was in violation of the Hague Convention and domestic laws implementing this convention, and the ECtHR found a failure to make use of the powers in the Hague Convention to enforce the court orders in the mother's favour.[69] Moreover, although the Court held that the domestic court's interpretation of the law relating to international arrests was reasonable, the legislation itself was inadequate: this is because the father's criminal contempt of court was not sufficiently serious to satisfy the domestic requirements for such an order.[70] The Court 'noted' (seemingly with approval) that Spain had implemented reforms increasing the criminal liability of a parent guilty of abducting a child from another person who had lawfully been granted custody.[71] Ultimately, however, the Court found the violation in relation to the failure of the state to take 'adequate and effective measures' to respect the mother's family ties with her child rather than due to the inadequacy of its domestic framework.[72]

We can see from this case the two basic insights highlighted above: that this right is fundamentally *relational* and that it concerns the dynamics within *systems* of family life. First, in order for Article 8 to be engaged at all, the applicant must show that they enjoy a 'family life' with another person. The existence of 'family life' depends on both the parent's relationship to the child and their relationship

[63] *Iglesias Gil and AUI v Spain* (n 7) at [10].
[64] ibid [13]; see also at [46] for a summary of actions taken by the state including phone tapping and asset freezes. At the point of the father's return to Spain, the applicant dropped civil and criminal actions, so there was no request for his imprisonment.
[65] ibid [11]–[20].
[66] ibid [23].
[67] ibid [50].
[68] ibid [52].
[69] ibid [59].
[70] ibid [61].
[71] ibid.
[72] ibid.

with the other adults, as determined by the court.[73] Article 8 is engaged where a parent shows 'commitment to the family', or 'attachment' to the child or 'motivation' to establish such a relationship.[74] Once the existence of 'family ties' has been demonstrated, the states owes both positive and negative duties to respect these ties. It is notable that although the courts will identify a violation against a person, it is the *relationship* that person has with their child that is the justification for Article 8 applying. Equally, it is the relationship that forms the true *object* of the state's duty. The state comes under a duty to act in a manner calculated to allow for a 'normal family life'.[75] The Court has reiterated on many occasions that this includes the 'mutual enjoyment by parent and child of each other's company' as a 'fundamental element' of normal family life.[76] Self-evidently, 'mutual enjoyment' reflects the fact that more than one party must be engaged in order for the family ties to exist. Measures that are designed to respect those ties cannot, in themselves, undermine or harm the relationship to an unjustified extent. When these family ties are disrupted, the state has positive obligations to respect and restore this relationship, but those same measures may themselves operate to harm that relationship. Although most cases are framed in terms of the parent's rights in relation to the child, the rights of the child (including their welfare) to the involvement of their parents in their upbringing is also, necessarily, implicated. One useful approach to understanding this relational dimension is by reference to the concept of the self-in-relationship with others. This conceptualisation can preserve a sphere of individual action, and the core idea of individual rights holders, whilst simultaneously recognising the vital interest in creating, maintaining and – in some instances – curtailing relationships with others. Thus, Kittay argues that we are 'selves that are always selves-in-relationship' and that the perception of individuality might only be relevant to limited spheres of action,[77] certainly not, in this instance, cases expressly concerned with respecting 'ties' or 'relationships' between individuals. In some cases, the child is joined in the proceedings as an applicant, yet in other cases the focus remains on the parent's rights, with a more indirect role for the child's rights.[78] As will be examined below, the primary limitation to the use of coercion is the welfare of the child. The child's welfare is relational because coercion may directly harm the child or may harm the child's relationship with others. This reflects the idea that a relational account

[73] T Koivula, 'What Makes a Father: Differentiation of Unmarried and Divorced Fathers in the Context of Custody under the Jurisprudence of the European Court of Human Rights' (2024) 38(1) *International Journal of Law, Policy and the Family* 1; see also C Fenton-Glynn, *Children and the European Court of Human Rights* (Oxford University Press, 2020) section 8.2.

[74] Fenton-Glynn (n 73) 222.

[75] *Marckx v Belgium* (n 41) at [31].

[76] *McMichael v United Kingdom* App No 16424/90 (1995) 20 EHRR 205 at [86].

[77] E Kittay, 'Searching for an Overlapping Consensus: A Secular Care Ethics Feminist Responds to Religious Feminists' (2007) 4(3) *University of St Thomas Law Journal* 468, 475.

[78] For example, in *Marckx v Belgium* (n 41), the child, Alexandra, was also an applicant and the Court held that her rights under art 8 and art 14 were violated by Belgium's regulation of parent–child ties.

is dependent on the interests of more than one person and that a 'relational self' forms a subject of human rights law.[79]

Second, for the systems of family life, the 'boundaries and structures' of the family are those which become 'meaningful' for the individuals who 'identify themselves as members' of a family.[80] Thus, the idea that the Article 8 constructs its own conception of 'family ties' based on formal classification such as with mothers and married fathers or parental commitment, attachment or motivation for other parents, is somewhat in tension with the internal identification of family connections within the systems of the family. It is worth recalling that systems are semi-autonomous in the sense that they determine their own boundaries and respond to externality through their own internal logic. From this perspective, direct legal regulation by command and control leads to irrelevant or 'disintegrating effects' on family life, or, because of the failure of the law to make good on its demands, the law suffers 'disintegrating effects' itself.[81] This is why there is a fundamental limitation to the state's ability to enforce family ties between individuals: those ties are external to the law and dependent on the dynamics of each family. As in *Iglesias Gil*, the case law consistently demonstrates the contingency of state power: in *Kosmopoulou v Greece*, the applicant argued that her Article 8 rights were violated when, having left her husband and daughter to live in the UK, the Greek courts granted the father custody of their child.[82] The ECtHR found that the mother enjoyed a de jure family relationship with her daughter (on account of the fact that she was the legal mother of the child) and that this right included, at its core, the 'mutual enjoyment' of company between parent and child. At the same time, the applicant mother sought and was granted access and contact such that her daughter would spend time with her once a week and during the holidays. However, before long, this arrangement broke down. The daughter refused to stay with the mother, leading to an instance in which the applicant caused her daughter physical harm.[83] Nonetheless, the Greek courts held that the child's welfare required her to have contact with her mother and that the father was obligated to facilitate this contact.[84] The father failed to comply with this order on occasions, but the courts also found that the child absolutely refused to stay with the applicant and that the father was 'doing all he could'.[85] From a systems theoretical perspective, this outcome is predicable: direct measures of enforcement of the mother's access rights, with her relationship defined based on formal

[79] J Nedelseky, 'The Relational Self as the Subject of Human Rights' in D Celermajer and A Lefebvre, *The Subject of Human Rights* (Stanford University Press, 2020).

[80] J Rodger, 'Luhmann's Theory of Psychic Systems and Communication in Social Work Practice' (2022) 22(3) *Journal of Social Work* 595, 642.

[81] Teubner (n 36) 21.

[82] *Kosmopoulou v Greece* (n 8) at [10]–[13].

[83] ibid [20]–[21].

[84] ibid [23].

[85] ibid [28].

criteria, are always dependent on cooperation. The daughter's absolute refusal to engage with her mother cannot be overcome by force of law.

Ultimately, in *Kosmopoulou*, both sides brought numerous criminal complaints against one another concerning non-compliance with court orders.[86] The ECtHR focused on the procedural aspect of the state's obligations because the mother had not received important information during the proceedings which led to an initial suspension of her access rights at a crucial time in the dispute.[87] It was, in the end, the unjustified disruption of her access rights by the Greek courts, rather than any explicit failure to ensure the father's compliance with court orders, that formed the basis of the violation of Article 8.[88] The shift from the substantive question examined in detail by the ECtHR to the procedural irregularities concerning the suspension of the mother's access rights is arguably reflective of the difficulty in respecting family ties in circumstances where the child is reluctant to engage with the non-resident parent.

B. Personal Responsibility

An unusual aspect of the case law is that whether the state is in violation of its duties is dependent on the *engagement and cooperation* of the family members and the *active* efforts of the applicant to enforce their rights. We have already seen that the non-cooperation of a child in *Kosmopoulou* was central to the human story, although the ECtHR ended up by identifying a procedural failure as the basis of the violation. Although the state must do its 'utmost' to *facilitate* cooperation, the duty to 'apply coercion' is inherently limited because of the need to encourage conciliation and cooperation to achieve practical results.[89] The reason given for this limitation, grounded on the need for cooperation, is also based on the idea that the interests of *all* parties are engaged.[90] As shown in section III.A above, the matter is distinctly relational: it is not the rights of one party, in isolation from others, that is in play, but the web of interests that form family ties. This context means that coercive measures are particularly risky as they have a tendency to threaten the interests of one party, thereby also undermining the child's welfare.

However, it is not only that cooperation is inherent in the effective realisation of Article 8, but that parents cannot rely on the state alone: they must take personal responsibility and be an active enforcer of their rights. In *Hokkanen*, the Finnish government highlighted the applicant's conduct, noting the father's failures to visit his daughter or request the imposition of fines, or to review

[86] ibid [30]–[31].
[87] ibid [49]–[50].
[88] ibid [50].
[89] *Iglesias Gil and AUI v Spain* (n 7) at 50].
[90] ibid.

enforcement decisions without delay.[91] The Court considered the complaints of the Finnish government to be 'improbable' and instead referred to the 'reasonable steps' which the father had taken to have his parental rights enforced by the state authorities.[92] Without these reasonable steps, there is an implication that the state's ineffective responses might not amount to a violation of his rights.[93] This is because, in effect, the applicant's behaviour would have been framed as the *cause* of the difficulties, with the father taking 'responsibility' for the results.[94] Yet, in this context, the responsibility of the non-resident parent is engaged in a more specific way: as Fenton-Glynn remarks, parents 'must themselves be proactive and involved in the enforcement attempts'.[95] This is a unique 'contortion' of the responsibility back on to individuals.[96] This is why in *Glaser*, the Court rejected a father's contention that the state must take the lead in enforcing rights of contact: 'active participation can hardly be dispensed with in the normal course of events'.[97] On the other hand, as explained in *Fourkiotis v Greece*, as will be further discussed below, a father's failure to seek criminal sanctions against the mother did not mean that he failed to proactively enforce his rights; in fact, the Court noted that such measures would have likely exacerbated the situation.[98]

So, parental involvement is essential in the enforcement of family rights. It is a striking recognition that both the applicant must be an active enforcer of their own rights and that the state's enforcement powers are contingent and limited by the cooperation of the other adults and the child. Fenton-Glynn is critical of this shift in responsibility.[99] Yet, there is also a certain systemic logic: the state cannot compel compliance effectively without cooperation because the object of the enforcement proceedings is the relationship between parent and child. Without the active involvement of the applicant, the relationship with the child could not be sustained and respected. It is also worth recalling that when law is understood as no longer hierarchically superior within the scheme of systems of social life and unable to directly make good on its own claims without the destruction of its target system, it is clear why cooperation and active involvement are necessary. Thus, although the Court is wrong to censure parents for lack of engagement with enforcement,[100] the cases examined in this article demonstrate not only the contingency of state power but also the complex systemic relationship between law and family life.

[91] *Hokkanen v Finland* (n 3) [57].
[92] ibid [56].
[93] ibid [60].
[94] ibid.
[95] Fenton-Glynn (n 73) 280.
[96] ibid 281.
[97] *Glaser v United Kingdom* at [70].
[98] *Fourkiotis v Greece* App No 74758/11 unreported, ECHR (6 Jun 2016) at [69] and [74].
[99] Fenton-Glynn (n 73) 281–82.
[100] As was the case in *GB v Lithuania* (36137/13) (2016).

C. Sanctions and the Need for Cooperation

The ECtHR reiterates in each case that although the state's positive duties are not absolute and are contextually malleable, the positive duty to 'facilitate reunion' requires the 'understanding and cooperation of all concerned' as an 'important ingredient.'[101] This is reflective of the basic fact that regulating family life exposes the practical limitations of state power: efforts to compel compliance are liable to result in ineffective outcomes, unresponsiveness or even harm to the family ties that are at the centre of the right. Indeed, in *Fourkiotis v Greece*, the ECtHR recognised expressly that coercive measures can be self-defeating: criminalising the obstructive parent might slow the reunion between the other parent and their child, harm the children and alienate the other parent further. This is why the Court stated that a 'deprivation of liberty' is an 'exceptional measure' that can only be considered once other means have been explored.[102] The Court in *Fourkiotis* was clear about the complex relationship between sanctions, cooperation and the welfare of the child: coercive measures might interfere with facilitating a cooperative attitude between parents and carers, which in turn may prolong the resolution of custody and access disputes. Yet, even if sanctions are not always appropriate to ensure compliance, a lack of cooperation 'cannot exempt' the state from implementing 'all measures' that are liable to maintain the family ties between parent and child.[103] This means, as the cases of *Amănălăchioai* and *Santos Nunes* demonstrate, coercive means are a subsidiary measure, with the state needing to act diligently to avoid alienation and cooperatively. These ideas are further explored in section III.D below, but are also discussed in this section as it pertains to the broader need to foster cooperation and balance this with the use of sanctions. This reflects that although indirect means of realising positive human rights duties might better navigate the systemic challenges outlined in this chapter, ultimately, the *background* availability of sanctions remains necessary in some cases as a means of encouraging compliance, as externalities intended to indirectly alter the internal logic of the family.[104]

In *Amănălăchioai v Romania*, a child was left with her maternal grandparents for holidays following the death of her mother. This arrangement was initially supported by the father until the grandparents asserted that they would not return the child to the father's custody.[105] The father sought the return of his daughter and obtained an order to this effect from the District Court.[106] However,

[101] *Iglesias Gil and AUI v Spain* (n 7) at [50].
[102] *Fourkiotis v Greece* (n 98) at [69].
[103] ibid [72].
[104] Fredman (n 4) 150 and 157.
[105] *Amănălăchioai v Romania* (n 6) at [6]–[8]. As such, there are some notable similarities with the leading case of *Hokkanen*.
[106] ibid [12]–[13].

enforcement was unsuccessful and the father's attempts to return his daughter to his custody were met with physical resistance and physical harm to the child.[107] Subsequent judicial decisions supported the grandparents, with whom the child had developed a close attachment, and the Romanian Court of Appeal ultimately decided that, for the present time, the child would remain with them.[108] This outcome was upheld by the Supreme Court,[109] which reasoned that changes in the father's living arrangement, including his re-marriage to a woman with a child of her own, meant that the daughter's best interests were served by remaining with the grandparents.[110] Moreover, it held that the initial permission given by the father had always been open-ended and that the father had acted violently in pursuit of restoring custody of his daughter. The applicant's wife, being young and already responsible for the care of another child, would not give care as well as the maternal grandparents would do.[111] The grandparents did not obtain legal custody of the child and nor were the father's parental rights terminated.[112] Over time, the child became increasingly attached to their carers and their relationship with the father deteriorated. This fact gives rise to a special duty of exceptional diligence.[113]

The father argued that the authorities had not taken sufficient steps to ensure the integrity or unity of his family by its failure to effect the immediate return of his child. As discussed above, one aspect of the state's duty is to punish non-compliance with court orders where these interfere with the parent's Article 8 rights. In *Amănălăchioai*, the Court held that the simple 'passage of time' which led to the child developing ever-closer bonds with her grandparents could not, of itself, justify further inaction on the part of the state; indeed, to allow the father's rights to be undermined by the passage of time would be to render these rights ineffective and illusory.[114] Moreover, the Court held that the measures taken must be speedily implemented: a 10-week delay between the father's request for state enforcement of his parental rights and the first hearing of his case was not sufficiently urgent, nor did it secure against a change of factual circumstances that would make re-establishing parental bonds more challenging over time.[115] Thus, the state comes under a positive duty to 'take appropriate measures to sanction a lack of cooperation' on the part of the child's carers.[116] Whilst the Court recognised

[107] ibid [17]–[18].
[108] ibid [29].
[109] ibid [36].
[110] ibid.
[111] ibid.
[112] ibid [37]–[40].
[113] The concept of parental alienation is controversial, but has been referred to by the ECtHR in a number of cases, including *Pisica v Moldova* (n 15).
[114] *Amănălăchioai v Romania* (n 6) at [89]: 'respect effectif de la vie familiale commande que les relations futures entre parent et enfant se règlent sur la seule base de l'ensemble des éléments pertinents, et non par le simple déroulement du temps'.
[115] ibid [93].
[116] ibid [94]: 'il appartient aux autorités compétentes de prendre les mesures adéquates afin de sanctionner ce manque de cooperation'.

that coercive measures are not preferable, sanctions must 'not be ruled out' in cases of manifestly unlawful conduct by the persons with whom a child is living.[117] It is clear, then, that the Court views sanctions as an important aspect of the effective regulatory scheme for family relationships, albeit that coercion is not to be the first measure where there is repeated non-cooperation. However, it is notable that criminal proceedings in this case 'proved futile' because of the lack of effective implementation of these measures which 'facilitated' the child's integration into her new environment with the grandparents.[118]

In another case, *Santos Nunes v Portugal*, the ECtHR found a violation of Article 8 in a case where the court had granted the father custody of his child in circumstances where the child's mother had placed his daughter with a couple, MG and G. The couple refused to hand over the child to the father in defiance of the court order.[119] The court eventually classified the case as urgent and transferred it to the judicial police division. Despite efforts to negotiate an agreement, no progress was made. Eventually, the domestic court ordered a transitional arrangement whereby E would live with the couple, with the father having rights of contact.[120] More than four years after the initial order granting the father custody, E was finally handed over. The couple were prosecuted for child abduction and made to pay damages.[121] The Court held that the uncooperative and obstructive attitude of the couple did not excuse the state for its failure to effectively protect the family ties between the father and E. The state had not taken 'all measures necessary' to facilitate the reunion between the father and his daughter which could be 'reasonably expected' in all the circumstances.[122] Despite the involvement of the police, there was little progress in tracing E and enforcing the court's orders until a custodial sentence was passed against MG.[123] In the period prior to the transfer of the case to the criminal division, the Court held that the lack of urgency and insufficiency of the efforts to trace E meant that there was a serious absence of diligence in respecting the applicant's Article 8 rights, which amounted to a violation.

D. Preparatory Measures and Exceptional Diligence

As introduced in the previous section, the Court employs two important doctrinal devices: 'preparatory measures' and 'exceptional diligence'. These, however, often act in tension with one another: on the one hand, the state is obligated to act with 'exceptional' diligence in enforcing rights of contact and custody, acting to restore these expeditiously so as to avoid parental alienation, but on the other

[117] ibid: 'le recours à des sanctions ne doit pas être écarté …'.
[118] ibid [95].
[119] *Santos Nunes v Portugal* App No 61173/08, unreported, ECHR (2012) at [12] and [18]–[19].
[120] ibid [32]–[40].
[121] ibid [44]–[51].
[122] ibid [68].
[123] ibid [75].

hand, enforcement of these rights without prior measures being taken is unlikely to be effective and may result in harm to the child's welfare. The family context means that the ECtHR employs a distinct framework, cognisant of the principled and pragmatic limits to enforcing parent–child relationships. The duty to maintain contact between parents and children is qualified not only by reference to the concept of 'reasonableness' but also with regard to the more specialised conception of 'exceptional diligence'.[124] This is because of the need to ensure enforcement action is effective and timely, so as to address the phenomenon of 'parental alienation' (unduly undermining the parent–child relationship). Indeed, in *Santos Nunes*, the Court stated that the passage of time may have 'irremediable consequences' and that the 'breakdown of contact with a very young child may lead to a growing deterioration' to the parent–child relationship.[125] This idea is more fully and sharply articulated in the cases of *Ignaccolo-Zenide v Romania* and *Pisica v Moldova*. Preparatory measures were first developed in *Hokkanen*, where the ECtHR held that the state is under a duty to promote the reunion of parent and child expeditiously. These preparatory measures show that enforcement is contingent on first taking steps to enable the relationship to develop; this means that the state comes under an initial facilitative duty.[126] These two duties may at times be in tension, but the effective and diligent enforcement of custody and contact is a way of avoiding the lapse of time and parental influence from de facto resolving the case.[127]

In *Ignaccolo-Zenide v Romania*, the ECtHR considered the case of a mother who complained of a breach of her rights of contact when the father, who had sole parental responsibility, removed their two daughters to the US without informing the mother of this development.[128] The parents entered into court proceedings in the US and in Europe, respectively, with a French court ultimately convicting the father of child abduction and sentencing him to a term in prison.[129] The mother sought to enforce these orders in California, at which point the father once again relocated the children to Romania.[130] The mother secured an order that the children be returned to her in the Romanian courts under the Hague Convention. The father continued to resist the court's orders and in the end his appeals against the order to return the children were dismissed. The mother made numerous attempts to have the Romanian court orders enforced, all without success. This resulted in a criminal complaint against the father. However, it was alleged that the Romanian police were 'turning a blind eye' to the father's conduct. At a conference with the mother and her children, both girls strongly expressed their desire not to reside

[124] *Pisica v Moldova* (n 15) at [66]; *Ignaccolo-Zenide v Romania* (n 5) at [102].
[125] *Santos Nunes v Portugal* (n 119) at [69]; *Fourkiotis v Greece* (n 98) at [61].
[126] *Hokkanen v Finland* (n 3) at [62].
[127] *LB v Slovakia* App No 5541/22, unreported, ECHR (12 September 2024) at [26]–[27].
[128] *Ignaccolo-Zenide v Romania* (n 5) at [10]–[12].
[129] ibid [20].
[130] ibid [27].

with her and the mother subsequently decided no longer to pursue their return.[131] The 'obstinate refusal' of the children to see their mother was the basis for the Romanian government's decision not to have the children returned to France.[132] The mother contended that Romania was in violation of her rights under Article 8 on account of its refusal to take sufficient steps to rapidly execute the court decisions.[133] The ECtHR held that the state was required to take 'preparatory measures', taking account of the 'understanding and cooperation' of all parties.[134] This means that Article 8 requires, prior to the use of coercive interventions, other 'soft' measures as a means of inducing compliance (and ensuring the welfare of the children is considered). Normatively, this is preferable: it recognises the state's inherent limitations in securing compliance in private arrangements, especially where the child's welfare is linked with the welfare of his or her parents and relies on their cooperation. Indeed, *Ignaccolo-Zenide* shows that to act without preparatory measures would be a violation of the Convention itself.

In *Pisica*, the applicant mother divorced the father of her son, but cohabited together and gave birth with the father to two further children (twins). However, the father, P, became aggressive towards the applicant and forcibly removed the children at various points until all three boys lived with the father, in defiance of an agreed custody schedule and a protective order.[135] In the end, all three children ended up in the father's custody and the mother was prevented from seeing them. A psychological report found that P had strongly influenced the attitude of the children to their mother and that denying access was a form of emotional abuse, but that meeting the mother at that time would be 'traumatising' while they continued to live with P.[136] The mother obtained an order granting her rights of custody and access, but P refused to comply, and so she sought urgent police intervention to enforce the order.[137] The children refused to leave because they wished to stay with the father, and subsequent attempts at enforcing these orders all failed, including a final effort at which P encouraged the children to comply.[138] The child's welfare and their expressed wishes are discussed below; however, at this stage, it is important to note that the child's views are a weighty concern, but are not a 'veto', and a broader assessment of their welfare is required.[139] The Court subsumed the failure to enforce the applicant's custody rights and the state's failure to prevent parental alienation as 'essentially the same issue' of whether the state complied with its positive obligations under Article 8 as a whole.[140] The Court highlighted a

[131] ibid [69]–[72].
[132] ibid.
[133] ibid [89].
[134] ibid [94].
[135] *Pisica v Moldova* (n 15) at [7]–[11] and [14]–[15].
[136] ibid [29].
[137] ibid [33]–[34].
[138] ibid [48].
[139] ibid [65].
[140] ibid [67].

series of failures of the state to enforce custody or act on the mother's complaints and recognised that the children's refusal to stay with the mother 'caused a difficult situation', meaning that the state needed to take measures in preparation for their reunification.[141] Without first enforcing the custody rights expeditiously and then failing to psychologically prepare the children for reunion with their mother, the state was in violation of its positive duties.

The concept of 'preparatory measures' reflects the fact that the state cannot make good on its primary duty without the cooperation of the parties involved. The failure in *Pisica* is particularly acute. However, we can also see this aspect in *Amănălăchioai* (see above), where the Court held that preliminary steps must be taken to facilitate the successful reunion of parent and child. The Court stated that once a family tie has been established, subsequent 'lack of contact' and the passing of time cannot be reasons not to enforce the order; instead, the state is obligated to take measures to allow for the parent–child relationship to develop, for example, by way of supervised contact between the non-resident parent and the child.[142] Preparatory measures exemplify the fact that in the context of family relationships, the state must rely on a range of strategies to facilitate the enjoyment of Article 8, many of which necessarily cannot be coercive. This also reflects a basic premise of the systems theoretical account of law and society: law does not assume a hierarchically superior position in relation to other systems, with legal commands needing to be internalised within other systems according to their functionally differentiated internal logic. Moreover, as already explained in section III.A above, family life is defined self-referentially, with the boundaries of the family determined by individuals. Those boundaries cannot be judicially moved, although the state might facilitate the circumstances in which the parent–child relationship can be maintained or restored.

E. The Child's Welfare

The constraining feature of the Court's analysis of Article 8 is the child's welfare: this is the single most important principle which imposes an imperative limitation on the use of coercive means to enforce court orders which uphold Article 8 rights.[143] As stated in *Pisica*, parents are not entitled to have measures taken that would harm the child's 'health and development'.[144] Thus, the state's duty to do its 'utmost' to respect and restore family ties is always limited by the child's welfare. This principle was established in *Hokkanen*, where the Court stated that any 'obligation to apply coercion' is 'limited' in particular by the 'best interests of the child'

[141] ibid [78].
[142] *Amănălăchioai v Romania* (n 6) at [97].
[143] *Ignaccolo-Zenide v Romania* (n 5) at [94].
[144] *Pisica v Moldova* (n 15) at [65].

and his Article 8 rights.[145] Equally, in *Amănălăchioai*, the Court explained that the child's welfare takes precedence[146] but this has two aspects: the welfare of the child requires a healthy family environment, whilst at the same time, child welfare will usually require maintaining ties with their family members, except in exceptional cases where breaking those ties is justified.[147]

There are two ways in which child welfare becomes important. First, coercion against a parent may expose the child to harm, which not only undermines the child's relationship with the parent being sanctioned but may also defeat the purpose of the enforcement action to restore contact with their non-resident parent. In many of the cases discussed, this idea is illustrative of the risk, identified by Teubner, that command and control regulation can lead to the destruction or collapse of the target system. An example is *Fourkiotis v Greece*, in which the mother had been threatened with imprisonment and fines each time she failed to comply with a judgment in favour of the father having contact with their children.[148] However, the Greek authorities did not implement these coercive measures and the Court found that it was justified in not doing so.[149] The Court reasoned that such measures establishing criminal liability are not necessarily appropriate because coercion is 'rarely effective'.[150] Criminal liability tends to be 'slow' to achieve a desired result, but also, and more crucially, criminalising a parent might have a 'deleterious effect' on a child's 'psyche', in turn undermining the needed cooperation between parents in the child's best interests.[151] Indeed, the applicant noted himself that the pursuit of criminal measures could be self-defeating or unpredictable, offering a new 'pretext' for alienating the children from their father.[152] From a system theoretical perspective, *Fourkiotis* exemplifies the regulatory trilemma which sees legal commands resulting in unresponsiveness, ineffectiveness or destructive outcomes, all of which are identified by the ECtHR in its discussion of the Greek measures available, but not employed, to secure compliance.[153] Thus, although failure to seek criminal sanctions was not a violation, the state nonetheless made procedural errors and failed to proactively facilitate a resolution, resulting in a violation of Article 8.

The second way in which welfare becomes important is because the views and wishes of the child form a key part of assessing the child's welfare. Therefore, contact and access without taking sufficient account of the child's views may not strike a fair balance. The child's wishes and feelings are a primary consideration

[145] *Hokkanen v Finland* (n 3) at [62].
[146] *Amănălăchioai v Romania* (n 6) at [81]: 'l'intérêt des enfants doit passer avant toute autre considération'.
[147] ibid.
[148] *Fourkiotis v Greece* (n 98) at [67].
[149] ibid [68].
[150] ibid: 'rarement souhaitables ou efficaces'.
[151] ibid: 'elles risquent d'avoir un effet délétère sur le psychisme de l'enfant mineur'.
[152] ibid [69].
[153] ibid.

when striking a fair balance between the different rights and the state's interests in upholding the rule of law. Indeed, following the principles in *Neulinger and Shuruk v Switzerland*, the child's welfare is 'paramount' and may 'override' the rights of their parents, depending on the 'nature and seriousness' of each case.[154] So, although the ECtHR states that the concept of 'reasonableness' and a 'fair balance' are employed so as to articulate the limits of the state's positive duties, these are inherently constrained by the cooperation of all parties and the child's welfare. This creates an unusual form of balancing exercise: it is one in which the child's welfare takes some degree of normative priority. Indeed, in *Pisica*, the Court stated that there is a 'broad consensus' that the child's rights are paramount.[155] However, although the Court recognised that the views of the child are to be taken into account, they are 'not necessarily immutable' and objections on their own will not be 'necessarily sufficient' to override parental interests, including the parent's right to regular contact.[156] Put even more strongly, the Court explained that the child's views are not an 'unconditional veto' and a broader consideration of their best interests is necessary in each case.[157]

The case of *N.TS v Georgia* illustrates these issues well. The applicant was the maternal aunt of three children whose father was convicted of drug offences and was also diagnosed with serious mental health difficulties. The mother of the three children died in unrelated circumstances. The children began living with their aunt. In the meantime, their father started treatment and was in remission, and requested the return of the boys to his care, which was resisted by the aunt and the maternal family.[158] The family circumstances of both the father and aunt were later assessed to both provide suitable environments, although issues were noted in relation to some psychological conflict on the part of the three boys towards their father.[159] The court ordered that the children be returned to their father, which was successfully appealed by the aunt and reached the Supreme Court, which remitted the case for a further hearing at the Court of Appeal.[160] Upon a rehearing, the Court of Appeal held that the children should be returned to their father.

The principal issue in *N.TS* concerned the psychological preparedness of the children to rejoin their father. The eldest child had been diagnosed with an anxiety disorder and the contact with their father during the intervening time had been minimal. Indeed, the children had assumed a 'negative' attitude to their father, which the Court of Appeal had considered a consequence of the maternal aunt and her family.[161] Enforcement of this order failed: the boys refused to be handed over

[154] *Neulinger and Shuruk v Switzerland* App No 41615/07), unreported, ECHR (6 July 2010) at [135]; *Strand Lobben v Norway* App No 37283/13, 70 EHRR 14 at [179].

[155] *Pisica v Moldova* (n 15) at [65].

[156] ibid.

[157] ibid.

[158] *N.TS v Georgia* (n 8) at [6]–[9].

[159] ibid [17].

[160] ibid [17]–[26].

[161] ibid [30]–[31].

to their father, with the children expressing fear of the use of force.[162] A psychologist reported that the father ought to attempt other ways of 'regaining their trust and re-establishing a relationship with his children'.[163] As a consequence, after two unsuccessful attempts to enforce the court's order, the children remained with their aunt. At the ECtHR, the case was brought by the aunt on behalf of the children; thus, it was not the aunt's rights which were argued to be violated, but those of the three boys. The Court repeated the important principle that the child's welfare is a 'primary' consideration and may override the rights of other persons.[164] Moreover, children have a right to be consulted and represented, in accordance with their maturity, so that they can express a view.[165] In *N.TS*, these principles, alongside the more specific principle that preparatory measures are necessary before giving effect to a significant change in circumstances, meant that the Court found a violation of Article 8. It stated that 'ordering such a radical measure without considering a proper transition and preparatory measures aimed at assisting the boys and their estranged father in rebuilding their relationship appears to be contrary to their best interests'.[166]

IV. Conclusion

The state's positive duties to seek the reunion of parents and children with exceptional diligence and appropriate 'measures' to facilitate contact and enforce family rights present a unique context for evaluating the contingency of state coercive power. On account of the family context, and the inter-systemic dynamic between law and family life, the use of direct, command and control measures is liable to result in the trilemma: families may be unresponsive, for example, where the attitudes of the parties make the involvement of each parent difficult; or it may be ineffective, as where coercion delays the process or leads to counterproductive outcomes; or even destructive, as where state measures undermine the parent–child relationship or further alienate a parent from their children. The ways in which these measures are constructed employs a quite distinctive analytic framework. The 'more vulnerable' the individual is to systemic pressures, such as children or parents seeking to re-establish access or custody in the face of unjustified, persistent obstruction, the 'more society has to develop protection mechanisms for the self-presentation and mobility of the individual'.[167] The various and complex ways in which the state

[162] ibid [34].
[163] ibid.
[164] ibid [71].
[165] ibid [71]–[72]. The ECtHR interprets this duty in light of art 12 of the United Nations Convention on the Rights of the Child, which embodies a right to be heard according to a child's capacity.
[166] *N.TS v Georgia* (n 8) at [83].
[167] G Verschraegen, 'Human Rights and Modern Society: A Sociological Analysis from the Perspective of Systems Theory' (2002) 29(2) *Journal of Law and Society* 258, 270.

comes under positive duties in the context of family relationships reflects not only the essentially *relational* quality of these rights but also the broader idea that 'obligations are not universal, and they are certainly not unlimited in scope'.[168] Indeed, a key thread in the cases and a core argument of this chapter is that the 'the nature and extent' of the state's duties will 'depend on the circumstances of each case'.[169] This chapter has carried out an analysis of the Convention that is both doctrinal *and* informed by a systems theoretical account of rights to evaluate the limitations of positive duties and the power of the state to make good on its obligations. In large part, the ECtHR tacitly and explicitly recognises these limitations through its focus on facilitating cooperation and personal responsibility, both of which reflect the need for behaviour change to be internalised within the family. In contrast, coercion is liable to put these objectives at risk.

[168] Stoyanova (n 42) 9.
[169] *Kosmopoulou v Greece* (n 8) at [45].

PART II

Identifying Limits

6

Causation, Reasonableness and Positive Obligations

SOPHIE TREACY

I. Introduction

When an applicant comes before the European Court of Human Rights (ECtHR) alleging that a state has failed to fulfil its positive obligations under the European Convention on Human Rights, she is asserting, either implicitly or explicitly, the existence of a causal link between the harm she suffered and the state's omission to fulfil the positive duties owed to her.[1] Subject to certain exceptions,[2] establishing causation is central to the imposition of legal liability, from the law of tort[3] to the rules of state responsibility under international law.[4] Whilst state liability for breach of positive obligations under the European Convention seems to be no different in this regard, the role of causation in connecting applicant harm to state omission to fulfil its positive obligations remains under-examined and undertheorised.[5] In her recent book,[6] Vladislava Stoyanova responds to this lacuna by teasing out certain elements of how causation functions in the context of positive obligations adjudication.[7] The central contribution of this chapter is to further explore both the concept of causation that is employed in this area of law and the role it plays

[1] See V Stoyanova, 'Causation between State Omission and Harm within the Framework of Positive Obligations under the European Convention on Human Rights' (2018) 18 *Human Rights Law Review* 309 at 311.

[2] See S Steel, *Proof of Causation in Tort Law* (Cambridge University Press, 2015) chs 4–6.

[3] See JJ Thomson, 'Remarks on Causation and Liability' (1984) 13 *Philosophy & Public Affairs* 101.

[4] Articles on the Responsibility of States for Internationally Wrongful Acts are reproduced in the *Yearbook of the International Law Commission*, 2001, vol II (Part Two). See also V Lanovoy, 'Causation in the Law of State Responsibility' (2022) *British Yearbook of International Law*, https://doi.org/10.1093/bybil/brab008; and T Davenport, R Mackenzie and N Craik, *Liability for Environmental Harm to the Global Commons* (Cambridge University Press, 2023) 96.

[5] L Lavrysen, 'Causation and Positive Obligations under the ECHR: A Reply to Vladislava Stoyanova' (2018) 18(4) *Human Rights Law Review* 705.

[6] V Stoyanova, *Positive Obligations under the European Convention on Human Rights* (Oxford University Press, 2023).

[7] ibid ch 3.

within the Court's wider determination of whether a state has breached its positive obligations under the Convention. The chapter makes two central claims. The first claim relates to the particular concept of causation that is invoked by the ECtHR. It is argued that causation in this context is necessarily less granular than how it manifests in other areas of the law, such as in the law of tort. The unworkability of the 'but for' test in this context is explored and it is shown how a Necessary Element of a Sufficient Set (NESS) test of causation can be seen to operate within the Court's jurisprudence. The second claim is that the concept of causation in this context should not be considered either an independent or normatively neutral head of inquiry when it comes to establishing state liability for omissions to fulfil positive obligations. Rather, the issue of causation is bundled into one single overarching question, usually related to the issue of reasonableness. This is because, it is submitted, the Court adjudicates positive obligations cases from a dual viewpoint, in that it is aware not only of providing a remedy for state omissions of the past, but also dictating state actions for the future. It is this proximity of the Court's adjudication to the stipulation of Convention duties that stokes its awareness of the broader reasonableness of expecting states to fulfil certain duties, regardless of whether causation is retrospectively established by the applicant.

II. The Standard of Factual Causation in Positive Obligations Cases

Causation is typically a threshold question of legal liability[8] – whether that be an individual's liability for her negligent actions or a state's liability for failing to fulfil its positive obligations under international law.[9] Whilst the role of causation in the former context has been the subject of sustained academic and judicial scrutiny, literature regarding the latter is comparatively thin on the ground.[10] In fact, international law courts are often criticised for being unclear or rudimentary in their causal analyses,[11] particularly in the area of international human rights law.[12] As Sulyok notes, the 'disturbing absence of clarity'[13] in this area creates difficulty and frustration for those seeking to understand the causal nexus that exists between state action or inaction and applicant harm under international law.

[8] WL Prosser, *Handbook of the Law of Torts*, 4th edn (West Publishing Co, 1971) at 41.
[9] Lanovoy (n 4).
[10] Lavrysen (n 5).
[11] I Plakokefalos, 'Causation in the Law of State Responsibility and the Problem of Overdetermination: In Search of Clarity' (2015) 26 *European Journal of International Law* 471 at 472–73.
[12] D McGrogan, 'The Problem of Causality in International Human Rights Law' (2016) 65 *International and Comparative Law Quarterly* 615.
[13] K Sulyok, *Science and Judicial Reasoning: The Legitimacy of International Environmental Adjudication* (Cambridge University Press, 2020).

In the spirit of bringing greater clarity to this area, this chapter examines causation as it features in the case law of the ECtHR, specifically within the Court's positive oblgiations jurisprudence. The reason for this particular focus is that, first, the positive obligations jurisprudence of the ECtHR is in need of greater analytical clarity generally speaking.[14] As Stoyanova observes, the methodology employed by the Court when determining whether a positive obligation arises under the Convention, or whether a state has breached its positive duties, may appear incoherent or even arbitrary.[15] This chapter aims to respond to the impetus for greater theoretical and doctrinal clarity in terms of how positive obligations are adjudicated as far as the issue of causation is concerned. Second, this chapter focuses on casuation within positive obligaitons cases specifically as, it is argued, there are some unique and interesting features of the causal inquiry as it operates within this particular context.

It is important to flag from the outset that the concept of *causation* in the law has, traditionally, represented two separate lines of inquiry. The first is the issue of factual causation, which refers to the question of whether the actions of a particular defendant caused, as a matter of fact, the harm suffered by the plaintiff. The second is the issue of legal causation (or proximity or remoteness) which essentially determines the *extent* to which a defendant should be liable for the factual events resulting from their acts or omissions. As we will explore later on, this is a distinciton that the ECtHR has not clearly drawn in its positive obligations jurisprudence. However, in order to square this chapter within the broader field of causation and the law, it is important to flag that the section that follows is concerned with the issue of *factual* causation – in other words, the question of whether the state's omission in failing the fulfil its positive obligations under the Convention is a factual cause of the damage incurred by the applicant.

We begin by examining the *standard* of factual causation that is used in positive obligations case law. As Stapleton notes, the term 'causation' is invoked for many different purposes to represent a whole range of different inquiries.[16] What constitutes 'causation' for a lawyer will differ from what the concept means for a scientist, or for a historian, or for somebody engaged in ordinary conversation. This has led to the division of causation as a concept into various categories, such as 'natural' or 'common-sense' causation, each corresponding to a different standard of percision.[17] What this reveals is that the concept of 'causation' can exist on different planes of metaphysical robustness, depending on the context within which it is invoked.[18] Accordingly, the following four subsections sketch out some

[14] B Dickson, 'Positive Obligations and the European Court of Human Rights' (2020) 61(3) *Northern Ireland Legal Quarterly* 203.

[15] Stoyanova (n 6) 2.

[16] J Stapleton, 'Choosing What We Mean by Causation in the Law Symposium: A Tribute to Professor David Fischer' (2008) 73 *MLR* 433.

[17] T Byrne, 'Legal Causation' (2023) 14 *Jurisprudence* 55.

[18] E Adams, 'The Flexibility of Description and NESS Causation' (2010) 10 *Journal of Philosophy, Science & Law* 12 at 13.

of the features of factual causation as it exists within positive obligations jurisprudence that dictate the standard of causation utilised by the Court when causally connecting a state failure to applicant harm.

A. Causation by Omission

The kind of causality at issue in positive obligations cases is causation by omission. The applicant must demonstrate that the inaction of the state in not fulfilling its positive duties caused their Convention rights to be violated. However, establishing causality by omission is no easy task. McGrath sums up the central difficulty as follows: either there is no such thing as causation by omission or there is far more than common sense says there is.[19] For example, imagine Sarah crosses the road, caused by her desire to get from one side to the other. Yet, if a speeding car knocked her down midway, or a bolt of lightning struck her before she could reach the other side, she would not have successfully done so. If we accept omissions as being causes, then responsible driving and pleasant weather are no less causes of her crossing the road than her intention to do so. This leaves us with a potentially infinite set of 'causes' for any one event, a difficulty that has led certain theorists to reject that omissions should ever be considered genuine causes.[20]

However, when there is a failure to fulfil a legal duty, the law needs a concept of causation to link the omission to liability for consequent harm, no matter how metaphysically flimsy it may be. The law is not interested in a potentially infinite body of counterfactual actions that might have prevented the harm; it is only concerned with the omission to which a legal duty attaches. This means that when determining whether an omission to fulfil a legal obligation caused harm, the law has to be *biased* towards it, purposefully ignoring the infinite other omissions that might have also prevented it from occurring.[21] The law's causal analysis of a certain harm will always be biased towards omissions to fulfil legal duties, such as the failure of a landlord to provide fire escape routes or the failure of a seller to warn a buyer of product risks.[22] Whilst such a biased perspective on causation would be unacceptable in other disciplines,[23] it has demonstrably succeeded in the law.[24]

[19] S McGrath, 'Causation by Omission: A Dilemma' (2005) 123 *Philosophical Studies* 125.

[20] See P Dowe, 'A Counterfactual Theory of Prevention and "Causation" by Omission' (2001) 79 *Australasian Journal of Philosophy* 216. See also D Ehring, 'Causal Relata' (1987) 73 *Synthese* 319.

[21] HLA Hart and T Honoré, *Causation in the Law*, 2nd edn (Clarendon Press, 1985) at 14.

[22] Examples taken from JD Rue, 'Returning to the Roots of the Bramble Bush: The "But for" Test Regains Primacy in Casual Analysis in the American Law Institute's Proposed Restatement (Third) of Torts' (2003) 71 *Fordham Law Review* 2679 at 2680.

[23] See Y Ben-Menahem, 'From Causal Relations to Causal Constraints' in *Causation in Science* (Princeton University Press, 2018) at 1–21 for a sense of what the natural sciences demand from a causal analysis.

[24] M Scordato, 'Three Kinds of Fault: Understanding the Purpose and Function of Causation in Tort Law' (2022) 77 *University of Miami Law Review* 149.

The law is, after all, no stranger to the lax use of causative language.[25] As Hart and Honoré observe, causal problems in the law tend to depend more on common sense than anything.[26] The strong justificatory force[27] and common-sense appeal[28] of invoking causative language when imposing liability for omissions means that the law is prepared to 'settle'[29] for a reductive account of causation in this context.[30]

Thus, the first thing to note about the standard of causation in positive obligations cases is that it is necessarily biased and reductive on account of it establishing causal relationships solely by omission. For example, in the case of *Hiller v Austria*,[31] the applicant's son escaped from a psychiatric hospital and subsequently committed suicide. The applicant alleged that the state had failed to fulfil its positive obligations to protect her son's right to life under Article 2 of the Convention as he 'would not have been able to commit suicide if he had been prevented from leaving the hospital grounds'.[32] Liability in this case therefore hinged, inter alia, on the causal significance of one particular omission, namely the failure of the state to fulfil its duties under Article 2, even if this harm was the product of any number of omissions. In cases such as this, the Court's causal analysis will be biased towards those potentially causal omissions that are underwritten by legal obligation. When an applicant alleges that the state's failure to fulfil its positive duties under the Convention *caused* her harm, the Court must overlook an infinite supply of other hypothetical omissions that might have counterfactually prevented the harm from occurring and focus exclusively on the causal significance of the state's omission.

B. The Specificity of Causative Events

Allowing the causal analysis to be biased towards an omission to fulfil a legal duty is not the only way in which the law has tailored its concept of causation in order to render it a workable line of inquiry for imposing liability. For instance, as Stapleton argues, the law purposely describes causal events at the level of specificity that matches its concern.[33] For example, if someone was to burn down a house, this

[25] Stapleton (n 16).

[26] Hart and Honoré (n 21) 9.

[27] S Steel, 'Legal Causation and AI' in E Lim and P Morgan (eds), *The Cambridge Handbook of Private Law and Artificial Intelligence* (Cambridge University Press, 2024) 189.

[28] See Thomson (n 3) 108.

[29] This is not to say that it is universally accepted. See, for instance, MS Moore, *Causation and Responsibility: An Essay in Law, Morals, and Metaphysics* (Oxford University Press, 2009), arguing that causation in the law should only ever be invoked when it maps onto a viable philosophical account.

[30] LA Paul and N Hall, 'Causation Involving Omissions' in *Causation: A User's Guide* (Oxford University Press, 2013) 173.

[31] *Hiller v Austria* (App No 1967/14).

[32] ibid para 21.

[33] J Stapleton, 'An "Extended But-for" Test for the Causal Relation in the Law of Obligations' (2015) 35 *Oxford Journal of Legal Studies* 697, 700.

could be described in either a coarse-grained or fine-grained way. We could say that a defendant started a fire (Event A) which burned down a house (Event B). Alternatively, we could say that they struck a match (Event A), which interacted with oxygen in the atmosphere to light a flame (Event B), which lit up piece of tinder (Event C), which caught fire to the grass surrounding the house (Event D), which destroyed the house (Event E) and so on. There are different levels of granularity according to which we can divide up the causative events leading to a particular effect. The trouble with framing events in a more fine-grained way is that it becomes increasingly challenging to draw hard and fast causative links between causes and their effects. This is why the law tends to gravitate towards coarse-grained accounts of antecedent causative events at the expense of metaphysical precision.[34]

It is clear to see why a coarse-grained framing of events would be critical for establishing causative links between a state's failure to fulfil its positive obligations and an applicant's harm. The kinds of omission that states are charged with before the ECtHR, like failures to put in place effective frameworks to safeguard life,[35] or failures to ensure the protection of vulnerable persons,[36] need to be construed along very coarse-grained lines if they are to be causally linked directly to specific harms suffered by individual applicants. In reality, the 'omission' of the state to fulfil its positive duties under the Convention is actually an endless stream of sub-omissions. For example, in the case of *Kolyadenko and Others v Russia*,[37] the Court held that Russia had breached the applicants' right to life under Article 2 of the Convention by not taking effective measures to prevent and warn them against the risk of flooding, leading to the destruction of their property and possessions. The applicants' damage was caused, first and foremost, by the flood. What the applicants sought to demonstrate was that the failure of the state to fulfil its positive obligation 'to put in place a legislative and administrative framework designed to provide effective deterrence against threats to the right to life'[38] was a cause-by-omission of the harm they suffered, which they successfully managed to do.[39] Notice what a coarse-grained framing of the causative event the Court allowed. The cause of the harm – the combined omissions of the government to establish a clear legislative and administrative framework to assess the risks of the river, to implement effective urban planning, to supervise, protect and inform the surrounding population, and to set in place an emergency warning system[40] – are all bundled together under the heading of one compounded cause-by-omission of the damage to the applicants' property and possessions. The state's omission to

[34] L Stapleton, 'Unnecessary Causes' (2013) 129 *LQR* 39.

[35] See *Öneryildiz v Turkey* (App No 48939/99); *Budayeva and Others v Russia* (App Nos 15339/02, 21166/02, 20058/02, 11673/02 and 15343/02).

[36] See *X and Others v Bulgaria* (App No 22457/16); *RB v Estonia* (App No 22597/16).

[37] *Kolyadenko and Others v Russia* [2012] ECtHR 338 (App No 17423/05).

[38] ibid 157.

[39] ibid 187.

[40] ibid 185.

fulfil its obligations under Article 2 in this case is really an innumerable number of omissions of all its administrative boards, commissions, committees etc not to have taken any meaningful preventative steps to counteract the risk of flooding at any point in time before it transpired. Of course, a degree of vagueness in how a state fulfils its positive obligations is inevitable and, indeed, desirable,[41] given that it allows states a margin of appreciation in terms of fulfilling what the Convention demands of them.[42] The upshot, however, is that omissions must be framed in a very coarse-grained way in order to render the causative inquiry a feasible endeavour.

C. Abandoning the 'But for' Test of Causation

We have seen that positive obligations cases necessarily adopt quite an imprecise and blunt test of causation, at least in metaphysical terms, as these cases establish causation by omission between very coarse-grained framings of events. However, this is no different from how the issue of causation works across many other areas of the law.[43] Yet, when it comes to translating this standard of factual causation into a test, the positive obligations cases part company with the standard approach of the law. Typically, when it comes to establishing causation, the 'but for' test is the first port of call for judges when deciphering a factual causal link between a breach of a legal duty and consequent harm.[44] The question is whether *but for* the act or omission of the defendant, would the plaintiff have sustained the harm? If the answer is no, then the act or omission of the defendant can be considered the factual cause for the plaintiff's damage, and liability can be attributed accordingly. Of course, the actual significance and utility of the 'but for' test as the primary test of causation in the law is greatly disputed on account of the difficulties it creates,[45] which we will return to shortly. The point for now is that the ECtHR has explicitly rejected the 'but for' test as the test for establishing causation in its positive obligations jurisprudence.[46] As the Court held in *E and Others v United Kingdom*,[47] 'the test under Article 3 however does not require it to be shown that "but for" the failing or omission of the public authority ill-treatment would not have happened'.[48] Instead, the Court stated, it mattered whether there was a 'real prospect' that the harm would have been avoided or mitigated had the state taken

[41] V Stoyanova, 'Framing Positive Obligations under the European Convention on Human Rights Law: Mediating between the Abstract and the Concrete' (2023) 23(3) *Human Rights Law Review* 1.

[42] *Fadeyeva v Russia* (App No 55723/00) at para 96.

[43] Byrne (n 17).

[44] NJ McBride and R Bagshaw, *Tort Law*, 6th edn (Pearson Education, 2018) 260.

[45] See M Moore, 'Causation in the Law' (2019) Winter Edition The Stanford Encyclopedia of Philosophy at 5.1, arguing that the supposed dominance of the 'but for' test is superficial and in reality judges modify or abandon it in a variety of ways.

[46] Stoyanova (n 1) 316.

[47] *E and Others v United Kingdom* (App No 33218/96).

[48] ibid para 99.

reasonably available measures in accordance with its positive obligations.[49] The 'but for' test was again rejected by the Court in the case of *O'Keefe v Ireland*,[50] in favour of an inquiry into whether there was a 'real prospect' that had the omissions not occurred, nor would the harm.[51]

This is not to say that the 'real prospect' test of causation has come anywhere close to universal application across the Court's positive obligations case law. For example, in *Tugar v Italy*,[52] the Court asked whether the applicant's harm was a 'direct consequence'[53] of the state's omission to fulfil its positive obligations, whilst in *Draon v France*,[54] the Court sought to establish a 'direct and immediate link'[55] because the omission and harm. Yet, as Stoyanova has argued, the 'real prospect' test may be considered a line of best fit through the doctrine in terms of representing the test of causation that the Court has opted for.[56]

There seem to be at least two reasons why the Court would abandon the 'but for' test in this context. First, positive obligations cases often have overdetermined causes,[57] meaning that applying the 'but for' test will throw up answers that affront common sense.[58] Second, if such cases were to adopt a 'but for' test of causation, it would create virtually insurmountable burdens of proof for applicants. In terms of the former, overdetermined causation occurs, broadly speaking, when a single event has multiple causes so that it is not possible to say *but for* one event, the outcome would not have happened.[59] For example, imagine that it takes a minimum of 50 ml of poison to kill a person and consider the following three scenarios;

- Kate and Johnny pour 25 ml of poison each into Barry's tea;
- Kate and Johnny pour 50 ml into Barry's tea at exactly same time;
- Kate pours 50 ml of poison into Barry's tea, but right before he is about to drink it, Johnny shoots him.

Each of these three scenarios are examples of overdetermination, as if we were to apply the strict 'but for' test of causation, it would not be possible to establish that Kate's actions are a 'but for' cause of Barry's death.[60] The same issue can

[49] ibid.
[50] *O'Keefe v Ireland* (App No 35810/09) at para 149.
[51] ibid.
[52] *Tugar v Italy* (App No 22869/93).
[53] ibid para 29.
[54] *Draon v France* (App No 1513/03).
[55] ibid para 106.
[56] Stoyanova (n 1) 317.
[57] I refer to overdetermination in the *legal* sense of the concept.
[58] A Burrows, *Remedies for Torts and Breach of Contract*, 3rd edn (Oxford University Press, 2004) 41.
[59] ibid.
[60] The kinds of overdetermination described are cumulative, complementary and pre-emptive respectively. See B Bollecker-Stern, *La préjudice dans la théorie de la responsabilité internationale* (Éditions A Pedone, 1973) at 267ff. Pierre d'Argent also adopts the same categorisation in 'Reparation Cessation, Assurances and Guarantees of Non-repetition' in A Nollkaemper and I Plakokefalos (eds), *Principles of Shared Responsibility in International Law: An Appraisal of the State of the Art* (Cambridge University Press, 2014) 208–50, at 224.

arise in positive obligations cases when the state's omission to fulfil its positive obligations is an overdetermined cause of the applicant's alleged harm and thus the 'but for' test cannot establish it as a factual cause of the harm. The Court acknowledged the unworkability of the 'but for' test in this context in its ruling in *Verein Klimaseniorinnen Schweiz and Others v Switzerland*,[61] wherein it held that the Swiss government had caused a violation of the applicant's rights under Article 8 by failing to take positive steps to mitigate the adverse effects of climate change. The harm that the applicants faced as a result of rising global temperatures is a paradigmatic example of an overdetermined cause. The failure of the Swiss government to fulfil its positive obligations to counteract climate change can only ever be considered a cumulative cause working in tandem with many other acts and omissions by both public and private actors. The Court recognised this, holding that the causative relationship between the harm suffered by the applicants and the omissions of the state could not be construed along the lines of a 'but for' test.[62]

The second issue with the 'but for' test of causation in this context is that it would create insurmountable probative difficulties for applicants. In the case of *E and Others v United Kingdom*,[63] for example, the applicants alleged that local authorities had not fulfilled their positive obligations under Article 3 by failing to take sufficient steps to prevent them from abuse they suffered as children. The state argued that it could not be proven that matters would have turned out any differently for the applicants had the local authorities been more proactive.[64] In other words, the omission could not be demonstrated to be a 'but for' cause of the harm. However, this line of reasoning created an impossible probative hurdle for the applicants' claim. An imagined counterfactual reality in which the state fulfilled its Convention obligations is far too uncertain to ground any probable conclusion that the harm would have been avoided had the state fully complied with its positive obligations. It is impossible to establish that *but for* the state's systemic failures to investigate instances of child abuse, the children would have been spared the harm they suffered as a matter of certainty. This was reason enough for the Court to explicitly reject the 'but for' test, as expecting the applicants to establish the counterfactual reality of the state having fulfilled its obligations was too burdensome.

Unlike other areas of the law in which the 'but for' test is more routinely applied, the kind of omissions that states are charged with in these cases are too vague to be subjected to such a strict counterfactual analysis. For example, in tort law it is clearly established that there is a common law duty not to defame your neighbour. If you breach this clearly stipulated duty and your neighbour loses her job as a result, you might be liable under tort law for having

[61] *Verein Klimaseniorinnen Schweiz and Others v Switzerland* (App No 53600/20).
[62] ibid §439.
[63] *E and Others v United Kingdom* (n 47).
[64] ibid para 99.

caused her this harm. By contrast, if a state is under a positive obligation to take reasonable measures to safeguard the reputation of those living within its jurisdiction under Article 8 of the Convention, for instance, this duty exists at a very abstract level of framing.[65] If an applicant comes before the ECtHR claiming that the state has breached its positive obligations by not protecting her from intrusive media coverage,[66] the Court would have to stipulate a highly concretised positive obligation of what exactly the state should counterfactually have done if a 'but for' test is to be implemented successfully. This is not something the Court is willing to do.[67] Unlike other areas of law, where it is desirable to have clearly stipulated legal duties, the same cannot be said for the law of positive obligations under the ECHR. This is an area of law, as Stoyanova notes,[68] where the positive duties that emanate from the Convention exist at different levels of framing, ranging from abstract to concrete. Typically, there are a variety of different measures that a state can choose from in order to fulfil its positive obligations. A 'but for' test of causation would require the Court to come down firmly on a highly specified means of fulfilling positive duties, which is not desirable from its perspective.[69] This provides yet another reason why 'but for' causation has been necessarily abandoned by the Court in its positive obligations jurisprudence.

D. The NESS Test of Causation

What the preceding analysis shows is that the 'but for' test of causation is analytically unworkable in the context of positive obligations, so the Court has abandoned it by necessity. In its place, however, there emerges no coherent or consistently applied alternative. Rather, there appears to be a patchwork of different tests for establishing the factual causative effects of state omissions, the most notable being the 'real prospect' test, which asks the following question: if the state had taken reasonable steps to fulfil its positive obligations, would there be a 'real prospect' of the applicant's harm being avoided or mitigated?[70]

What alternatives to the 'but for' test are there that the Court might implement in this context? In other areas of law, such as in the law of tort, the 'but for' test also inevitably runs into problems of overdetermination.[71] In order to deal with overdetermined causes in this context, the law has adopted an alternative test of causation, known as the NESS test. The NESS test, first formulated by Hart and

[65] Stoyanova (n 41).
[66] See, for instance, *Lindon and Others v France* (App Nos 21279/02 and 36448/02).
[67] Stoyanova (n 41).
[68] ibid.
[69] V Stoyanova, 'KlimaSeniorinnen and the Question(s) of Causation' (*Verfassungsblog*, 7 May 2024), https://verfassungsblog.de/klimaseniorinnen-and-the-questions-of-causation.
[70] Stoyanova (n 1).
[71] See, for instance *Fairchild v Glenhaven Funeral Services Ltd* [2002] UKHL 22.

Honoré[72] and developed by Wright,[73] establishes whether something is a cause by asking whether it is a necessary element of a sufficient set of conditions to bring about a particular event. The NESS test of causation is a 'weaker'[74] test because it accepts certain acts or omissions as causes that the strict 'but for' test would reject.[75] For example, if two fires are started simultaneously at opposite sides of a house by two separate defendants, and they converge to burn the house down, neither defendant's actions can be considered a 'but for' cause of the harm. On the other hand, both fires are NESS causes of the house burning down because although neither fire is a *necessary element* of the damage (ie, 'but for' causes), they are both necessary elements *of sufficient sets* for the harm to occur (ie, NESS causes).

It is clear why a NESS test of factual causation would work well in the context of positive obligations. Consider the case of *Traskunova v Russia*,[76] for example, which concerned an application under Article 2 on behalf of a woman who died whilst participating in a clinical trial of asenapine. The circumstances surrounding the exact nature of her death were not altogether clear, expect for the fact that she had pneumonia, which had been overlooked by her doctors, as well as a latent cardiovascular disease, and asenapine is known to have a cardiotoxic effect.[77] The Court held that the state was under a positive obligation under Article 2 to implement an effective framework to protect vulnerable individuals participating in clinical trials, particularly as this is a high-risk activity.[78] In terms of linking the omission of the state to fulfil this obligation to the death of the patient, it could not be shown to be a 'but for' cause because even if the state had effected better oversight over the clinical trials, it may well have made no difference, not least because the patient was already suffering from pneumonia that had been overlooked by her doctors. On the other hand, we can say that the state's omission to fulfil its positive obligations was a NESS cause of the patient's death because the lack of an effective framework to safeguard participants in clinical trials could be considered a sufficient set of conditions to give rise to the patient's death. The Court did not frame the issue of causation in this way – in fact, it scarcely dealt with the issue at all – but it seems that a NESS test of causation is implicitly implemented when deciphering a sufficient causative link between the state's omission and the consequent harm. The advantage of the NESS test is that it allows much looser causative links to be drawn between state omissions and applicant harm. In cases such as *Traskunova*,[79]

[72] Hart and Honoré (n 21).
[73] RW Wright, 'Causation in Tort Law' (1985) 73 *California Law Review* 1735.
[74] T Honoré, 'Necessary and Sufficient Conditions in Tort Law' in G Owen (ed), *Philosophical Foundations of Tort Law* (Oxford University Press, 1995).
[75] S Beckers, 'The Counterfactual NESS Definition of Causation' (2021) 35 *Proceedings of the AAAI Conference on Artificial Intelligence* 6210 at 6211.
[76] *Traskunova v Russia* (App No 21648/11).
[77] ibid para 38.
[78] ibid para 69.
[79] *Traskunova* (n 76).

where the harm is overdetermined, it seems that the Court adopts this NESS test of causation, even if not in name.

To summarise thus far, this section has sketched out four defining features of causation as it exists in positive obligations jurisprudence. The first is that causation in the context of positive obligations is always concerned with omissions, thereby demanding that the causative inquiry is biased towards only those omissions that incur a legal duty. The second is that the specificity with which the causative events are framed is quite coarse-grained. The third is that the 'but for' test has been necessarily abandoned by the Court. The fourth is that the NESS test seems to be both the most used and most useful test of causation, even if never referred to under this name.

III. The Role of Causation in Positive Obligations Cases

Now that we have explored the standard of factual causation in the Court's positive obligations jurisprudence, we turn to examine the role that it plays within the Court's wider reasoning of state liability under the Convention. In other words, what is the significance of the Court finding that the state's omission to fulfil its positive obligations caused of the applicant's harm in terms of finding a violation of the Convention?

The issue of causation is difficult to track through the Court's positive obligations case law, not least because it fails to conform to a single routinely applied analysis. The Court has sought to establish 'direct links',[80] 'causative links'[81] or 'immediate links'[82] between applicant harms and state omissions in the absence of further elaboration as to how this kind of analysis should proceed. In turn, this makes it difficult to ascertain the role that causation is playing in this context. Is it similar to causation as it functions in the law of tort, offering a determinator for where the loss for a particular harm should fall? Or does it have a unique role in this context? In the following two subsections, it is argued that causation is not a central liability-determining question in positive obligations cases, which distinguishes it from other areas of the law. Rather, the Court's finding of causation is heavily informed by its prior assessment of whether it is reasonable for the state to be under a positive obligation in the future to take actions that would have had a real prospect of mitigating or avoiding the applicant's harm in the past. Causation is therefore differently calibrated in the liability assessment than it is, for instance, in the law of tort:[83] first, unlike causation in tort law, the

[80] *Balmer-Schafroth and Others v Switzerland* (App No 22110/93) at para 40.
[81] *Janah v United Kingdom* (App Nos 19059/18 and 19725/18) at para 56.
[82] *Botta v Italy* (App No 21439/93) at para 34.
[83] See J Murphy, 'Unpicking Torts: Elements, Conditions of Actionability and Standing Rules' (2024) 87(6) *MLR*, https://doi.org/10.1111/1468-2230.12899.

entire issue becomes normatively charged in positive obligations cases; second, the issue of causation has low-determining power in terms of attributing liability to states; and, third, the distinction between factual and legal causation does not hold up in this context.

A. Causation and Reasonableness

It is clear from the Court's case law that causation is often merged with other issues, such as whether it is reasonable for a state to be held liable for a particular omission, or the degree to which the state had control or knowledge of the domain within which the applicant was harmed.[84] So, if it is unreasonable for the Court to have expected a state to take particular measures so that the applicant's harm was avoided or mitigated, it is likely that the Court will find the omission not to be a cause of the harm.[85] Likewise, if it is demonstrated that the state had sufficient knowledge that the applicant was at risk of harm, and failed to take positive steps to avoid or mitigate its occurrence, it is likely that the Court will find the omission to have caused the harm.[86] Allowing the question of causation to be coloured by these other considerations such as reasonableness and state knowledge is quite unique. Typically the question of factual causation is presumed to be normatively neutral, or at least as neutral as possible.[87] The law of tort, for instance, asks whether on the balance of probabilities, a particular failure to fulfil a legal duty is a 'but for' or NESS cause of a particular harm, regardless of normative considerations like whether it is *reasonable* to impose liability on the defendant. These questions remain sharply distinguished from the issue of factual causation. However, as Stoyanova notes, this is not the case in positive obligations jurisprudence, where issues such as state knowledge or reasonableness may bleed into the casual inquiry and usher it towards a particular finding.[88]

It is submitted that when it comes to the question of causation in positive obligations cases, the central and overarching assessment in which the Court is engaged is often one of reasonableness. If the Court finds it unreasonable, for whatever reason, to hold a state liable for breaching its positive obligations, this will retroactively drive it towards a negative finding in respect of causality. By the same token, if the Court believes that the state's actions are, all things considered, unreasonable, then this will result in a positive finding of causality to buttress its imposition of liability.

[84] Stoyanova (n 1) at 309.
[85] See, for instance, *Premininy v Russia* (App No 44973/04).
[86] See, for instance, *Brincat and Others v Malta* (App No 60908/11).
[87] Of course, the issue of causation in the law is necessarily tailored to provide a workable line of analysis. See Scordato (n 24).
[88] Stoyanova (n 1) at 309.

The decision in *LCB v United Kingdom*[89] is illustrative in this regard. While working for the British Royal Air Force, the applicant's father had been exposed to radiation during nuclear testing. The applicant was diagnosed with leukaemia at a young age, with her father's exposure to radiation citied as the potential medical cause. The applicant claimed inter alia that the state had failed to fulfil its positive obligations under Article 2 of the Convention by failing to monitor her and her father's health prior to her diagnosis. What is significant from a causation perspective is that, upon her admission to the hospital, the applicant's medical record listed under a 'Summary of Possible Causative Factors', 'Father – Radiation exposure'.[90] Thus, there was actual medical evidence proffered before the Court that the state's failure to reduce or monitor the negative impact of the nuclear testing was at least a possible cause of her illness. Nonetheless, the Court set out to determine whether 'given the circumstances of the case, the State did all that could have been required of it to prevent the applicant's life from being avoidably put at risk'.[91] It then proceeded to find that it was too 'uncertain' whether greater monitoring would have diminished the severity of her disease,[92] notwithstanding the evidence before it. What seems to be happening is that the Court is primarily concerned with the reasonableness of the state's efforts to comply with the Convention and is only then, informed by this assessment, driven to a causal analysis in support of this finding.

Issues such as state knowledge and control over the applicant's activities can be considered factors that indicate the reasonableness of the state's omission to protect them from harm. For example, in the case of *Karsakova v Russia*,[93] the question for the Court was whether Russia had breached its positive obligations under Article 2 of the Convention by failing to provide medical care to the applicant's brother while he was in detention, leading to his subsequent death. However, while the Court was conscious that 'the positive obligation [to protect human life] must be interpreted in a way which does not impose an impossible or disproportionate burden on the authorities',[94] it emphasised that a positive obligations arises under Article 2 when the state 'knew or ought to have known at the time of the existence of a real and immediate risk to the life of an identified individual'.[95] In this case, because the applicant's brother was in custody, the state should reasonably have known about his deteriorating condition and should have taken reasonable positive action to address it. The state's omission in this respect was therefore held to be a cause of the death.[96]

[89] *LCB v United Kingdom* (App No 23413/94).
[90] ibid para 13.
[91] ibid para 36.
[92] ibid para 40.
[93] *Karsakova v Russia* (App No 1157/10).
[94] ibid para 47.
[95] ibid.
[96] ibid para 43.

The question, then, is what is it *reasonable* to expect of states in terms of fulfilling their positive duties? If the Court is primarily concerned with negotiating liability for omissions based on its assessment of what can reasonably be expected of states, what sort of duties can reasonably be expected and what cannot? This question is not explored here, and indeed would prove methodologically challenging, not least because the standards of what is reasonable to expect of states vis-a-vis their Convention obligations are in a constant state of flux, and it is often impossible to decipher why certain cases were decided certain ways. The point for our purposes is that this overarching assessment of reasonableness is what seems to hold sway in the Court's ultimate determination of liability, and it is suggested that the question of causation is sometimes retroactively tailored to accord with this finding.

It is by no means suggested that the reasonableness of holding a state liable for an omission to fulfil its positive obligations is the only normative consideration that can shape the causation issue. In the cases of *LCB v United Kingdom*[97] and *Karsakova v Russia*,[98] this seemed to be the case, but equally, concerns such as the *effectiveness* of the Convention and the imperative to ensure that Convention rights are 'not theoretical and illusory but practical and effective'[99] can have a similar effect on the causation question. Indeed, positive obligations cases are an area of the Court's case law where the effectiveness mandate looms particularly large.[100] If the Court finds that a state should be held accountable for a certain failure in terms of its positive obligations under the Convention, this can often be steered by an impetus to render human rights protection effective.[101] Accordingly, the question of causation might be veered towards an affirmative finding regarding the link between the state's omission and the applicant's harm.

Why would the Court be so concerned with the reasonableness or effectiveness of imposing liability for a state's failure to fulfil its positive duties to such an extent that it would taint or skew its assessment of causation? The reason, it is submitted, comes down to the dual viewpoint of the Court in this specific context. When the Court is ruling whether a state should be held liable for a certain omission, it is only partially concerned with providing the particular applicant with a remedy for their particular grievance. Of much greater significance for the Court is that it is determining what compliance with positive obligations will look like into the future for *all* contracting states. So, on the one hand, the Court is adopting a retrospective view on the omission of the state and the harm suffered by the

[97] *LCB v United Kingdom* (n 89).

[98] *Karsakova v Russia* (n 93).

[99] *Artico v Italy* (App No 6694/74) at para 33.

[100] JG Merrills, *The Development of International Law by the European Court of Human Rights*, 2nd edn (Manchester University Press, 1993). See also AR Mowbray, *The Development of Positive Obligations under the European Convention on Human Rights by the European Court of Human Rights* (Hart Publishing, 2004) 221.

[101] L Wildhaber, "European Court of Human Rights' (2002) 40 *Canadian Yearbook of International Law* 310.

applicant in order to achieve justice between the two parties. On the other hand, however, because positive obligations are so open-ended,[102] the Court is engaged in an ongoing process of iterating the ever-evolving positive duties to which the Convention gives rise in light of present-day conditions.[103] This means that deciding whether a state is liable for a certain omission under the Convention is of much greater consequence than simply remedying the applicant's harm. It is also a matter of stipulating the parameters of an ever-expanding body of state obligations.[104] Indeed, the recent climate action cases such as *Klimaseniorinnen*[105] and *Duarte Agostinho*,[106] not to mention the modest damages awarded by the Court, would indicate that often the applicants themselves are more concerned with the Court's stipulation of prospective positive duties than with retrospectively providing remedies for harm.

This dual viewpoint of the Court, in looking backward at the omission and harm whilst also looking forward at the positive obligations that states should be expected to fulfil going forward, says something about the distinctiveness of this area of law. In tort law, the focus is solely retrospective in holding particular defendants liable for particular harms against the normative logic of corrective justice.[107] The concept of causation helps to achieve reparation for past acts or omissions that breach legal duties.[108] Thus, causation is inherently reparative. However, when it comes to positive obligations adjudication, the focus is equally, if not more so, on the reasonableness or effectiveness of imposing a certain positive duty on all contracting states going forward.[109] This means that the concept of causation, which is about reparative justice, can easily be outweighed by the Court's other central concern, which is to ensure the reasonable yet effective development of positive obligations under the Convention.

To demonstrate the dual viewpoint that the Court adopts when adjudicating on positive obligations, consider the case of *O'Keeffe v Ireland*.[110] In this case, the applicant suffered sexual abuse when she was a student at a state-funded primary school. She claimed inter alia that the state had failed to fulfil its positive obligations under Article 3[111] by failing to structure the primary education system so

[102] D Xenos, *The Positive Obligations of the State under the European Convention of Human Rights* (Taylor & Francis, 2011) 4.

[103] See *Tyrer v United Kingdom* (1978) Series A No 26 at para 3. See further Baroness Hale, 'Beanstalk or Living Instrument? How Tall Can the European Convention on Human Rights Grow?', 16 July 2011, www.gresham.ac.uk/watch-now/beanstalk-or-living-instrument-how-tall-can-european-convention-on-human.

[104] Council of Europe, 'The European Convention on Human Rights – A Living Instrument' (2020), https://edoc.coe.int/en/european-convention-on-human-rights/8528-the-european-convention-on-human-rights-a-living-instrument.html.

[105] *Verein Klimaseniorinnen Schweiz and Others v Switzerland* (n 61).

[106] *Duarte Agostinho and Others v Portugal and Others* (App No 39371/20).

[107] EJ Weinrib, *The Idea of Private Law*, revised edn (Oxford University Press, 2012) xiv.

[108] MS Moore, 'Causation and Moral Blameworthiness' in Moore (n 29).

[109] Brice Dickson encapsulates this sentiment when he writes that 'as Dickson notes, the Convention is a building project not a fire-fighting operation.' See Dickson (n 14) at 204.

[110] *O'Keefe v Ireland* (n 50).

[111] Article 3 ECHR provides that 'no one shall be subjected to torture or to inhuman or degrading treatment or punishment'.

as to safeguard her against abuse.[112] In terms of causation, the Court echoed its assertion in *E and Others v United Kingdom*[113] that 'it is not necessary to show that "but for" the State omission the ill-treatment would not have happened.'[114] Rather, it mattered whether there was a 'real prospect' that if the state had taken reasonably available measures, the harm would have been avoided or mitigated. As we have explored in the first half of this chapter, this kind of analysis can be considered a kind of NESS test of causation.[115] Yet, in terms of the *role* that this causal analysis is playing in the wider determination of the state's liability, the Court is not focused solely on looking back in time at a link between state omission and applicant harm and seeking to achieve corrective justice between the two parties on the basis of causation. It is equally aware that its ruling of state liability in this context marks an articulation of the positive duties that flow from Article 3, affecting what *all* state-funded primary schools within the Council of Europe must be expected to do by way of safeguarding children. This other perspective that colours the Court's determination of liability is anchored in a broad assessment of what can reasonably be expected of states, having regard to the level of state knowledge and control, alongside the impetus to render the Convention practical and effective.

B. Implications for Causation

What the preceding analysis demonstrates is that causation in positive obligations cases can be influenced by the Court's prior assessment of what is reasonable to expect of contracting states in terms of complying with their positive duties under the Convention. Unlike in tort law, where causation operates within an exclusively retrospective inquiry into the link between a breach of legal duty and consequent harm, the question of causation in positive obligations cases may be influenced by the Court's other forward-looking concerns as to how far state liability under the Convention should stretch.

This sharply distinguishes causation from how it is understood in the law of tort. First, unlike in tort law, causation in this context is not a truly *determinative* head of inquiry. A successful tort claim requires that factual causation is necessarily established on the balance of probabilities, otherwise the claim will most certainly fail. This, as we have seen, is not necessarily the case in the law of positive obligations. The test of causation found in the doctrine surfaces in vague and inconsistent phrasing, and can be shaped to accord with the Court's assessment of what is reasonable to expect of state authorities, or what is necessary to make the Convention practical and effective. Second, unlike the law of tort, the distinction between factual and 'proximate' (or 'legal') causation is not nearly as distinct in this area. In tort law, the assessment of factual causation

[112] *O'Keeffe v Ireland* (n 50).
[113] *E and Others v United Kingdom* (n 47) at para 99.
[114] *O'Keeffe v Ireland* (App No 35810/09) at para 149.
[115] See Wright (n 73).

aims to be as neutral as is possible, with normative questions of whether liability should be imposed only penetrating the analysis when considering whether the defendant's actions were a 'proximate' cause of the plaintiff's harm. In the case of positive obligations, because the first question of factual causation is already influenced by normative concerns such as reasonableness and effectiveness, the question of 'proximate' causation is already subsumed into it, thereby blurring the distinction between the two.

IV. Conclusion

This chapter has covered two overarching questions that pertain to causation in the ECtHR's jurisprudence on positive obligations. The first question explored what causation in this context *is*. The fact that this area of law is always concerned with causation by omission and that the causative events must necessarily be framed in quite a coarse-grained manner were flagged as reasons why factual causation in this area is quite a metaphysically fragile concept to begin with. It was then demonstrated how the 'but for' test is unworkable in this area and has therefore been abandoned by the Court. In its stead, it was argued, the Court has adopted a test that resembles a NESS test of causation, even if not in name. The second question explored what *role* causation carries out in the Court's jurisprudence. It was argued that the assessment of causation can be swayed by broader concerns that the Court has, in terms of ensuring the reasonableness of imposing state liability whilst ensuring the effective protection of human rights. This has some significant consequences for the operation of causation, such as stripping it of determinative power and blurring the distinction between factual and legal causation.

7

Causation

Why and How for Establishing Breach of Positive Obligations under the European Convention on Human Rights?

VLADISLAVA STOYANOVA

I. Introduction

Causation can be regarded as an inherent feature of reasoning about legal responsibility. It underlines any legal inquiry about responsibility and the consequences flowing once responsibility is established.[1] Causation provides justification as to why a specific 'injurer' should be singled out and held responsible for the specific 'victim's' harm.[2] At the same time, causation has been difficult to define.[3] These difficulties are perhaps ever greater when the legal inquiry is about omissions as causes.[4] Here causal inquiry is understood as the analytical effort to establish *a link* (a connection) between an omission (or omissions/failures to take measures) by the state and harm in the system of state responsibility under the European Convention on Human Rights (ECHR or 'the Convention'). In this sense, the omission is the claimed cause (A), and the harm is the claimed effect/outcome/result (B). For the purposes of this chapter, the symbol (A) will be used to denote the alleged cause (ie, the omission), while the symbol (B) will denote the alleged effect (ie, the harm). This link between (A) and (B) is crucial for establishing

[1] TM Honoré, 'Causation and Remoteness of Damage' in A Tunc (ed), *International Encyclopaedia of Comparative Law: Torts*, vol 11, ch 7 (Mohr, 1983) 1–156 at 21–22.

[2] C Sartorio, 'Causation and Responsibility' (2007) 2 *Philosophical Compass* 749.

[3] R Wright, 'Causation, Responsibility, Risk, Probability, Naked Statistics, and Proof: Pruning the Bramble Bush by Clarifying the Concepts' (1987–88) 73 *Iowa Law Review* 1001.

[4] TM Honoré, *Responsibility and Fault* (Hart Publishing, 2002) 41; C Sartorio, 'How to Be Responsible for Something without Causing it' (2004) 18(1) *Philosophical Perspectives* 315; M Moore, *Causation and Responsibility: An Essay on Law, Morals, and Metaphysics* (Oxford University Press, 2009) 129–30; J Schaffer, 'Causes Need Not Be Physically Connected to Their Effects: The Case for Negative Causation' in C Hitchcock (ed), *Contemporary Debates in Philosophy of Science* (Blackwell Publishing, 2004) 197. For a recent study on omissions, see S Steel, *Omissions in Tort Law* (Oxford University Press, 2024).

responsibility for harm, as it rests on the expectation that in the hypothetical world where the omission did not occur – meaning the state had taken measures – the harm would (or at least would likely) have been prevented.[5] The link therefore can be characterised as one of prevention.[6]

My objective is to explain this link in light of the case law of the European Court of Human Rights (ECtHR or 'the Court'). The reasoning of the Court in judgments where omissions are invoked as a basis for state responsibility is therefore of key importance for achieving this objective. All judgments delivered in 2023 and 2024 addressing arguments about breach of substantive positive obligations under Articles 2, 3 and 8 ECHR are considered,[7] so that a sufficiently representative sample is covered. Any standards or considerations used in the Court's reasoning that emerge from the case law are contextualised so that they can be better understood. In particular, they are contextualised within philosophical discussions about causation and how causation has been addressed in other areas of law. Such comparative parallels allow a better understanding of the role of the causal link in the human rights law reasoning employed by the Court and the justifications of this role.

The following path will be followed. Section II explains what is considered as cause and effect in the human rights law reasoning where positive obligations are invoked, and how causes and effects might be framed and specified. In particular, it explains that the causal inquiry is actually an inquiry about the existence of positive obligations and about the interpretation of their content and scope. By invoking explicitly or implicitly causal links between harms and omissions, the Court in fact determines the existence of obligations, their content and scope, and simultaneously determines breach.

Section III attempts to review the Court's practice through the lens of the distinction between factual causation and legal causation. This distinction and its rationale have been addressed in other areas of law,[8] and have been an object of rich theoretical discussion.[9] Given that the ECHR is an international treaty and

[5] Alternatively, the risk of harm could have been avoided or reduced. Another alternative is that the harm could have been mitigated. All these alternatives and modifications of the effect (B) will be addressed below. The required degree of likelihood to prevent the harm (B) or the risk of harm is also another relevant question.

[6] This chapter does not engage with the meaning of prevention – as opposed to, for example, precaution – in the context of the ECtHR case law. Prevention is invoked in a broad-brush manner to signal that omissions form the basis of breaches of obligations, grounded in the assumption that, had the omissions not occurred, the harm would either not have materialised or would have been less likely to occur.

[7] I do not consider judgments where the only argument raised is a breach of the procedural positive obligation to investigate. For this obligation, see K Kamber, *Prosecuting Human Rights Offences* (Brill, 2017). Admissibility decisions have also been excluded from the analysis. In the forthcoming analysis, I do not cite *all* the 2023 and 2024 judgments that I have identified in the HUDOC database as judgments where positive obligations under arts 2, 3 and 8 have been invoked.

[8] See, eg, R Goldberg (eds), *Perspectives on Causation* (Hart Publishing, 2011).

[9] See, eg, R Fumerton and K Kress, 'Causation and the Law: Preemption, Lawful Sufficiency, and Causal Sufficiency' (2001) 64 *Law and Contemporary Problems* 83; D Hamer, '"Factual Causation" and "Scope of Liability": What's the Difference?' (2014) 77(2) *MLR* 155.

that responsibility under the ECHR is an international responsibility, international law is therefore an important area of law to draw parallels with. However, as Plakokefalos and Lanovoy have noted, causation has remained under-explored in international law.[10] The codification process of the law of state responsibility in international law has left the question of causation aside by concluding that it is the relevant primary rules (ie, the primary obligations) that determine causation.[11] This justifies the engagement with the ECtHR's case law where primary obligations, including positive obligations, have been developed and standards for determining breach have been advanced. However, as sections II and III show, the case law is erratic; it therefore needs to be juxtaposed against some more developed and consistent systems of legal responsibility.[12] Since the existing scholarship and international law have been underpinned by comparative parallels with tort law, tort law responsibility can offer a comparative framework. In addition, domestic tort law also aims to protect important individual interests, which reveals a normative similarity with human rights law.[13] The domestic counterpart of tort law is thus used in section III to offer insights as to the distinction between legal and factual causation and its rationale. The analysis in section III is thus guided by the question of whether the Court has distinguished the different considerations of respectively factual and legal causation (sections III.A and III.B).

Since the answer to this question is negative, section III.C explains that the mixture of factual and legal causation is inevitable. This inevitability is related to the role of the causation inquiry that simultaneously serves the analytical steps of establishing the existence, the content and the scope of the obligation, and establishing its breach. Factual causation is used for articulating reasoning and conclusions in terms that shroud normative convictions about whether the state should have positive obligations to intervene and how interventionist it should have been. Therefore, the causal inquiry with its mixture of factual and normative elements is ultimately an inquiry about the existence of positive obligations,

[10] I Plakokefalos, 'Causation in the Law of State Responsibility and the Problem of Overdetermination: In Search of Clarity' (2015) 26(2) *European Journal of International Law* 471; V Lanovoy, 'Causation in the Law of State Responsibility' (2022) *British Yearbook of International Law* 1, https://doi.org/10.1093/bybil/brab008.

[11] *Yearbook of the International Law Commission*, 2001, vol II, Part Two: Commentary to Art 31, para 10 ('the requirement of a causal link is not necessarily the same in relation to every breach of an international obligation'). J Crawford, *Brownlie's Principles of Public International Law* (Oxford University Press, 2019) 559: 'ARSIWA pragmatically avoids the issue [of causation], leaving specific determinations to the particularities of each case.'

[12] On this comparison, including the development of international law in comparison with domestic counterparts for establishment of legal responsibility, see A Nolkaemper, 'Constitutionalization and the Unity of the Law of International Responsibility' (2009) 16(2) *Indiana Journal of Global Legal Studies* 535.

[13] J Varuhas, *Damages and Human Rights* (Hart Publishing, 2016), 474: 'Both human rights law and tort law 'perform similar functions in protecting the most fundamental of interests'; D Nolan, 'Negligence and Human Rights Law: The Case for Separate Development' (2013) 76(2) *MLR* 286, 293–97; V Stoyanova, 'Common Law Tort of Negligence as a Tool for the Deconstruction of Positive Obligations under the European Convention on Human Rights' (2020) 24 *International Journal of Human Rights* 632.

about the interpretation of their content and scope, and about the determination of breach. By invoking explicitly or implicitly causal links between harm and omissions, including links framed as factual, the Court masks normative determinations about the existence of obligations and their breaches. Determining the existence of positive obligations places the Court on the path of becoming a law maker, a task reserved for the states' legislatures.

II. What is the Cause and What is the Effect in the Human Rights Law Reasoning?

In the system of state responsibility under the ECHR for breaches of positive obligations, the causal inquiry examines whether a *link* can be established between a state's omission (A) and the resulting harm (B).[14] Sections II.A offers a better understanding of (B) by explaining that it concerns choices about the definitional scope of the relevant ECHR right. Section II.B clarifies that (A) has to be limited to *legally* relevant omissions. Yet, as section II.C further clarifies, the specification of these legally relevant omissions collapses with the determination of breach of the positive obligations. As a consequence, as section II.D explains, causation is a tool for determining both the existence of positive obligations (including their content and scope) and their breach. Finally, section II.V more concretely shows how by making certain choices in the framing and the specification of the causes and effects, the Court can 'control' the conclusion about breach that follows from the reasoning in the judgment.

A. The Effect: Harm to Important Interests as Protected by the ECHR

(B), ie the harm,[15] is understood as the negative effects upon the interests protected by the rights that are enshrined in the different provisions of the Convention. In the context of the ECtHR judgments, this harm, understood as negative effects upon interests, is an object of inquiry in the determination of the definitional scope of the right.[16] This definitional inquiry aims to answer the question of whether these effects pass the threshold for being defined as an *interference* with the right to

[14] This very sentence can be accepted as containing an incongruity – there might be no obligation to be possibly breached if there is no link, while at the same time, the link is a consideration for determining breach of an obligation that is already assumed to exist. The reasons for this incongruity will be explained below.

[15] In the risk-based reasoning for establishing breach, it is no longer (B) that matters, but the risk of (B), which modifies the causation inquiry. See section II.E below.

[16] J Gerards and E Brems, 'Introduction' in E Brems and J Gerards (eds), *Shaping Rights in the European Convention on Human Rights* (Cambridge University Press, 2013) 1.

life, the right to private life etc. The usage of the term 'interference' here might be confusing, since it does not refer to breaches of any obligations. The question of obligations is not relevant at this stage of the human rights law review performed by the Court. The establishment of 'interference' simply means that the definitional scope of the right is engaged, since the harm done to the applicant is of such a nature that it has negatively *affected* the important interests protected by, for example, the right to life or the right to private life and so on.

It could be therefore accepted that there is a causal inquiry at play at the definitional stage of the review; but this inquiry is different from the causal inquiry concerning the link between (A) and (B). The former is not a causal inquiry about obligations, which implies that it is not about omissions of taking measures as possible causes for harm. It is not about the required conduct of the state. The former pertains to the definitional scope of the right, and it is about the link between the factual condition of the individual applicant (ie, the physical state of the external world) and the interests protected by the ECHR provisions.[17] It is about the normative (ie, value-based) assessment whether this factual condition should be considered as affecting these ECHR interests. This implies a normative assessment as to how expansively these interests should be interpreted. The more expansive and more factual conditions – claimed by applicants to have been harmful to them – can be covered by the definitional scope of the right.

The causal inquiry pertaining to the link between (A) and (B) is an inquiry about measures (arguably that form the content of positive obligations) for elimination (ie, prevention) or mitigation of the harmful condition that has been already found worthy of protection at the definitional stage of the review. Once found worthy of protection, since the harmful condition is considered as having negatively affected the relevant ECHR interests, this already necessarily implies that the state's conduct will be subjected to review by asking whether and what measures have been in place to prevent or mitigate the harm (or the risk of harm). This means that once the definitional step of the inquiry is successfully passed with the conclusion that the factual condition of the applicant was harmful and therefore worthy of ECHR protection, it is easier to make the assumption that the state had some obligations as a matter of the ECHR. In essence, then, the human rights review can easily proceed under the assumption that the state was expected to adopt certain conduct *as a matter of ECHR obligations*. Because of this assumption, in its human rights review, the Court can proceed to identify and concretise possible omissions as being legally relevant for finding breaches of positive obligations.

An example to illustrate the above clarified distinction between the causal inquiry at the definition stage, on the one hand, and the causal inquiry for

[17] I use the term 'condition' here since it is neutral, as opposed to the term 'harm', which already has a negative connotation. However, in the rest of the chapter, I use the term 'harm' under the assumption that the factual condition of the application have been found to fall within the definitional scope of the ECHR right invoked.

determining the existence, scope and breach of obligations, on the other hand, is provided by *Locascia and Others v Italy.* In this case the applicants complained about the inability of the state to ensure the proper functioning of waste collection in the region where they lived.[18] As part of the definitional review as to whether the applicants' factual condition could be considered as negatively affecting interests protected by Article 8, the Court noted:

> [A] *causal link existed* between exposure to waste treatment and an increased risk of developing pathologies such as cancer or congenital malformations, even though other factors such as family history, nutrition and smoking habits in the area might also have influenced the mortality rate.[19]

It also added that 'living in the area marked by extensive exposure to waste in breach of the applicable safety standards made the applicant more *vulnerable to* various illnesses'[20] and that 'the environmental nuisance that the applicants experienced in the course of their everyday life *affected, adversely and to a sufficient extent, their private life* during the entire period under consideration'.[21] Having established the link between the applicant's condition and the Article 8 interests, the Court continued to examine the question of obligations.[22]

In *Locascia and Others v Italy*, therefore, the definitional inquiry implied the establishment of a link between, on the one hand, the factual reality that included existence of waste and pollution in the region and, on the other hand, the Article 8 interests of the applicants. This is different from the question of what conduct the state should have adopted (ie, what measures that might form the content of positive obligations) to protect the affected interests under Article 8 of the Convention.

Admittedly, the Court does not always make the above clarified distinction between the definitional inquiry and the obligation inquiry. The reasoning in *Locascia and Others v Italy* regarding the waste collection problem after 1 January 2010, when the state of emergency ended, is illustrative. The Court observed that:

> [T]he applicants have not demonstrated whether and to what extent the *shortcomings* in the management of waste treatment and disposal services in Campania in the period following the end of the state of emergency *had a direct impact on their home and private life.* Although the presence of large quantities of 'ecobales' shows the persistence of a general deterioration of the environment in Campania, this is not in itself sufficient

[18] *Locascia and Others v Italy* App No 35648/10, 19 October 2023.
[19] ibid para 127 (emphasis added).
[20] ibid para 130 (emphasis added).
[21] ibid para 132 (emphasis added).
[22] ibid para 133. For another relevant example, see *Moldovan v Ukraine* App No 62020/14, 14 March 2024, para 30, where the applicant argued that '[t]here therefore existed a direct link between the establishment of paternity and the applicant's private life'. At para 35 of the judgment, the Court agreed by considering that 'the right claimed by the applicant discloses sufficient relevant elements to fall within the concept of "private life"'. See also *Vlaisavlevikj v North Macedonia* App No 23215/21, 25 June 2024, paras 37–39.

> to establish that the situation specifically *affected* the population of the municipalities of Caserta and San Nicola La Strada and, if so, *the extent of the interference with the applicants' right to respect for their home and private life*.[23]

The reasoning in this paragraph reveals a confusion.[24] If the deterioration of the environment could not be causally linked to the interests protected by Article 8, then Article 8 would not be relevant to begin with. If this were to be the case and contrary to what the above quoted paragraph suggests, the question of any obligations and therefore any 'shortcomings in the management' would not be relevant either.

Verein Klimaseniorinnen Schweiz and Others v Switzerland is another judgment that can be used to illustrate how the Court invokes and uses the distinction explained above (ie, the causal inquiry at the definitional stage versus the causal inquiry for determining the existence and breach of obligations). A full appreciation of the causal inquiry performed in this judgment is not attempted here.[25] My point here is limited to highlighting the distinction made between the following two links. On the one hand:

> [T]he link between the various adverse effects of the consequences of climate change, and the risks of such effects on the enjoyment of human rights at present and in the future. In general terms, this issue pertains *to the legal question of how the scope of human rights protection* is to be understood as regards the impacts arising for human beings from an existing degradation, or risk of degradation, in their living conditions.[26]

On the other hand, the Court also formulated 'the link, at the individual level, between a harm, or risk of harm, allegedly affecting specific persons or groups of persons, *and the acts or omissions of State authorities* against which a human rights-based complaint is directed'.[27]

The first link pertains to the definitional limits of the interests protected by the rights enshrined in the Convention. Posing this question exposes the limits

[23] *Locascia and Others v Italy* (n 18) para 135 (emphasis added).

[24] In its case law, the ECtHR does not consistently follow the distinction between definitional review and the review of the violation of obligations. For an analysis related to negative obligations, see J Gerards, 'How to Improve the Necessity Test of the European Court of Human Rights' (2013) 11(2) *International Journal of Constitutional Law* 466; J Gerards and H Senden, 'The Structure of Fundamental Rights and the European Court of Human Rights' (2009) 7(4) *International Journal of Constitutional Law* 619.

[25] See V Stoyanova, 'In Search for the Content of States' Positive Obligations under the European Convention on Human Rights: *KlimaSeniorinnen* and Climate Change' in C Amado Gomes, H Oliveira, A Roch and M Fermeglia (eds), *Climate Change before International Courts: A Comparative Study* (Routledge, 2025); V Stoyanova, '*KlimaSeniorinnen* and the Question(s) of Causation', *Verfassungsblog* (7 May 2024), https://verfassungsblog.de/klimaseniorinnen-and-the-questions-of-causation. See also M Geistfeld and S Steel, 'Causation and Climate Change in Tort' in D Kysar and E Lim (eds), *The Oxford Handbook on Climate Change and Private Law* (Oxford University Press, forthcoming).

[26] *Verein Klimaseniorinnen Schweiz and Others v Switzerland* [GC] App No 53600/20, 9 April 2024, para 425 (emphasis added). See also para 515: 'The question of "actual interference" in practice relates to the existence of a direct and immediate link between the alleged environmental harm and the applicant's private or family life or home.'

[27] ibid para 425.

of human rights law, in that certain harms may fall outside its scope and therefore remain unaddressed by this specific body of law. As the quotation suggests through its use of the term 'legal question', determining which harms – though factually present – should be recognised as falling within the scope of human rights protection is ultimately a normative question. The second link pertains to obligations themselves and shows that even if the harm affects important interests as protected by the ECHR, this does not necessarily mean that there are obligations on the state to do something about this harm as a matter of human rights law. It is this second link that will be in the focus of the following analysis.

A final clarification is due here regarding the first link that pertains to the definitional limits of the interests protected by the rights enshrined in the Convention. As mentioned earlier with reference to relevant quotations, in the Court's reasoning, this link is presented as a link between the applicant's physical condition and the interests protected by the Convention. As also suggested earlier, given that the determination of the scope of the interests is based on values that the Court might choose to endorse, the determination about the existence of the link is also normative. Accordingly, the proposition that the definition scope includes some sort of causal inquiry, understood as an inquiry as to how one factual event leads to another one, might be inapt. Although the Court refers to 'direct impact' and 'link', it is not really a *factual* inquiry that is at stake. Normative choices are instead made as to which harms that exist in the physical, factual state of the world should be addressed by the ECHR.[28]

B. The Cause: Legally Relevant Omission(s)

Normally, harm is easy to demonstrate – we just need to focus on the factual reality and observe loss of life, injuries, deterioration of human health etc. However, whether this harm can be called (B), meaning effect/outcome/result of something identifiable and specifiable as (A), is a separate question. Whether and how different areas of law (for example, tort law, public law and human rights law) establish any links between (A) and (B) in order to determine responsibility for (B) is also a separate query.[29]

This brings us to the need to better understand (A). As noted above, it is an omission or multiple omissions, which complicates the analysis and to which I will return below. In general, it is quite uncontroversial that states can be held responsible under the Convention for omissions.[30] More generally in international law, it

[28] This relates to the wider discussion about facts and law, and how the perception and the description of facts reflects the observer's subjective interests. For relevant references, see Hamer (n 9) 159.

[29] For a useful comparison between public law and private law, see E Rock, 'Causation in Public Law' (2023) 30 *Australian Journal of Administrative Law* 56; G Turton, 'Causation and Risk in Negligence and Human Rights Law' (2020) 79(1) *Cambridge Law Journal* 148. See also A Sangiuliano, 'Causation and Exposition' (2025) *International Journal of Constitutional Law* (forthcoming).

[30] V Stoyanova, *Positive Obligations under the European Convention on Human Rights: Within and Beyond Boundaries* (Oxford University Press, 2023).

is also accepted that states can incur international responsibility for omissions.[31] However, omissions are difficult to identify, perceive and specify unless we have some baseline expectations about the counterparts of these omissions, ie, *the measures that need to be taken*.[32] At this point, the consensus that generally omissions can be the basis for establishing breach of an obligation, which could lead to international responsibility, is not helpful. There needs to be some understanding about the conduct that should have been performed in the hypothetical world where action could and should have been taken. Therefore, there needs to be some understanding about the counterparts to these omissions so that the omissions themselves can be perceived, formulated and articulated.

Omissions can also become perceivable and possible to identify and specify once the harm materialises, which also raise questions about the link between (A) and (B). The link is understood to be historical/chronological – first is (A) and then (B) in terms of temporal sequence. The issue then that arises is how we can know what is (A) (ie, the cause understood as omission(s) to take measures) when we still do not know (B), given that (B) has not yet occurred. Here it is relevant to note that the establishment of legal responsibility is *post factum* since (B) has already occurred.[33] As the harm has already materialised, the possibility to perceive and specify omissions also arises (or at least becomes easier), and therefore the possibility for applicants to formulate and specify omissions for the sake of arguing that the state is responsible. All of this means that the harm (B) affects the perception about (A) and accordingly the possibility to identify (A). This seems to defy the temporal sequence and the logical temporal link between (A) and (B).[34]

It is not only the case that, by the time legal responsibility is reviewed *post factum*, the harm has already factually occurred. It is equally important that, as previously noted, for the review to proceed to the question of whether a breach of an obligation has taken place, that harm must have already been normatively assessed as affecting interests protected by the Convention. As explained in section II.A, this normative assessment pertains to the determination of the definitional scope of the right – the normative determination that the scope is engaged and thus the normative assessment of the harm (B) affects the perception about (A) and accordingly the possibility to identify (A). In particular, it makes it easier to argue that there must be (A) – ie, omissions by the state – and that counterparts

[31] A Ollino, *Due Diligence Obligations in International Law* (Cambridge University Press, 2022).

[32] Even the mere distinction between positive and negative obligations is determined with reference to certain baseline expectations in the particular societal context. For a clear illustration, see *Diaconeasa v Romania* App No 53162/21, 20 February 2024, para 49, where the Court reasoned that since the applicant did not ask for a new measure, but was deprived by the state of a measure (ie, personal assistant) from which she could previously benefit, her art 8 claim was reviewed as a possible breach of a negative obligation.

[33] This is also reflected in the admissibility requirement for a victim status under the ECHR.

[34] Rhetorically the ECtHR seems to have solved this problem by consistently stating in its case law that breach of positive obligations is assessed without the benefit of the hindsight. See, however, the Partly Dissenting Opinion in *O'Keeffe v Ireland* [GC] App No 35810/09, 28 January 2014.

to these omissions should be possible to identify and specify in order to determine state responsibility.

Are there any limits as to which omissions are relevant at all? In the context of establishing state responsibility, it is not the case that any possible counterpart to the omission(s) matter and, in this sense, that any possible measure is relevant. It would be utterly unacceptable to claim that every conceivable omission, simply because it can be detected, identified, perceived and linked to the harm an individual has endured (or the risk of such harm), grounds state responsibility under the ECHR. There must be limits *on what omissions are legally significant*, demanding analytical tools to navigate the complex analytical landscape for establishing legal responsibility.[35] Such a tool is the distinction between the existence of an obligation and the breach of that obligation. As Crawford has observed:

> [O]mission is more than simple 'not-doing' or inaction: it is legally significant only when there is a legal duty to act which is not fulfilled, and its significance can only be assessed by reference to the *content of that duty* … the absence of any primary obligation 'to do' will mean that no omission may be complained of.[36]

Put simply, there must first be an obligation to take measures (ie, to avoid the omission) that has not been complied with. This obligation serves as the basis for determining breach that leads to responsibility. The cause is not simply a cause (ie, factually a cause); the law recognises it as a cause for the purpose of determining responsibility. The cause must be a breach of an *already existing* and identifiable obligation.[37]

C. The Specification of a Legally Relevant Omission (or Omissions) Collapses with the Determination of Breach

All of this brings us to the important questions about the framing of positive obligations in human rights law, the specification of the content of these obligations

[35] V Stoyanova, 'Framing Positive Obligations under the European Convention on Human Rights Law: Mediating between the Abstract and the Concrete' (2023) 23(3) *Human Rights Law Review* 1.

[36] J Crawford, *State Responsibility. The General Part* (Cambridge University Press, 2013) 218 (emphasis added).

[37] By 'already existing' obligation, I mean an obligation that bound the state at the relevant point in time when the harm (or the risk of harm) materialised and when the state should have taken measures to fulfil this very obligation. Given that the human rights law review is *post factum*, this point in time is in the past. It follows that omissions should be assessed as legally relevant only with reference to the law that bound the state at the relevant point in time in the past. The ECtHR itself has confirmed that breach of positive obligations is assessed without the benefit of the hindsight (V Stoyanova, *Positive Obligations under the European Convention on Human Rights* (Oxford University Press, 2023) 31). This corresponds to the requirement in the law of state responsibility that a determination is made of whether a state was bound by an international obligation that was 'in force' when the conduct allegedly leading to the breach occurred. See Responsibility of States for Internationally Wrongful Acts, *Yearbook of the International Law Commission*, 2001, vol. II, Part Two, art 13.

in their framing, and the determination of breach of the obligations once these are specified. The text of the ECHR does not frame and specify such obligations.[38] Their content, understood as the concrete measures that states are required to undertake, is only specified in the context of the reasoning in a concrete judgment where the question of breach needs to be decided. As a result, the question of whether there was an obligation (and therefore a legally relevant omission) *collapses* with the question whether there was a breach of the obligation.[39] It is thus difficult to maintain the separation between the determination as to whether a positive obligation existed at the relevant point in time in the past and the determination of whether it was breached in the specific case.

The reasoning in *Biba v Albania* can be helpful to illustrate this collapse. A 13-year-old pupil used a catapult to shoot a projectile into the right eye of another pupil. This caused almost total blindness of the eye. The incident happened at the premises of a private school in Albania, during a break between classes. The father of the injured child argued *inter alia* that the state 'failed to adequately supervise the licensed private school', which implied an argument that the state could have prevented the accident by taking certain measures.[40] The Court agreed with the applicant. It observed that 'an educational institution is in principle under an obligation to supervise pupils during the entire time they spend in its care'.[41] It added that '[e]ducational institutions are expected to take *appropriate* measures to prevent the use of dangerous objects by pupils on school premises or custody'.[42] According to the Court's reasoning, the accident occurred, therefore the state did not take 'appropriate' measures to prevent it, and therefore Albania breached its positive obligations under Article 8. The latter were never specified beyond the invocation of the standard of appropriateness. It then follows that there are no two distinct analytical steps in the reasoning: first, specification of the 'appropriate' measures and then review whether any were undertaken. In fact, the 'appropriateness' is judged in combination with the identification, the articulation and the specification of the omissions.

The reasoning in *Validity Foundation on Behalf of TJ v Hungary* offers another valuable example to demonstrate this collapse of the analysis about existence of a positive obligation and the analysis about breach of the obligation. The case

[38] Besides the abstract framing in art 1 of the Convention that states 'shall *secure* to everyone within their jurisdiction the rights and freedoms defined in Section I of this Convention' (emphasis added).

[39] For a detailed analysis, see Stoyanova (n 35).

[40] *Biba v Albania* App No 24228/18, 7 May 2024, para 52. The applicant invoked also procedural omissions. For how the Court mixes procedural omissions/deficiencies and substantive omissions in its reasoning, see V Stoyanova, 'Biba v Albania: Positive Obligations under Article 8 and the Question of Causation', *Strasbourg Observers* (10 July 2024), https://strasbourgobservers.com/2024/07/10/biba-v-albania-positive-obligations-under-article-8-and-the-question-of-causation.

[41] *Biba v Albania* (n 40) paras 52 and 71, with reference to *Kayak v Turkey* App No 60444/08, 10 July 2012, para 60.

[42] *Biba v Albania* (n 40) paras 52 and 72 (emphasis added). See also *AE v Bulgaria* App No 53891/20, 23 May 2023, para 89, where the standard of 'appropriateness of the authorities' response' was also invoked.

concerned the death in a social care home of a woman with severe disabilities. According to the applicant organisation that represented her, although the direct cause of death was pneumonia, 'long-term neglect was the decisive factor leading to her death'.[43] By specifying the measures in the determination that they were *not* undertaken,[44] the Court simultaneously performs the two analytical operations/steps: first, the determination of the existence of an obligation to take measures; and, second, the determination that the obligation was breached, since the measures were not taken. In other words, the omissions are made legally relevant and assessed as a basis for responsibility for breach of an obligation via their specification.

A third illustration is *EK v Latvia*. The applicant argued that Latvia breached its positive obligations under Article 8 since it did not help him to enforce his contact rights with his daughter in view of the mother's opposition. In particular, the applicant argued that Latvia had not taken measures to facilitate his contact and to ensure the mother's cooperation.[45] The Court stated that Article 8 imposes on the state 'an obligation to take measures that would reconcile the conflicting interests of the parties, keeping in mind the paramount interests of the child'.[46] According to the Court's reasoning, the 'key consideration' for determining breach is 'whether the authorities have taken *all necessary steps* to facilitate contact as can reasonably be demanded in the special circumstances of each case'.[47] Like *Biba v Albania*, where, as mentioned above, the 'appropriate' measures remained initially unarticulated, 'all the necessary steps' in *EK v Latvia* were never identified and specified as a first step so that a second analytical step of reviewing the actual state conduct could then be performed. By specifying measures in the determination that they were *not* undertaken,[48] the Court concurrently determined the existence of an obligation to take measures and breach since the measures were not taken. As to the standard of necessity (ie, 'necessary steps'), no inquiry is performed in the reasoning regarding the question of whether any specified measures were actually *necessary*. What is necessary can be understood as that which is indispensable for achieving the desired outcome (ie, facilitation of the contact between the father and the child).

[43] *Validity Foundation on Behalf of TJ v Hungary* App No 31970/20, 10 October 2024, para 81.

[44] These included shortage of medical staff, insufficient medical and therapeutic care, inappropriate living conditions and the excessive use of means of restraint: ibid paras 91–94.

[45] *EK v Latvia* App No 25942/20, 13 April 2023, para 70. For a detailed analysis of this case, see Cummings, ch 5 in this volume.

[46] *EK v Latvia* (n 45) para 75.

[47] ibid para 76 (emphasis added). See also *IS v Greece* App No 19165/20, 23 May 2023, para 84.

[48] *EK v Latvia* (n 45) paras 86–97 (eg, the domestic court not ordering 'the other steps sought by the applicant with a view to facilitating contact and reconciling the conflicting interests of the parties, including the obligation on I.B. [the mother] to attend psychological support sessions' (para 87); no consequences for the mother for disregarding the exercise of contact rights (para 90); therapy or medication, inter alia, 'educating the parents on the effect of their behaviour on the child, or imposing a fine on the uncooperative parent' (para 91) and 'ordering specialist help' (para 92)).

D. Causation as a Tool for Determining Both the Existence of Positive Obligations and their Breach

What does this collapse of the analysis about existence of a positive obligation and the analysis about breach of the obligation imply for the causal inquiry? The link between the omission that is the claimed cause (A) and the harm that is the claimed effect/outcome/result (B) is relevant for both. In other words, the determination that an obligation existed at the relevant point in time and the determination that it may have been breached are conflated. Therefore, the causal inquiry is relevant at the same time to both analytical steps: first, the existence, the framing and the specification of the obligation; and, second, the determination of breach of the obligation. It then follows that the causal inquiry is actually an inquiry about the interpretation of the content and scope of the primary positive obligations.[49] By invoking explicitly or implicitly causal links between harm and omissions, the Court therefore *determines the existence of obligations*, and determines and reasons about their content and scope. The Court also concurrently makes conclusions about breaches of these obligations. To be clear, the invocation of causal links is not the sole analytical took in the reasoning. Other tools are also used in combination,[50] such as compliance with the national legal framework or with relevant international legal rules.[51]

Let's revert to the three judgments mentioned in section II.C above to better explain the point made in the previous paragraph about the role of the causal inquiry. As already noted, in *Biba v Albania*, the Court stated that '[e]ducational institutions are expected to take *appropriate* measures to prevent the use of dangerous objects by pupils on school premises or custody'.[52] The standard of 'appropriate' is suggestive that the measures are expected to somehow contribute to prevention. Via the invocation of this standard (ie, 'taking appropriate measures'), the Court determined that there was a positive obligation and that it was breached, since the state conduct (in the form of omissions) was not 'appropriate'.

In *Validity Foundation on Behalf of TJ v Hungary*, the Court also drew upon the standard of 'appropriate measures to protect' life.[53] It also invoked the standard of 'adequate response', where adequacy can be perceive as expressing the idea of a causal link between omitted measures and harm.[54] A third standard was also

[49] For a very similar argument, see Lord Hoffmann, 'Causation' in Goldberg (n 8) 3, 5: 'anyone is entitled to say that in treating X in some particular context as having caused Y, the courts are stretching the ordinary meaning of "cause". But this is *engaging in a legitimate argument over interpretation* and not introducing the concept of "real" causation as a preliminary test which has to be satisfied before the question of interpretation arises' (emphasis added). See also L Green, 'Are There Dependable Rules on Causation?' (1929) 77(5) *University of Pennsylvania Law Review* 601.

[50] See Plakokefalos, ch 8 in this volume.

[51] Stoyanova (n 30) 63.

[52] *Biba v Albania* (n 40) paras 52 and para 72 (emphasis added).

[53] *Validity Foundation on Behalf of TJ v Hungary* (n 43) paras 72 and 88.

[54] ibid para 94: 'The Government however failed to demonstrate that the authorities had provided an adequate response to the generally difficult situation in Topház.' See also *AE v Bulgaria* (n 42) para 100,

referred to in the reasoning in *Validity Foundation on Behalf of TJ v Hungary*: the state 'failed to demonstrate that the domestic authorities had had the *requisite standard of protection* that would have enabled them to prevent the deterioration in health and ultimately death of Ms T.J.'.[55] By using the standards of 'appropriate', 'adequate' and 'requisite' that hint at the idea of causation, the Court's reasoning formulates the obligation and determines its breach.[56]

The standard of 'all necessary steps' used in *EK v Latvia* introduces some nuances in the causation inquiry in comparison with the standards of 'appropriate measures' and 'adequate response'. First, the adjective 'necessary' implies that the content of the positive obligation consists only of necessary (understood as indispensable) measures. This seems to limit the scope of measures that might be legally relevant for the content of the obligation and the determination of its breach. Second, the word 'all' in the expression 'all necessary measures' implies that any conceivable measure that passes the threshold of being defined as 'necessary' must be taken by the state. This seems to expand the scope of the obligation since even if one necessary measure was not undertaken, breach should follow.[57]

The Court's reasoning does not suggest that it has fully considered the nuances of the 'all necessary steps' standard or how this affects the scope of the state's obligations. Nor does it appear that the Court's use of different standards in other judgments reflects a conscious or deliberate decision about the extent of those positive obligations. For example, in *Biba v Albania*, the standard was *not* 'all appropriate measures', which would imply that even if one 'appropriate measure' was not taken by the state authorities, breach should follow.

Finally, it should be mentioned that in *EK v Latvia*, the Court qualified the standard of 'all necessary steps' in the following way: 'all necessary steps to facilitate contact *as can reasonably be demanded in the special circumstances of each case*'.[58] The standard of 'reasonable' can also be understood as reflecting a causal

where the standard of adequacy was used: 'the applicable legal provisions are not fully capable of responding to domestic violence'. See also *Abbasaliyeva v Azerbaijan* App No 6950/13, 27 April 2023, para 37: 'Taking into account the domestic courts' reasoning and conclusions in the present case, it cannot be established that they conducted an *adequate* balancing exercise between the applicant's right to respect for her private life and the newspaper's freedom of expression' (emphasis added). See also *GTB v Spain* App No 3041/19, 16 November 2023, para 128.

[55] *Validity Foundation on Behalf of TJ v Hungary* (n 43) para 96 (emphasis added).

[56] Other standards, such as sufficiency, have been also invoked. See *Alhowais v Hungary* App No 59435/17, 2 February 2023, para 117. 'Due diligence' has been also invoked. See *GTB v Spain* (n 56) para 124: 'The authorities were thus under a positive obligation stemming from Article 8 to act *with due diligence in order to* assist the applicant in obtaining his birth certificate and his identity documents, so as to ensure effective respect for his private life' (emphasis added).

[57] *IS v Greece* (n 47) para 93 illustrates the impact of the 'all' standard: 'Admittedly, the authorities faced a very difficult situation which stemmed in particular from the tensions existing between the parents of the children, as highlighted by the Government. However lack of cooperation between the separated parents cannot exempt the competent authorities from implementing *all the means likely* to allow the maintenance of the family bond' (emphasis added).

[58] *EK v Latvia* (n 45) para 76 (emphasis added). The standard of 'reasonable', although initially invoked at para 76, is not mentioned in the actual determination of breach in the specific case. See also *Janočková and Kvocera v Slovakia* App No 39980/22, 8 February 2024, para 44; *Zavridou v Cyprus* App No 14680/22, 8 October 2024, paras 78 and 81.

link between the measures expected from the state and the prevention of the harm. Since the measures have to be reasonable, these measures should be possible to causally link with the prevention of the harm given the circumstances. Notably, what is reasonable is always context-dependent,[59] and therefore dependent on the particular combination of circumstances that has arisen. This supports the position about the collapse of the analytical operations meant to determine the existence of a positive obligation and the breach of this obligation.[60] More specifically, the positive obligation – whose content is some reasonable measures – could not be more specifically identified and formulated prior to the existence of the particular combination of circumstances. This combination of factual circumstances is only *post factum* assessed and reviewed for the purposes of determining breach of the Convention. In such a *post factum* assessment, a breach cannot be determined by relying on a predefined set of measures established before the emergence of the factual situation and before the assessment of breach of the Convention.

E. Choices in the Framing and Specification of the Harm and the Causes

So far, section II has aimed to clarify the cause (A) and the effect (B) that are linked for the purpose of establishing state responsibility for breach of positive obligations under the ECHR. This section aims to explain that any links between (A) and (B), and therefore the framing of the content and scope of positive obligations, can be expressed with different levels of specification by modifying (A) and (B). In other words, there are choices that the Court can make in its reasoning as to how (A) is formulated and *with what level of specification* (A) is expressed. More precisely, the measures that are the alleged counterparts to the omissions might be formulated as measures to prevent harm. Alternatively, the measures might be articulated as measures of mitigating harm. Mitigation might have different degrees that might not be even specified in the reasoning, in which case it might be difficult to even understand what (A) is.[61] Precaution might be also invoked as the standard for specifying the measures. Similarly, there are choices to be made in the reasoning as

[59] See O Corten, 'The Notion of "Reasonable" in International Law: Legal Discourse, Reason and Contradiction' (1999) 48 *International and Comparative Law Quarterly* 613; Stoyanova (n 30) 73. See also Plakokefalos, ch 8 in this volume.

[60] In some judgments, the Court does not even invoke the standards of 'appropriate' or 'necessary'. See *Moldovan v Ukraine* (n 22) para 44, where the Court formulated its task in the following way: 'The Court will therefore examine whether the respondent State, in handling the applicant's action for judicial recognition that a late person was his father, has complied with its positive obligation under Article 8 of the Convention.' In other cases (eg, *AE v Bulgaria* (n 42) para 93), instead of 'appropriate' or 'necessary' measures, the Court refers to the standard of efficiency.

[61] See, eg, *AP v Armenia* (n 61), which concerned sexual abuse of a pupil with intellectual disability at school: 'A failure to take readily available measures that could have had a *real prospect of altering the outcome or mitigating the harm* caused is sufficient to engage the responsibility of the State' (at para 121, emphasis added).

to how (B) is framed and specified. A notable example here is the modification of (B) as not being the harm itself, but the *risk* of harm or the potential risk.[62] In addition to risk-based harm,[63] the Court can resort to other choices in how to frame (B), ie, how to frame the negatively affected interests.[64]

Daraibou v Croatia can be used as an illustration.[65] The case concerned a fire that broke out in a detention centre, in which three detained migrants died, and the applicant suffered severe injuries. The applicant complained about the authorities' failure to protect his life and their failure to properly investigate the incident under Article 2 of the Convention. The Court's reasoning was characterised by the invocation of the standard of precaution, which indeed in the prison setting appeared warranted.[66] In particular, the Court noted that:

> [E]ven where it is not established that the authorities knew or ought to have known about any such risk, there are certain basic *precautions* which police officers and prison officers should be expected to take in all cases in order to minimise *any potential risk* to protect the health and well-being of the arrested person.[67]

The Court was clear that it could not 'discern sufficient evidence to show that the authorities knew or ought to have known that there had been a real and immediate risk that the applicant and other detainees would try to set fire or injure themselves in any other way'.[68] This means that no actual or putative knowledge about the specific type of risk (ie, real and immediate) from the specific harm (ie, fire) could be established. However, the Court chose to reframe the knowledge standard and make it one of precaution.[69] It also chose to reframe the harm as

[62] ibid para 116 (risk of sexual abuse); *Alhowais v Hungary* (n 56) para 117: 'Whenever a State undertakes or organises dangerous activities, or authorises them, it must ensure through a system of rules and through sufficient control that *the risk* is reduced to a reasonable minimum' (emphasis added).

[63] When the harm is reframed as risk, this has implications for the content of the positive obligation. The Court has formulated the positive obligation 'to put in place regulations geared to the specific features of the activity in question, particularly *with regard to the level of risk potentially involved*' (emphasis added). *Verein Klimaseniorinnen Schweiz and Others v Switzerland* (n 26) para 538.

[64] The reframing of the harm as risk of harm, which implies looser causation and consideration of wider counterfactuals and thus a wider scope of the obligation, can be distinguished from cases where the Court has decided to formulate a separate procedural positive obligation upon the state to perform risk assessment. For the latter, see *Gaidukevich v Georgia* App No 38650/18, 15 June 2023, para 57 ('autonomous, proactive and comprehensive lethality risk assessment' in the context of domestic violence).

[65] *Daraibou v Croatia* App No 84523/17, 17 January 2023.

[66] For another setting where precaution was used by the Court, see *Kotilainen and Others v Finland* App No 62439/12, 17 September 2020, a case about shooting at school. The applicants in *Verein Klimaseniorinnen Schweiz and Others v Switzerland* (n 26) invoked precaution, but the Court chose not to use this standard in its reasoning.

[67] *Daraibou v Croatia* (n 65) para 84 (emphasis added).

[68] ibid para 87.

[69] See also ibid para 88: 'In the Court's view, there were certain basic precautions the police should have been expected to take in respect of the persons held in their custody in order to minimise any potential risk of grave accidents such as the one in the present case.'

one of 'potential risk of grave incidents'.[70] It chose not to consider the standard of imminence.[71]

Once these choices in the framing were made, a wider set of circumstances could be considered. To elaborate, a wider set of omissions could be included in the analysis without much specificity as to how each articulated omission could have caused the harm. As already noted, the Court chose to reformulate the harm as that of 'potential risk of grave incidents', which allows further expansion of the possibly relevant omissions. In particular, the following omissions were articulated in the reasoning in *Daraibou v Croatia:* (1) lights (that probably started the fire) were not taken from the detainees; (2) there was no proper monitoring of the detainees; and (3) there was no expert report as to the fire-protection measures in the building.[72] The Court concluded that 'the Bajakovo police station building and its personnel were rather ill-prepared to deal with a fire outbreak on their premises'.[73] This conclusion appeared to be very much warranted; all that I try to highlight here is that there are choices that the Court can make as to how to formulate the harm, its causes and the link between these two.

The judgment in *Mitrevska v North Macedonia* can be also used to exemplify certain choices as to the framing of the harm and the omissions.[74] The applicant, who was adopted as a child, complained about her inability to obtain information about her biological origins and health information about her biological parents. For the purposes of the definitional scope of Article 8 (see section II.A above), the harm was formulated in the following way:

> The Court reiterates that persons who, like the applicant in the present case, seek to establish their parentage have a vital interest, protected by the Convention, *in receiving the information* necessary to discover the truth about an important aspect of their personal identity. In addition, the applicant also had *an interest in obtaining information relevant to her health*, given that she argued in the domestic proceedings that she was seeking information concerning the medical history of her parents in order to determine whether she had a hereditary disease.[75]

The harm was therefore framed as the failure to receive information. However, the omission for the purposes of establishing the obligation and its breach was re-articulated in the Court's reasoning as 'absence of a *possibility* to obtain access to

[70] ibid. See also the domestic violence case of *AE v Bulgaria* (n 42) para 96, where the harm is framed as risk.

[71] For the dilatation of this standard in the case law of the Court, see Stoyanova (n 37) 205.

[72] It can be also observed that the various omissions mentioned in the reasoning were of a different nature, which also means that their possible causal contribution to the harm is of a different nature and different degree. For example, not taking lights from the detainees can be more easily accepted as causing fire in general and as causing the specific fire. In contrast, the absence of an expert report appears to be a cause of a lesser degree. In particular, the existence of an expert report as such does not mean that in reality there were fire-protection measures. Neither does it mean that the report as such could have prevented the fire.

[73] *Daraibou v Croatia* (n 65) para 92.

[74] *Mitrevska v North Macedonia* App No 20949/21.

[75] ibid para 50 (emphasis added).

non-identifying information'.[76] Given this choice of framing, the articulated omission is causally distanced from the harm as formulated by the applicant and the Court (ie, providing her with information) at the definitional scope of the analysis (see section II.A above). The omission could be remedied, which means that she might be provided with the possibility, but this would not necessarily lead to actual provision of information. In this sense, the causal chain between the omission and the harm is obscured.[77] This appears to be a warranted way to reasoning, since the actual provision of information might come in tension with the interests of other individuals. My objective here is simply to illustrate how the Court can make different choices in the specification of the harm and the causes.

III. Distinguishing Factual and Legal Causation

An important conclusion from the analysis in section II is that the establishment of state responsibility for omissions under the ECHR is marked by conceptual difficulties and the availability of different choices that the Court can make in its reasoning. To better understand these difficulties and choices, comparative parallels with more developed and consistent systems of legal responsibility can offer relevant insights.[78] In particular, legal systems try to make a distinction between the multiplicity of possible factually relevant causes from legally relevant causes for the harm.[79] In this sense, at least theoretically, the causal inquiry has been explained as consisting of two consequent steps.[80] The first one is factual causation that seeks to establish the factual link between an omission and the harmful outcome. This is meant to reflect the historical picture of the events leading to the

[76] ibid para 85 (emphasis added).

[77] See also *Vlaisavlevikj v North Macedonia* (n 22) paras 37–39 and 45. In this case, the harm that was found to fall within the scope of art 8 was collection and use of personal data. However, a breach was found not because of the failure by the national authorities to order the private company to delete the data; it was found because the domestic courts failed to examine the question whether 'the continued retention and use of the applicant's data corresponded to that legitimate aim'.

[78] While being aware of the warning about the inappropriateness of domestic analogies, it has been also demonstrated that responsibility in international law has similarities with domestic private law and public law. See A Nolkaemper, 'Constitutionalization and the Unity of the Law of International Responsibility' (2009) 16(2) *Indiana Journal of Global Legal Studies* 535.

[79] J Spier, *Unification of Tort Law: Causation* (Kluwer, 2000); M Infantino, 'Causation Theories and Causation Rules' in M Bussani and AJ Sebok (eds), *Comparative Tort Law: Global Perspectives* (Edward Elgar, 2021) 264–83; Honore (n 1); HLA Hart and AM Honore, *Causation in the Law* (Clarendon Press 1985); S Steel, *Proof of Causation in Tort Law* (Cambridge University Press, 2015); Goldberg (n 8).

[80] J Stapleton, 'Unpacking "Causation"' in P Cane, T Honoré and J Gardner (eds), *Relating to Responsibility: Essays in Honour of Tony Honoré on His 80th Birthday* (Hart Publishing, 2001) 145, 166–67; FD Busnelli et al, 'Causation' in *Principles of European Tort Law. Text and Commentary* (Springer, 2005) 43, 59: 'For practical purposes, every (European) legal system (under review) accepts that the mere fact that a condition sine qua non-relation between a loss and an activity is established, does not mean that every and all consequent losses have to be compensated by the liable person.' Some legal systems perceive the issue as part of causation, 'whereas others perceive it an unrelated legal vehicle'.

outcome. This picture can be very wide, which can make the inquiry overly inclusive. The inquiry may be also hampered by scientific complexity and uncertainty.[81]

Once the first step of factual causation is performed, the second step follows. This second step has been framed as legal causation. Other possible framings that have been used are remoteness,' proximate cause' assessment or scope of responsibility.[82] This second step seeks to determine for which effects (ie, harms) of the wrongful act the defendant is to be held legally responsible and, accordingly, is to ensure remedies.[83]

This section attempts to review the practice of the Court by applying the distinction between factual and legal causation. The analysis is guided by the question of whether the Court has distinguished the different considerations of respectively factual and legal causation (sections III.A and III.B). The response to this question is negative. Section III.C explains that the mixture of factual and legal causation is inevitable. The inevitability is related to the role of the causation inquiry that, as explained in section II, includes both analytical steps that are performed simultaneously in the reasoning: first, the establishment of the content and the scope of the obligation; and, second, the establishment of its breach. My aim is not to criticise the Court, but rather to expose and to better understand the reasoning.

A. Factual Causation

The inquiry into factual causation is restrained, given the specific facts of the case and the arguments raised by the parties. Omissions have to be identified and specified; in the ECtHR's proceedings, this is normally done by the applicant.[84] Possible

[81] In such cases, a normative approach to the inquiry might have to be applied, which questions the distinction between factual and legal causation. See J Stapleton, 'Cause-in-Fact and the Scope of Liability for Consequences' (2003) 119 *Law Quarterly Review* 388, at 388.

[82] It is more accurate to describe this second step as scope of responsibility rather than a test of 'causation' per se. See ibid.

[83] The second step is therefore intrinsically linked to the remedial function of the law and the idea that remedies (including monetary compensation) should not be afforded for all possible loses/harms. In this chapter, I do not address the question of remedies. The link, however, between the approach to causation for determining breach of primary obligations and the nature of the secondary obligations (ie, the remedies) needs to be acknowledged. See V Stoyanova, 'Causation and Breach of Positive Obligations under the European Convention on Human Rights: Correcting the Past, Preventing the Future' in V Stoyanova and M Andenæs (eds), *The Role of the Causal Inquiry under the European Convention on Human Rights* (Cambridge University Press, forthcoming).

[84] *Daniel Karsay v Hungary* App No 32312/23, 13 June 2024, paras 94 and 136; *Moldovan v Ukraine* (n 22) para 39; *Vagdalt v Hungary* App No 9525/19, 7 March 2024, para 44; *Biba v Albania* App No 24228/18, 7 May 2024, para 52; *Validity Foundation on Behalf of TJ v Hungary* (n 43) para 60; *Varyan v Armenia* App No 48998/14, 4 June 2024, paras 77–79; *Vlaisavlevikj v North Macedonia* (n 22) para 35; *Zavridou v Cyprus* (n 58) paras 71–72; *AE v Bulgaria* (n 42) para 63 (minor bodily harm was not an offence subject to public prosecution); *Kilic v Austria* App No 27700/15, 12 January 2023, para 138. Omissions can be also identified based on the reasoning of the domestic courts. See *AP v Armenia* (n 61) (failure to protect a pupil from sexual abuse by a teacher at the school).

alternatives as counterparts to the omissions (ie, measures actually taken) might be identified and specified by the respondent state.[85]

In the identification of omissions and counterparts to omissions, there might be certain restraints coming from the determination of the definitional scope of the right (see section II.A). In particular, given how the Court has chosen to frame the definitional scope (ie, which interests are considered affected and how), only certain harms can be considered as relevant.[86] There might be also restraints from certain admissibility requirements, such as victim status.[87] It might be objected that these two restraints (ie, formulation of the definitional scope and the victim status requirement) are not actually factual since they are *legally* and therefore *normatively* imposed. These restraints indeed impose certain limits on the factual causal inquiry. Since these limits are normative, they seem to defy the distinction between factual causation and legal causation. I will, however, follow Plakokefalos, who has argued that the normative character of the above-mentioned restraints does not make them legal/policy tools and considerations. What they do is ensure that the factual causation is investigated within 'particular – legal – boundaries'.[88]

Having introduced this clarification, we can focus on the identification and the specification of omissions for the purposes of the factual causation inquiry. To factually link harm to the omissions that might be invoked by the applicant, different tests can be applied. In the context of tort law, the 'but for' test has been applied.[89] According to this test, an omission is considered *the* cause of the harmful outcome, when this outcome would not have occurred without the omission. The 'but for' test asks whether the outcome would be the same if the abnormal factor (ie, the omission) is removed from the set of historical facts. In this sense, the factor has to be the necessary precondition.

The problem here is that there are multiplicity of omissions and none of them might be possible to factually *exclusively* link to the harm, so that the specific omission can be considered as *the* cause that satisfies the 'but for' test.[90] These might be concurrent omissions. Each one of them on its own might be normatively

[85] *AP v Armenia* (n 61) para 102 (the teacher who sexually abused the applicant received severe punishment). See also *Biba v Albania* (n 84) paras 56–57; *Varyan v Armenia* (n 84) paras 80–86; *Vlaisavlevikj v North Macedonia* (n 22) para 36; *Zavridou v Cyprus* (n 58) paras 73–76; *AE v Bulgaria* (n 42) paras 74–80. Other parties, including interveners, can also specify measures. See *Kilic v Austria* (n 84) para 144.

[86] Equally important, in choosing how to frame the definitional scope of the right, the harm that is the object of the review can be expanded and, accordingly, the scope of counterfactuals and possible causal omissions are also expanded. See *Alhowais v Hungary* (n 56) para 112: 'the Court has considered that the sphere of application of Article 2 of the Convention cannot be interpreted as being limited to the time and direct cause of the individual's death. Chains of events that were triggered by a negligent act and led to loss of life may also fall to be examined under Article 2'. There is a circularity at play in this statement: the establishment of negligence is assumed for the purpose of triggering the definitional scope of art 2.

[87] *Verein Klimaseniorinnen Schweiz and Others v Switzerland* (n 26) paras 478–88 and 533–35.

[88] Plakokefalos (n 10) 476. Plakokefalos relies on Hamer (n 9).

[89] See generally Steel (n 79).

[90] The nature of omissions is such that usually they are always many that can be identified.

worthwhile to assess as basing legal responsibility. This reveals how the choice of test is affected not only by factual/evidential challenges (ie, evidential difficulties in proving exclusivity), but also by normative considerations.[91] In light of such normative consideration, an alternative to the 'but for' test has been advanced. This is the necessary element of a sufficient set (NESS) test,[92] which requires the identification of *a* cause, not *the* cause, which makes it more inclusive.[93]

The ECtHR has never explicitly referred to the NESS test. It has, however, explicitly rejected the 'but for' test. This was made explicit for the first time in *E and Others v United Kingdom*:

> The test under article 3 however does not require it to be shown that 'but for' the failing or omission of the public authority ill-treatment would not have happened. A failure to take reasonably available measures which could have had a real prospect of altering the outcome or mitigating the harm is sufficient to engage the responsibility of the state.[94]

The last sentence in this quotation contains indicators that can be perceived as implying the idea of causation: 'real prospect of altering the outcome'. The Court, however, does not use consistently the 'real prospect' test.[95] Overall, the Court has never indicated a causation test of general relevance in its positive obligations case law.[96] Terminologically there is also a huge diversity of terms and concepts in the case law that can be understood as expressing the idea of factual causation. For example, in *Dimaksyan v Armenia*, which concerned the death of applicant's son during compulsory military service following an accidental shooting by a fellow serviceman, after rejecting the 'but for' test, the Court held that:

> [W]hat is important, and sufficient to engage the responsibility of the State under Article 2, is to show that the deficiencies in the operation of the relevant regulatory

[91] For an excellent analysis of why the distinction between factual and legal causation ultimately breaks down, and how this occurs, see Hamer (n 9).

[92] According to this test, '[a] particular condition is a cause (contributed to) a specific result if and only if it was a necessary element of a set of antecedent actual conditions that was sufficient for the occurrence of the result'. R Wright, 'Causation, Responsibility, Risk, Probability, Naked Statistics, and Proof: Pruning the Bramble Bush by Clarifying the Concepts' (1987–88) 73 *Iowa Law Review* 1001, 1019. Another explanation of NESS is the following: whether the wrongful act was one among many other possible causes of the harm. See Treacy, ch 6 in this volume.

[93] Plakokefalos (n 10) 478.

[94] *E and Others v United Kingdom* App No 33218/96 (26 November 2002) para 99; *O'Keeffe v Ireland* (n 34) para 149. For more recent rejections of the 'but for' test, see *Dimaksyan v Armenia* App No 29906/14, 2023, para 83; *AP v Armenia* (n 61) para 108; *Verein Klimaseniorinnen Schweiz and Others v Switzerland* (n 26) para 444.

[95] V Stoyanova, 'Causation between State Omission and Harm within the Framework of Positive Obligations under the European Convention on Human Rights' (2018) 18 *Human Rights Law Review* 309. The choice of 'real prospect' test or whatever other concepts the Court has used to express the idea of causation has not been justified in the reasoning. This is not surprising since the Court does not engage with theoretical discussions. However, the question whether the 'real prospect' test should be the test used in human rights law can be an object of theoretical investigation.

[96] For a slight modification of the test, see, eg, *AP v Armenia* (n 61) para 121: 'A failure to take *readily available* measures that could have had a real prospect' (emphasis added). This implied that it was the easy availability of the measures that influenced the determination of breach.

> framework *worked to an individual's detriment*, which, in the Court's opinion, occurred in the present case.[97]

The standard of 'to an individual's detriment' seems to be looser than the NESS test, since it does not include an inquiry as to whether any identifiable deficiencies were actually necessary for the materialisation of the harm.

In *Alhowais v Hungary*, which concerned the death of F, a Syrian migrant and the applicant's brother, which occurred during a border control operation at a river on the Hungarian–Serbian border, the Court noted: 'It is confined to examining, among other things, whether in the present case, in the organisation and planning of the border control operation in question, failings occurred which can be *linked directly to the death* of F.'[98] Linking failings/omissions to the harm reveals an attempt to perform a causal inquiry. However, questions about the necessity of certain failings or the sufficiency of a group of failings are not asked, as demanded by the NESS test.

To conclude, although some causation tests (such as 'real prospect') can be identified in the Court's reasoning that are suggestive of the idea of factual causation, these are not consistently used. Just as important, as the next section will show, is that whatever omissions the Court chooses to identify and specify in its reasoning, they are not independent and separate considerations that can be isolated as factual causation applied as an initial isolated necessary step in the human rights review. These considerations are instead mixed with other considerations that are theoretically regarded as belonging to the toolbox of the legal causation.

B. Legal Causation

Legal causation requires 'some policy-based control over responsibility'.[99] It offers tools for determining causation in law that are normative in nature; these tools are not related to factual causes, many of which might not be epistemologically accessible in any case. The answer to the question 'what made a difference in bringing about a transition between states?' is therefore driven by normative considerations.[100] The reason is that the answer depends on the perspective taken by the decision-maker and the general objective of the responsibility system where the question is asked. Certain normative and policy choices therefore shape the answer as to whether the actor whose responsibility is at stake should be held legally responsible.

[97] *Dimaksyan v Armenia* (n 94) para 83 (emphasis added).

[98] *Alhowais v Hungary* (n 56) para 133 (emphasis added).

[99] Lanovoy (n 10) 61. Lanovoy refers to Judge William Andrews in *Helen Palsgraf v The Long Island Railroad Co* (1928) 248 NY 339: 'What we do mean by the word "proximate" is, that because of convenience, of public policy, of a rough sense of justice, the law arbitrarily declines to trace a series of events beyond a certain point. This is not logic. It is practical politics.'

[100] J Stapleton, 'Perspectives on Causation' in J Horder (ed), *Oxford Essays in Jurisprudence* (Oxford University Press, 2000) 61, 62.

It then follows that not only is the choice of a test for factual causation affected by normative and policy considerations (that might defy the characterisation of the test as 'factual'), but additional normative and policy considerations are also relevant for the assessment of breach.[101] Given their normative nature, it is questionable whether they should be called causation at all. Such considerations can be summarised as foreseeability of the harm, the reasonableness of taking measures, the closeness in time and space between the omission and the harm, the severity of the harm and violation of any existing rules.[102]

All of these have been used by the Court in its case law. In particular, the Court has consistently invoked the foreseeability of the harm,[103] and actual[104] or putative knowledge[105] of the state about harm (or risk of harm) to determine responsibility for omissions. Similarly, the standard of reasonableness is consistently invoked.[106] 'Disproportionate burden' can be understood as a reformulation of the reasonableness standard.[107] The immediacy of the harm[108] and the location of the harm have also been relevant considerations.[109] The nature of the harm in terms of gravity is also pertinent.[110] In addition, the Court consistently refers to domestic[111] and international[112] legal standards to assess whether omissions should lead to

[101] Stapleton (n 80) 173.

[102] 'Causation' in *Principles of European Tort Law. Text and Commentary* (Springer, 2005) 43, 59.

[103] See V Stoyanova, 'Fault, Knowledge and Risk within the Framework of Positive Obligations under the European Convention on Human Rights' (2020) 33 *Leiden Journal of International Law* 601.

[104] *AP v Armenia* (n 61) para 130; *GTB v Spain* (n 56) para 126; *Hovhannisyan and Karapetyan v Armenia* App No 67351/13, 17 October 2023, para 101.

[105] *Varyan v Armenia* (n 84) para 93, where the Court summarises the various factors in order to determine actual or putative knowledge.

[106] Stoyanova (n 30) 73; See, for example, *Hubert Howak v Poland*, App No 57916/, 16 February 2023, para 78-79, where there was a clear causal link between the omission of the doctor who examined the applicant after the car crash and the harm suffered by the applicant. Yet, no violation of Article 2 ECHR was found since the Court did not consider it reasonable that isolated incidence of medical malpractice, should lead to responsibility under the ECHR.

[107] See *Verein Klimaseniorinnen Schweiz and Others v Switzerland* (n 26) para 538 for further references.

[108] ibid para 417: 'immediate danger to humans'. See also, eg, *Alhowais v Hungary* (n 56) paras 94, 136 and 143; Stoyanova (n 30) 203.

[109] See, eg, *AP v Armenia* (n 61), which concerned the school setting and where the Court held that states have an 'inherent obligation … to ensure their [the children's] protection from ill-treatment, especially in a primary-education context'. See also *Biba v Albania* (n 84) for the school setting. See, eg, *Varyan v Armenia* (n 84) for the military/army setting. See more generally I Plakokefalos, 'The Scope of Responsibility in the Jurisprudence of the European Court of Human Rights' in Stoyanova and Andenas (n 83).

[110] See, eg, *GTB v Spain* (n 56) para 115: 'certain factors have been considered relevant for the assessment of the content of those positive obligations on States. Some of them relate to the applicant. They concern the *importance of the interest at stake* and whether "fundamental values" or "essential aspects" of private life are in issue' (emphasis added). *Verein Klimaseniorinnen Schweiz and Others v Switzerland* (n 26) para 417: 'In the longer term, some of the consequences risk destroying the basis of human livelihoods and survival in the works affected areas.'

[111] *Hovhannisyan and Karapetyan v Armenia* (n 104) para 109 ('contrary to military rules'); *Locascia and Others v Italy* (n 18) para 141 ('the landfill site was operated – in breach of the relevant legislative provisions administrative authorisations').

[112] See *Verein Klimaseniorinnen Schweiz and Others v Switzerland* (n 26), which contains references to international environmental law. See generally A van Aaken and I Motoc (eds), *The European Convention on Human Rights and General International Law* (Oxford University Press, 2018).

a breach of positive obligations. In some judgments, the Court might choose to foreground some of these considerations and to diminish the role of others. As explained in section II.E above, the Court can make choices in the framing of the harm and the causes, which also implies choices as to whether, for example, immediacy of the harm should be highlighted or how stringently to interpret the standard of immediacy.[113]

While some of these considerations might be *masked* as causation in this way, suggesting an inquiry about causation,[114] they ultimately imply *concurrent* inquiries about the existence of a positive obligation, the content and the scope of such an obligation, and its breach.[115] As already suggested in section II.D above, these three inquiries collapse into each other when the claimed basis for responsibility is omission. Since omissions have no definitive counterparts regarding the discretion of states how to 'ensure' the rights protected by the ECHR[116] and, accordingly, since the content of the primary positive obligation is never specified in advance, the *post factum* determination of breach has to resort to certain tools of reasoning that create the impression that the Court does not simply *invent obligations* for the determination of breach in specific cases. The impression needs to be created that in the concrete case, obligations with some more specific content and scope actually existed in the past, prior or at least at the time of the materialisation of the harm (or the risk of harm). The impression needs to be created that the whole analysis does not entirely collapse into normativity and policy-making through the creation of rules and standards (ie, the invention of obligations) that states have never explicitly agreed with. The mixture between what theoretically has been framed as factual and legal causation is therefore inevitable for ensuring the perception that the Court's reasoning does not invent obligations, but reviews compliance with arguably already-existing obligations.

C. The Inevitable Mixture of Factual and Legal Causation

One tool for creating such a perception is resort to logic, rationality, analytical validity and correctness, which is achieved by the inclusion of factual causation in the reasoning. Factual causation and references to scientific studies, regardless

[113] For the standard of immediacy of the harm, see FC Ebert and R Sijniensky, 'Preventing Violations of the Right to Life in the European and the Inter-American Human Rights Systems: From the *Osman* Test to a Coherent Doctrine on Risk Prevention?' (2015) 15 *Human Rights Law Review* 343.

[114] Terms used by the Court that can be perceived as expression the idea of causation are proximity, remoteness and foreseeability.

[115] In agreement with Plakokefalos (n 10). See also Green (n 49).

[116] V Stoyanova, 'The Disjunctive Structure of Positive Rights under the ECHR' (2018) 87 *Nordic Journal of International Law* 344; R Alexy, 'On Constitutional Rights to Protection' (2009) 3 *Legisprudence* 1, 5; V Wibye, 'Beyond Acts and Omissions: Distinguishing Positive and Negative Duties at the European Court of Human Rights' (2022) 23 *Human Rights Review* 479; M Klatt, 'Positive Obligations under the European Convention on Human Rights' (2011) *Heidelberg Journal of International Law* 691, 694.

of their inconclusiveness and possible selectivity in the choice of studies,[117] legitimise the Court's decision-making process and its discretion in inventing obligations. The Court's reasoning, decisions and discretion gain the appearance of being easier to justify since they are presented as being based on science and logic. In this sense, the invocation of factual causation masks the obligation-making function of the Court and, consequently, the normative role of the Court that it unavoidably assumes when it has to apply abstract standards to concrete facts. The reasoning is presented as not being exclusively normative, but as being based on rationality, logic and analytical rigour.[118]

When the Court uses concepts and terms that somehow express the idea of a factual causation, it achieves the following. The Court might be actually addressing the normative questions about the scope and content of the obligation and the breach of the obligation, when in fact *this is presented* as a discussion about factual causality. Why would the Court do this? When it is presented as a factual causality, the argumentation appears to be based on reason (ie, rational thinking), on facts and evidence. The reasoning appears rational. In this way, any normative considerations might remain hidden or obscured, and the judgment is presented as being based on evidence and rationality. All of this means that normative considerations might not be explored separately; they might not even be recognised as being normative.

The above explanations are not meant to be a critique against the Court and its reasoning. Indeed, it might be in the interest of legal certainty to distil the normative considerations in the reasoning (ie, legal causation/scope of responsibility) from factual causation and to have a clear test for factual causation.[119] Along the same lines, it can be also advanced that it is one question to address the factual involvement of the state in the harm (ie, factually whether omissions by the state caused the harm) and it is a separate normative question to consider *whether* the state should have acted and *how* it should have acted to prevent the harm. However, the two questions collapse in the same way as the question about the existence of

[117] Generally, the procedural question of evidence and which studies the Court chooses to accept is under-studied. See M-B Dembour,' The Evidentiary System of the European Court of Human Rights in Critical Perspective' (2023) 4 *European Convention on Human Rights Law Review* 363. For a more detailed exploration about selectivity in the Court's choices as to which medical studies to rely on and how this impacts the framing of the case and consequently the determination of responsibility, see, eg, F van Leeuwen, 'Epistemic Blind Spots, Misconceptions and Stereotypes: The Home Birth Jurisprudence of the European Court of Human Rights' (2024) 35 *European Journal of International Law* 153.

[118] For a similar argument applied to the context of civil law and criminal law, see Green (n 49) 601, where it is argued that while the inquiry might be stated 'in what seems to be terms of *cause* is in fact whether the defendant should be held responsible' (emphasis in original).

[119] J Stapleton, 'Choosing What We Mean by Causation in the Law' (2008) 73 *MLR* 463; I Plakokefalos, 'Causation in the Law of State Responsibility and the Problem of Overdetermination: In Search of Clarity' (2015) 26(2) *European Journal of International Law* 471, 490: 'an effort to differentiate between the issue of factual involvement of the respondent in the harmful outcome (cause in fact) and the issue of the scope of responsibility that is dictated by broader concerns regarding the proper scope of the primary rule breached'.

a positive obligation collapses with the question of its breach (see section II.D above). There is a conflation of the questions, since omission(s) become *legally* and normatively relevant with the identification and the specification of the conduct (ie, the measures) that should have 'corrected' the omissions. To put it differently, the measures – that should have been undertaken in the hypothetical world as alternatives to omissions so that they somehow 'made up' for the omissions – become legally relevant with their designation as being part of the content and the scope of the positive obligation.

It then follows that the mixture of factual causation and legal causation is inevitable in the reasoning. It is inevitable since the Court has to reason about omissions that have no definitive counterparts. It is inevitable since the Court has to reach a conclusion by invoking rationality to legitimise its judgments so that it can present the finding of a breach of a positive obligation as being in line with the demands of this obligation, even though the content of the obligation remains vague.

IV. Conclusion

The judgments of the ECtHR manifest a mixture of factual and legal causation, when the Court reasons whether omissions should be the basis for breach of positive obligations under the Convention. However, considerations that can be generally framed as normative govern its reasoning, which implies that it is legal causation that dominates. Yet, the Court still invokes factual causation to maintain an appearance that its judgments are based on logic, rationality, analytical validity and correctness. Factual causation is invoked for creating the impression that the Court does not simply invent positive obligations. The causal inquiry with its mixture of factual and normative elements is ultimately an inquiry about the existence of positive obligations, about the interpretation of their content and scope, and about the determination of breach. By invoking explicitly or implicitly causal links between harm and omissions, the Court therefore determines the existence of obligations and makes conclusions about their breaches. In this light, it adopts a quite-legislative function performed with the usage of what might appear to be neutral factual language.

8

The Standard of (Un)Reasonableness in Human Rights Positive Obligations

ILIAS PLAKOKEFALOS*

I. Introduction

Reasonableness in the law of human rights appears as a standard by which states are expected to fulfil their duty to protect and promote the rights of individuals within their jurisdiction. This standard lies within the realm of positive obligations.[1] The case law of the European Court of Human Rights (ECtHR) is replete with references (explicit or implicit) to that standard of reasonableness. On the one hand, the ECtHR, in applying the European Convention on Human Rights (ECHR),[2] employs a reasonableness standard in the process of determining causal concepts and in shaping the scope of the responsibility of the respondent State.[3] At the same time the Court recognises that states have limited resources and competing priorities, but they still have obligations to take measures to protect, ensure and respect human rights to all individuals under their jurisdiction or control.[4] The determination of what constitutes a reasonable measure is context-specific and may

* I wish to acknowledge with thanks the editors, Vladislava Stoyanova and David McGrogan, for their illuminating comments on earlier drafts of this chapter. I would also like to thank Linos-Alexandre Sicilianos, Harry Platanakis, Maria-Louiza Deftou, Markos Karavias and Ioanna Pervou for their comments, insights and suggestions. The usual disclaimer applies.

[1] A Clapham, *Human Rights in the Private Sphere* (Clarendon Press, 1993) especially at 89–133; A Mowbray, *The Development of Positive Obligations under the European Convention of Human Rights by the European Court of Human Rights* (Hart Publishing, 2004) 152–53, 168; V Stoyanova, *Positive Obligations under the European Convention on Human Rights* (Oxford University Press, 2023) 73–94. See also F Sudre, 'Les "obligations positives" dans la jurisprudence Européene des droits de l'homme' (1995) *La Revue trimestrielle des droits de l'homme* 363; B Conforti, 'Reflections on State Responsibility for the Breach of Positive Obligations: The Case-Law of the European Court of Human Rights' (2003) *Italian Yearbook of International Law* 3, 8.

[2] Convention on the Protection of Human Rights and Fundamental Freedoms (concluded 4 November 1950, entered into force 3 September 1953) 213 UNTS 221.

[3] Stoyanova (n 1).

[4] Mowbray (n 1) 3–4; L-A Sicilianos, 'Reviewing Violations of the Right to Life: Positive Obligations under the ECHR', (2014) 3 *Cyprus Human Rights Law Review* 117, 118–19.

vary depending on factors such as the severity of the violation and the resources available.[5]

The standard of reasonableness in the context of human rights positive obligations appears in the reasoning of the Court when it engages in a causal analysis, but the application of the standard unfurls in several stages. Starting from causation, the application of causal analysis in the law can be best described as a two-step approach.[6] First, the decision-maker – whether a judge, arbitrator or member of a committee – must determine factual causation.[7] Factual causation is essentially the historical relationship between the wrongful act and the resulting harm.[8] Various tests of causation ('but for', *causa adequata* and the like) come into play here.[9] Then the decision-maker establishes the scope of the defendant's (or respondent's, whatever the case may be) responsibility.[10] The term 'scope of responsibility' is meant to substitute the non-helpful term proximity.[11] It denotes the operation whereby a court decides for which consequences of her wrongful act the defendant will be responsible.[12] To determine the scope of responsibility courts take into account factors such as reasonableness, knowledge, proximity, remoteness and other similar elements.[13] Reasonableness is a key component of the scope of responsibility analysis.[14] The ECtHR employs reasonableness, alongside other criteria and standards, to shape the scope of responsibility of the state.[15]

The reasonableness standard is applied by the Court (while establishing the scope of responsibility) to the examination of the measures adopted by the state that are causally connected to the harm complained of by the applicant. The measures adopted by the state vary from case to case and include legislation,[16]

[5] *Marckx v Belgium* App No 6833/74, 13 June 1979 para 31; *McCann and Others v United Kingdom* [GC] App No 18984/9 27, September 1995, para 151. The pre-eminent reference on the considerations the ECtHR must consider is *Osman v United Kingdom* [GC] 28 October 1998, para 116, Reports 1998-VIII, para 11.

[6] I Plakokefalos, 'Causation in the Law of State Responsibility and the Problem of Overdetermination: In Search of Clarity' (2015) 26(2) *European Journal of International Law* 471, 473–76.

[7] On factual causation, see, among many others, WX Malone, 'Ruminations on Cause in Fact' (1956–57) 9 *Stanford Law Review* 60; J Stapleton, 'Factual Causation' (2010) 38 *Federal Law Review* 467.

[8] J Stapleton, 'Legal Cause: Cause in Fact and the Scope of Liability for Consequences' (2001) 54(3) *Vanderbilt Law Review* 941, 951.

[9] Malone (n 7).

[10] On the scope of responsibility, see Stapleton (n 8).

[11] For the difficulties of the definition of proximity, see L Green, *Judge and Jury* (Vernon Law Books, 1930) 202–05.

[12] Stapleton (n 8) 945.

[13] For an excellent (and unsympathetic to proximity) account, see L Green, 'Are There Dependable Rules on Causation?' (1928–29) 77(5) *University of Pennsylvania Law Review and American Law Register* 601.

[14] Stoyanova (n 1) 88–89. To be sure, reasonableness is also present in various contexts in the ECHR, notably in arts 5 and 6. This chapter does not address the use of reasonableness in terms of 'reasonable time' (art 6) and 'reasonable suspicion' and 'reasonable necessity' (art 5).

[15] Stoyanova (n 1) 88–89.

[16] See, for example, *Makaratzis v Greece* [GC] App No 50385/99, 24 December 2004, where the Court engages in a discussion on the Greek law regulating the use of force by the police (at para 57).

administrative decisions[17] and regulatory frameworks.[18] The standard of reasonableness has a place alongside various other standards, notions and concepts that are subsumed by a broad language that refers to 'priorities' and 'resources', as well as observations on the 'diversity of situations' and 'difficulties' on behalf of the state.[19] These are employed in an effort to encompass the vast number of relevant factors in the decision-making process of the Court. Using this broad terminological spectrum, the ECtHR seems to try and balance its subsidiary role in shaping and dictating the appropriate measures a state party to the Convention adopts and the need to reach a decision by actually passing judgment on these measures.[20]

Admittedly, it is difficult to separate the sequence in the reasoning of the Court (from factual causation to the determination of the scope of responsibility to the application of the reasonableness standard) because the Court does not always provide the necessary clues and because the conclusions cannot always be traced to a specific point in that sequence.[21] In practice, the Court blends these processes to reach its decision.

This chapter argues that the ECtHR uses a *Wednesbury* unreasonableness standard[22] as one of the factors relevant in deciding whether a state has violated its positive obligations to protect human rights. Similarly to the *Wednesbury* dictum of the UK High Court, the ECtHR is trying to see if the respondent state has adopted a course of conduct (be it normative or operational) that is patently and demonstrably unreasonable.[23]

Wednesbury is of course the progeny of UK administrative law and specifically judicial review. A few words on borrowing from a UK law precedent are in order. Initially UK law treated the shortcomings of the decisions of public bodies through tort law.[24] The case law took a different turn (mainly in the 1940s) and

[17] See, for example, *Giuliani and Gaggio v Italy* [GC] App No 23458/02, 24 March 2011, paras 114, 140, 197.

[18] See, for example, *Centre for Legal Resources on Behalf of Valentin Câmpeanu v Romania* [GC] App No 47848/08, 17 July 2014, para 130.

[19] In *Ribcheva and Others v Bulgaria* App Nos 37801/16, 30 March 2021 the Court expressly recognised that different factual situations call for the application of a different standard of reasonableness (at para 165). See also *Tanribilir v Turkey* App No 21422/93, 16 November 2000, para 71; *Öneryildiz v Turkey* [GC] 30 November 2004, para 107.

[20] The Court habitually holds that it cannot, in hindsight, substitute its opinion for that of the state. See, for instance, *Andronicou and Constantinou v Cyprus* App No 86/1996/705/897, 9 October 1997, para 181; *Ribcheva* (n 19) para 170.

[21] Stoyanova (n 1) 75. To be clear, Stoyanova here discusses the question of alternative measures of protection that the state could have adopted to abide by its obligations under the ECHR. Nonetheless, by analogy, the same is true for the judicial review process applied by the ECtHR. The Court looks at a measure adopted by the state and decides whether it was sufficient to safeguard the applicant's rights. This, according to Stoyanova, cannot be done without looking at alternative measures of protection. The two questions are intertwined.

[22] *Associated Provincial Picture Houses v Wednesbury* [1948] 1 KB 223.

[23] ibid 230.

[24] T Arvind and L Stinton, 'The Curious Origins of Judicial Review' (2017), https://hdl.handle.net/10779/uos.23427743.v1, 4.

began reviewing administrative decisions, an exercise that was to become judicial review.[25] It is within this context that the High Court delivered *Wednesbury*.[26] Judicial review has a long and convoluted history, and it is well beyond the scope of this chapter to delve in such an analysis.[27] Judicial review is also the subject of significant theoretical debates as to its function, purpose, and application, and these debates also lie outside the scope of this chapter.[28] Nor does this chapter seek to draw analogies between national constitutional orders and the supranational function of the ECtHR. For our purposes, judicial review is relevant only to the extent that the ECtHR indeed reviews legislation, administrative measures and decisions, and generally the regulatory framework put in place by states parties to the Convention.[29] It merely borrows the reasoning from a national court that reviews a decision of a public body. At its bare minimum, this is a type of review

[25] ibid especially 21–27.

[26] Judicial review in the constitutional law context can be traced back to US law and specifically to *Marbury v Madison* 5 US 137 (1803). For the view that *Marbury* was pre-dated by a few other cases and for an analysis of the reasons it became the most famous judicial review case, see JN Rakove, 'The Origins of Judicial Review: A Plea for New Contexts' (1997) 49(5) *Stanford Law Review* 1031.

[27] See, among many others, M Cappeletti and J Clarke Adams, 'Judicial Review of Legislation: Antecedents and Adaptations' (1966) 79(6) *Harvard Law Review* 1207; G Calabresi, 'The Global Rise of Judicial Review after 1945' (2020) 69(3) *Catholic University Review* 401.

[28] In the literature there are at least three identifiable strands regarding the nature of judicial review before UK courts. The classic ultra vires reasoning, meaning that the courts quash decisions of public bodies or officials because they lie outside the jurisdiction conferred to them (see C Forsyth, 'Of Fig Leaves and Fairy Tales: The Ultra Vires Doctrine, the Sovereignty of Parliament and Judicial Review (1996) 55(1) *Cambridge Law Journal* 122 and, *contra*, P Craig, 'Ultra Vires and the Foundations of Review' (1998) 57(1) *Cambridge Law Journal* 63), a rights-based approach (see TRS Allan 'Constitutional Dialogue and the Justification for Judicial Review (2003) 23(4) *Oxford Journal of Legal Studies* 563) and a legitimacy approach (see T Poole, 'Legitimacy, Rights and Judicial Review' (2005) 25(4) *Oxford Journal of Legal Studies* 697). This chapter will not engage in a similar exercise regarding the ECtHR. However, what is interesting is the effect of the ECHR on the judicial review system of the UK. The Human Rights Act 1998 gave courts the right, under s 4(2), to render a declaration of incompatibility between legislation and the ECHR. A fascinating debate ensued regarding the changes brought to the UK constitutional order and judicial review. See, for example, ATH Smith, 'The Human Rights Act 1998: The Constitutional Context' in Cambridge Centre for Public Law, *The Human Rights Act and the Criminal and Regulatory Process* (Hart Publishing, 1999); M Elliott, 'The Human Rights Act 1998 and the Standard of Substantive Review' (2001) 60(2) *Cambridge Law Journal* 301; A Kavanagh, 'What is So Weak about "Weak Form Review"? The Case of the UK Human Rights Act 1998' (2015) 13(4) *International Journal of Constitutional Law* 1008; R Masterman, 'The United Kingdom's Human Rights Act as a Catalyst on Constitutional Migration: Patterns and Limitations of Rights Importation by Design' (2023) 19(1) *European Constitutional Law Review* 88. It is also telling that the concept of judicial review has been one of the main arguments in the literature regarding the constitutionalisation of the EU. See the classic account in J Weiler, 'The Transformation of Europe' (1991) 100(8) *Yale Law Journal* 2403.

[29] There is, of course, literature on the constitutional aspects of the ECHR. See, for example, L Wildhaber, 'A Constitutional Future for the European Court of Human Rights?' (2002) 23 *Human Rights Law Review* 161; S Greer and L Wildhaber, 'Revisiting the Debate about Constitutionalising the European Court of Human Rights' (2013) 12(4) *Human Rights Law Review* 655; R Bellamy, 'The Democratic Legitimacy of International Human Rights Conventions: Political Constitutionalism and the European Convention on Human Rights' (2015) 25(4) *European Journal of International Law* 1019.

also performed by the ECtHR.[30] Whenever the term appears throughout this chapter, it appears in this narrow meaning.

The chapter also argues that the application of the unreasonableness standard has some significant implications as to the intensity and the type of the review of the conduct of the state. First, in terms of intensity, it leads to a less rigorous review. This standard sets a high bar for finding a violation, making the Court's review of state conduct less intense than a typical 'reasonableness' test would be. Second, in terms of the type of review, it involves a non-legal analysis. The Court's decision relies on a broad mix of policy, morality and factual considerations (not strictly legal parameters) allowing it to handle a wide variety of cases.

This chapter first pinpoints the relevance and interaction between the causal analysis and the reasonableness standard (section II). It then moves on to discuss the application of the standard by the ECtHR (section IV). Finally, it looks at the content of the standard in the jurisprudence of the Court. The chapter shows that the Court's reasoning resembles the *Wednesbury* unreasonableness test known to English courts and brings forward the point that that the type of analysis the Court employs is not strictly legal; instead, it incorporates a mixture of moral, policy and factual considerations. Here the chapter delves into the content of the unreasonableness standard as applied by the Court (section IV). This flexible approach is essential given the wide diversity of cases that the ECtHR adjudicates, as developing distinct legal parameters for every unique situation would be impractical. Finally, the chapter offers some concluding remarks.

II. Cause in Fact, Scope of Responsibility, and Reasonableness in the ECtHR Jurisprudence

The application of the standard of reasonableness is ubiquitous in a variety of legal fields.[31] The reasonableness standard appears in the following setting in the jurisprudence of the ECtHR. First, the Court uses reasonableness when it goes

[30] The ECtHR performs what the literature dubs as 'weak judicial review', meaning that it reviews the inconsistency of legislation (or the regulatory framework) against the ECHR, but it cannot strike it down. See JI Colón-Ríos, 'A New Typology of Judicial Review of Legislation' (2014) 3(2) *Global Constitutionalism* 143, 145; Bellamy (n 29).

[31] There are several uses of a reasonableness test in English tort and administrative law. In the former, it is about the reasonable person, while in the latter, it is about the reasonableness of a decision of a public authority. See J Gardner, *Torts and Other Wrongs* (Oxford University Press, 2019) especially ch 9, 'The Many Faces of the Reasonable Person' at 271; P Craig, 'The Nature of Reasonableness Review' (2013) 66 *Current Legal Problems* 131. Craig shows that in administrative law, reasonableness is applied in certain cases where the courts interpret the statute and decide whether the purpose for which the public authority acted is legal with reference to the statute in question (at 135–36). Besides its application in law and the distinction of the various uses of the term, there are also several distinctions in political philosophy regarding the terminology surrounding reasonableness overall. See, for example, L Krasnoff, 'The Reasonable and the Rational' in J Mandle and DA Reiny (eds), *The Cambridge Rawls Lexicon* (Cambridge University Press, 2014) 692.

into a causal analysis. Stoyanova offers a most useful classification of the use of the reasonableness test in the causal analysis of the ECtHR. Assuming that the factual causation question is already resolved, the Court uses a reasonableness test to address specific problems within the scope of responsibility limb of the causal analysis. It uses the test in the process of determining causation and, in particular, in the process of shaping the scope of responsibility of the respondent state.[32] Whenever the ECtHR uses a 'strong causation' test, reasonableness helps to reach a more equitable outcome.[33] Whenever it employs a 'weak causation' test where the test is more relaxed, it does the exact same thing only towards the opposite direction.[34] The equitable role of reasonableness in these situations either leads the Court to protect particular interests or take into consideration broader community interests than those dictated by factual causation.[35]

To understand how causation works in the case law of the ECtHR it is necessary to take a step back and move from the general to the particular. All courts, tribunals and quasi-judicial bodies at some point must grapple with causation. Courts accept that the relation of necessity between the breach and harmful outcome is one that the law should designate as causal. This is the case in human rights law as well.

The causal analysis and its numerous manifestations appear in tort, criminal and in certain circumstances administrative law. Causal theories are abundant and the subdivisions within these theories render their exhaustive mapping irrelevant for the purposes of the present chapter.[36] Nonetheless, a basic distinction between cause in fact and cause in law should be the basis for our discussion. Theory distinguishes between causation in fact (or 'factual causation' or 'actual causation')[37] and causation in law (or 'legal causation', 'proximity' or 'scope of responsibility'). The mainstream theory and practice view causal analysis as being informed first by an inquiry on the facts of the case.[38] This essentially means that the court looks (or should look) into the factual relationship between an act or on mission and harm free from any constraint of a legal concept or theory. The inquiry into factual causation is closely related to the subsequent and separate issue of the scope of responsibility. The scope of responsibility inquiry is usually termed legal causation, or proximity (*causa proxima*) or remoteness

[32] See, for instance, *Vilnes and Others v Norway* App Nos 52806/09 and 22703/10, 5 December 2013; *O'Keefe v Ireland* [GC] App No 35810/09, 28 January 2014, para 201 where the Court employed 'equity' and skipped the criterion for a 'clear causal link' to connect the violation to the damages claimed.

[33] Stoyanova (n 1) 76–79.

[34] Strong causation means that the Court requires a high level of causal connection, while weak causation means that the Court applies a more relaxed causal standard (ibid).

[35] ibid 78–79.

[36] See, among many others, RW Wright, 'Causation, Responsibility, Risk, Probability, Naked Statistics, and Proof: Pruning the Bramble Bush by Clarifying the Concepts' (1987–88) 73 *Iowa Law Review* 1001.

[37] See ibid 1011; C Morris, 'On the Teaching of Legal Cause' (1939) 7 *Columbia Law Review* 1087, 1088.

[38] Stapleton (n 8).

(*causa remota*) of damage.[39] The scope of responsibility essentially entails the following question: for which consequences of his conduct should the defendant be held responsible?

The next step is to see when such an analysis is necessary in international law in general and in the law of human rights in particular. In international law, causation appears through the operation of the law of state responsibility.[40] Even though causation appears in the law of state responsibility primarily at the stage of reparation, it also appears at the stage of breach. The discrepancy in prominence between reparation and breach is easily explained. The International Law Commission (ILC), in developing the Articles on the Responsibility of States for Internationally Wrongful Acts (ARSIWA), discussed the role of causation and reparation and made an explicit reference to it in two articles.[41] Conversely, it did not delve into the issue in its analysis of the relevant article on breach. This makes sense. Breach is primarily connected to the primary obligations of states.[42] Since the ILC had opted to develop secondary obligations, it did not veer off course and it did not move towards an analysis of causation connected to the breach.[43]

Since in international law, the breach is always connected to a primary obligation, the relevant categorisation among these obligations is the one that classifies primary obligations based on whether they are obligations of conduct or obligations of result.[44] Causation must also be studied in relation to the manner the obligation has been breached. This inquiry is rather straightforward, since the relevant distinction is between an obligation that has been breached by an act

[39] On the issue of remoteness or scope of responsibility, see Green (n 11); J Stapleton 'Choosing what we Mean by "Causation" in the Law' (2008) 73 *Missouri Law Review* 433; D Hamer, '"Factual Causation" and "Scope of Liability: What's the Difference?' (2014) 77(2) *MLR* 155; MA Geistfeld, 'Proximate Cause Untangled' (2021) 80(2) *MLR* 420.

[40] For a comprehensive analysis, see V Lanovoy, 'Causation in the Law of State Responsibility' (2022) *British Yearbook of International Law* 1, https://doi.org/10.1093/bybil/brab008. See also T Demaria, *Le Lien de Causalité et la Réparation des Dommages en Droit International Public* (Pedone, 2021); A Orakhelashvili, *Causation in International Law* (Edward Elgar, 2022).

[41] Articles 31, 34 and 36(1) of the Articles on Responsibility of States for Internationally Wrongful Acts, ILC *Yearbook* 2001/II(2); see Commentary to art 31 at p 92, para 9-13 and to art 34 at p 95, para 1.

[42] See B Bollecker-Stern, *La préjudice dans la théorie de la responsabilité internationale* (Pedone, 1973); 180; A Gattini, 'Breach of International Obligations' in PA Nollkaemper and I Plakokefalos (eds), *Principles of Shared Responsibility in International Law: An Appraisal of the State of the Art* (Cambridge University Press, 2014) 25.

[43] Conspicuously, the ILC made a brief, and confusing, reference to causation in the commentary to the articles on attribution. This might be simply an overzealous effort to clarify the, admittedly, convoluted notion of attribution in international law; see Commentary to the Articles on Responsibility of States for Internationally Wrongful Acts, A/CN.4/SER.A/2001/Add.1 (Part 2), ILC Ybk 2001 (Vol II, Part Two) p 38, para 4.

[44] Obligations of conduct, as opposed to obligations of result, require from states to make an effort towards the goal set by the obligation, and if the states make the effort – according to what the rule prescribes – then they have fulfilled their obligation. See generally J Combacau, 'Obligations de résultat et obligations de comportement : quelques questions et pas de réponse' in *Mélanges offerts a Paul Reuter, Le droit international: unité et diversité* (Pedone, 1981) 181; A Marchesi, 'The Distinction between Obligations of Conduct and Obligations of Result Following its Deletion from the Draft Articles on State Responsibility' in *Studi di diritto inernazionale in onore di Gaetano Arangio-Ruiz* (Editoriale Scientifica, 2004) 826.

and an obligation that has been breached by an omission.[45] These distinctions are important because the type of obligation usually has a bearing on the manner of breach. Turning back to the issue at hand, positive obligations are obligations of conduct,[46] and are usually, but not always, breached by omission and not by an act.[47] Therefore, even though the type of obligation and the type of breach are studied separately for reasons of methodological clarity, one should not be viewed in clinical isolation from the other.

The question now is how the ECtHR applies its causal analysis on the law of human rights. It seems that the Court is not particularly clear when it comes to the causal standard it applies to the factual causation limb. In *Vilnes*, the facts related to the use by deep sea divers of certain decompression tables that contained unsafely short times for decompression, leading to mental and physical harm to the applicants. The Court had to decide whether the state had taken the necessary measures to protect the divers. The ECtHR mentioned two different standards in its analysis. It first held that there was a 'strong likelihood' that the decompression sickness caused harm to the applicants.[48] It then went on to state that 'it is only with the benefit of hindsight that we know that the tables were a probable cause of the diver's health issues'.[49] While it seems that the Court applies a probabilistic test of causation (likelihood), this statement does not make a lot of sense, since all causal analysis takes place with hindsight.[50] Further, in the same judgment, the Court added the requirement for a 'sufficient causal link'.[51] It is not clear which one is the preference of the Court as it applied both (the probabilistic test and the sufficiency test) to reach the same result, finding no violation of the ECHR.[52] More often than not, the Court uses a variety of terms including 'direct' or 'clear' causal link.[53] This terminology is not very helpful as it does not clarify the actual test used by the ECtHR in each and every case.[54]

The reasonableness analysis comes in when the Court discusses the scope of responsibility of the state. In positive obligations cases, the Court, while establishing

[45] (n 41) p.35, para 4.

[46] Sicilianos (n 4) 120.

[47] On the difficult question of omissions, see T Honoré, *Responsibility and Fault* (Hart Publishing, 1999) 41–66; RW Wright, 'Once More into the Bramble Bush: Duty, Causal Contribution and the Extent of Legal Responsibility' (2001) 54 *Vanderbilt Law Review* 1071.

[48] *Vilnes* (n 32) para 233.

[49] ibid.

[50] The analysis is even more complicated if one takes into account that elsewhere in the judgment, the Court concluded that the knowledge of the risk in the process in question which was not regulated by the state was actually present at the relevant time. Therefore, the Court seems to have contradicted itself; see Stoyanova (n 1) 77.

[51] *Vilnes* (n 32) para 270. The 'sufficient link' standard is applied quite often by the ECtHR; see Demaria (n 40) 199.

[52] *Vilnes* (n 32).

[53] See, for example, *Öneryildiz* (n 19) para 166; *Albekov and Others v Russia* App No 68216/01, 9 October 2008 para 123. A direct causal link requirement is also implicit in *Budayeva and Others v Russia* App Nos 15339/02, 21166/02, 20058/02, 11673/02 and 15343/02, 20 March 2008, paras. 172–73. On the unprincipled terminology of the Court, see Stoyanova (n 1) 48–49.

[54] Stoyanova (n 1) 77.

the scope of responsibility, determines whether the state has adopted the requisite measures (if any) to protect the rights enshrined in the Convention.[55] In doing so, it employs (among other criteria) a reasonableness standard.[56] However, the Court does not confine itself only to the examination of the measures themselves, as it looks at broader issues as well as the resources and priorities of the state.[57]

It is crucial that in positive obligations, the scope of responsibility is examined against a factual background that lacks direct involvement of state authorities. There are cases involving positive obligations, such as *Mastromatteo*[58] and *Choreftakis*,[59] relating to the right to life where the state is not involved directly, at least prima facie, with the act in question. An individual pulls a trigger or draws a knife and commits murder. The state is not factually involved in the incident, in the sense that the incident takes place among individuals and there is no organ of the state present in the chain of events.[60] In other cases, it may be that the incident involves state organs, but again, the core issue is the adequacy and reasonableness of legislative and operational measures adopted by the state. In *Ribcheva v Bulgaria*, for example, the applicants were relatives of an agent of the anti-terrorist squad of Bulgaria. He was shot and killed by a man during an operation to arrest the shooter. The state was not directly involved in the killing of the agent at all. Here the Court examined the reasonableness of the measures because reasonableness is connected to the level of risk control during the operation of the state.[61] The question was whether the measures, or the decision of the state, as the case may be, were reasonable. The answer to this question, coupled with the result of the cause in fact test, guides the Court to decide whether there has been a violation of the Convention or not.[62]

III. The Application of the Reasonableness Standard

In the field of positive obligations, the Court examines the steps taken by the state to protect the applicant from the claimed violation of the ECHR. This examination contains several elements. The Court looks first at the national regulatory regime. It looks at whether national laws, regulations (including other regimes that have

[55] Triggering an obligation to fulfil; see Stoyanova (n 1) 73.

[56] See, for example, *Hutten-Czapska v Poland* [GC] App No 35014/9719 June 2006, para 167; *Lopes de Sousa Fernandes v Portugal* [GC] App No 56080/13, 19 December 2017, paras 166–67; *Lozovye v Russia* App No 4587/09, 24 April 2018, para 43.

[57] This is a commonplace phrase in the jurisprudence of the Court, but see, for example, *Öneryildiz* (n 19) para 107.

[58] *Mastromatteo v Italy* [GC] App No 37703/97, 24 October 2002.

[59] *Choreftakis and Choreftaki v Greece* App No 46846/08, 17 January 2012.

[60] A similar situation existed in *Biba v Albania* App No 24228/18, 7 May 2024, which involved an incident in a school where one pupil caused serious harm to another pupil's eye. Again, the state was not actively present with its organs when the incident took place; see paras 72–73.

[61] *Ribcheva* (n 19) paras 165–67.

[62] ibid paras 165, 175.

a regulatory impact) and the measures adopted should be criticised. It also looks at whether the authorities complied with the regulations adopted at the national level. The next move is to assess the causal relationship between the regulatory steps taken by the state and the alleged violation of the Convention in question. In this context, and particularly within the scope of responsibility limb of the causal analysis, a host of other considerations appear, such as the knowledge of the circumstances, the probabilities of harm and the foreseeability of the risk, if there is one according to the facts of the case.

In addition to these elements, the Court considers other relevant circumstances. These may vary depending on the case. In cases that concern police action by the state, they include 'the difficulties involved in policing modern societies, the unpredictability of human conduct and the operational choices which must be made in terms of priorities and resources'[63] and the positive obligation 'must be interpreted in a way which does not impose an impossible or disproportionate burden on the authorities'.[64] These elements are not always examined in isolation from one another and the Court does not strictly follow all the steps in sequence.

A separate yet equally important aspect of the Court's analysis is the content of the right in question. The Court makes it clear that, alongside all the other considerations, the content of the right itself plays a significant role. In international law, the prohibition of torture and slavery have already gained the status of peremptory norm.[65] The right to life has not attracted such a stature as of yet, although there is a lively academic discussion around it.[66] When it comes to the ECHR, a hierarchy of rights may be inferred through Article 15, where the right to life, the prohibition of torture or inhuman and degrading treatment, slavery, and the principle *nullum crimen, nulla poena sine lege* are deemed to be non-derogable.[67] The ECtHR does not treat all rights, or all aspects of rights, in the same manner when it comes to positive obligations. It has even gone as far as to distinguish between different violations of the same obligation. In relation to Article 8, it has held that it takes into account whether the specific violation involves '"fundamental values" or "essential aspects" of private life', the impact on the applicant, and whether there is discordance between social reality and the law.[68] In relation to

[63] *Osman* (n 5) para 116. The reference to policing of course speaks to the facts of cases that involve a violation of art 2 ECHR, while the rest of the considerations, such as those of priorities and resources, feature in other cases as well.

[64] ibid.

[65] Conclusion 23 and Annex paras (f) and (g), International Law Commission, Draft Conclusions on the Identification and Legal Consequences of Peremptory Norms of General International Law (Jus Cogens) with Commentaries, A/77/10 2022.

[66] For this discussion and for the view that the core of the right to life (that is, the deliberate deprivation of life) has already attained the status of *jus cogens*, see S Casey-Maslen, *The Right to Life under International Law: An Interpretative Manual* (Cambridge University Press, 2021) 17–18.

[67] On the hierarchy of human rights, see T Meron, 'On a Hierarchy of International Human Rights' (1986) 80(1) *American Journal of International Law* 1; T Koji, 'Emerging Hierarchy in International Human Rights and Beyond: From the Perspective of Non-derogable Rights' (2001) 12(5) *European Journal of International Law* 917.

[68] *Hämäläinen v Finland* [GC] App No 37359/09, 16 July 2014, para 66.

Article 2, it has accepted that a standard of strict necessity and proportionality applies to the second paragraph of the article[69] that expressly provides for such a standard.[70] Yet, it has also held that such a standard does not apply to the first paragraph of the article.[71]

Now it is apposite to turn to the case law to examine the application of the reasonableness standard in the reasoning of the Court. In most cases, there is a national regulatory regime in place that is relevant to the claim.[72] A good example is *Öneryildiz v. Turkey*. In this case, the question was whether Turkey had taken the necessary measures to protect the right to life of the applicants whose relatives were killed by a methane explosion. The Court readily found that there was a legal regulation in place and proceeded with deciding, first, on whether the authorities had complied with the legal measures in question and, second, whether the legal measures should be criticised.[73] Then the Court held that the Convention and the judgment must not impose a disproportionate burden to the government and that it must take into account the available resources and the choice of priorities of the state.[74] It first found that the authorities ought or ought to have known of the risk of methane explosion.[75] It held that the framework was defective because it did not provide for a supervisory mechanism to encourage the relevant authorities to comply with the technical standards.[76] It also held, under its reasonableness review, that there were reasonable alternative measures that would not entail any excessive cost.[77]

This type of analysis goes straight to the potential causal relationship of the measures taken (or not taken as the case was in *Öneryildiz*) to the harm. Yet, the analysis is not framed exclusively in factual causation terms. Awareness of the risk, the ineffectiveness of the measures in place and the reasonableness of alternative measures were part of the analysis of the scope of responsibility and the judicial review type assessment of the measures adopted by the states. The Court proceeded with a review of the legislation and its implementation, and it simultaneously did not lose sight of the factual causal inquiry, while not relying solely on it.[78] This is a crucial point. The Court did not clarify that it performs a reasonableness review

[69] The chapeau of art 2(2) reads as follows: 'Deprivation of life shall not be regarded as inflicted in contravention of this article when it results from the use of force which is no more *than absolutely necessary*' (emphasis added).

[70] *Ribcheva* (n 19) para 162.

[71] ibid para 165.

[72] There are cases where there is no legal framework in place that can be applied to the facts. For example, in *Söderman v Sweden* [GC] App No 5786/08, 12 November 2013, the ECtHR found a violation of the procedural limb of art 8 since there was absolutely no criminal or civil remedy for the applicant (at para 117). Then the Court found a violation of the ECHR and that it did not need to go any further in its inquiry.

[73] *Öneryildiz* (n 19) para 97.

[74] ibid para 107.

[75] ibid para 101.

[76] ibid para 109.

[77] ibid para 107.

[78] The causal connection was brought up in ibid paras 134–35.

of the measures adopted by the state in the context of the determination of the scope of responsibility and its relationship to the factual causation limb of the causal analysis. To be sure, if the Court was clearer, it would be easier to understand the sequence of its reasoning. Yet, this does not have a significant bearing on the outcome of the case as such.

The case law regarding the positive obligations where the state has granted conditional release or leave, or has decided to re-integrate inmates offers further insights into the operation of the Court's reasoning. The Court performs the scope of responsibility inquiry and the assessment of the measures that the state has adopted without much clarification. A decision to grant leave or to propose the re-integration of an inmate who then proceeds to commit a fresh crime is an act by the state (albeit a normative one) that, if a strict 'but for' test is used, would lead to the conclusion that the decision of the state is a cause of the result in question. But the Court does not apply such a 'but for' test; it promotes a 'direct causal link' test. Alongside this test, it assesses the conduct of the state in terms of knowledge of the circumstances, whether actual or constructive. On this basis, it applies a reasonableness standard. A case in point is *Choreftakis and Choreftaki v Greece*, in which the conditionally released from prison ZL murdered the applicants' son.[79] ZL had a substantial disciplinary record, yet the relevant legislation directed the Prison Council that had to decide on his release to not take this into account when deciding.[80] The ECtHR first repeated its ruling in *Osman*, stating that it must take into account several circumstances, such as the difficulties of policing and the like.[81] The Court also recognised that it must take into account both whether the state knew or should have known about the immediate risk to the life of a person, and whether it had taken reasonable steps to protect the right to life.[82]

The inquiry about the reasonableness of the steps taken by the state goes hand in hand with the issue of knowledge of the circumstances, as these may be, by the state. Knowledge of the circumstances is part of the scope of responsibility limb of causation.[83] The invocation of causation in *Choreftakis* in the assessment of the legal framework might appear inconsistent, particularly given that the Court had already concluded there was no direct link between the Council's decision and the murder of the applicants' son. However, this must be treated not as inconsistency, but rather as a way for the Court to show that causation (factual causation in this instance) alone is not enough.

Subsequently, the Court's analysis often becomes something of a mixture of an assessment of the adequacy and reasonableness of the legal framework in place. Then the Court includes the application of the legal framework by state officials

[79] *Choreftakis* (n 59) paras 6, 12.
[80] ibid paras 14–15.
[81] ibid para 46 citing *Osman* (n 5) para 116.
[82] ibid para 47.
[83] Stoyanova (n 1) 75–76.

and also takes into account a factual causal analysis that in some cases looks out of place.[84] In *Mastromatteo*, the Court, speaking on the application of the legal framework, held that the mere absence of disciplinary punishments is not sufficient to justify the grant of measure facilitating re-integration.[85] It also held that the abscondment of the inmate's accomplice was not the only circumstance to be taken into account. In *Choreftakis*, also speaking on the application of the legal framework, it held that the Prison Council could base its decision on other factors (such as the young age of the inmate), despite the fact that it had access to the full record of the inmate's terrible disciplinary record, and at the same time the relevant legislation prevented it from relying on this.[86]

What may be confusing is that the actual content of the reasonableness standard varies. This is not a mystery. If one is lost in the details of the reasonableness analysis, the view of the fundamental issue of the content of the obligation becomes obscure. It is one question to locate where a reasonableness standard is being employed. It is a different question to look into what the reasonableness standard actually contains. The following section responds to the second question.

IV. The Content of the Unreasonableness Standard

In the application of the standard of reasonableness, the Court shows a move towards something akin to the *Wednesbury* test as we know it from UK administrative law.[87] In *Wednesbury*, the King's Bench upheld a local council's by-law regarding age-restricted admittance to movie theatres.[88] However, Lord Greene articulated the test of unreasonableness, holding that the decision in question must be so unreasonable that no reasonable body would find it reasonable.[89] This dictum has not, as of yet, been overturned. It has come under scrutiny and criticism.[90] The

[84] The difficulty in disentangling causation from reasonableness is expertly explained in J Gerards, 'How to Improve the Necessity Test of the European Court of Human Rights' (2013) 11(2) *International Journal of Constitutional Law* 466, 474.

[85] *Mastromatteo* (n 58) para 72.

[86] This approach attracted a strong and principled dissent centred, carefully, on the point of the basis for the decision to the Council. The dissent pointed out that it was not certain that had the Council had access to the disciplinary record of the inmate, it would have certainly declined to grant him the status of conditional release. Nonetheless, the Council would have been able to make an informed decision providing a higher level of protection to the society, see *Choreftakis* (n 59) Joint Dissenting Opinion of Judge Sicilianos, Joined by Judges Steiner, and Lazarova Trajkovska (para 5).

[87] *Wednesbury* (n 22).

[88] ibid 224.

[89] ibid 230.

[90] See, for example, Lord Lester and J Jowell, 'Beyond *Wednesbury*: Substantive Principles of Administrative Law' (1988) 14(2) *Commonwealth Law Bulletin* 858; Craig (n 31) 161. For an attempt at clarification of the principle, see P Daly, '*Wednesbury*'s Reason and Structure' [2011] *Public Law* 238, 238–40.

case law following *Wednesbury* is not crystal clear either.[91] However, the principle has not yet been overturned.

The differences between common law and European human rights law are too many to discuss and go beyond the purposes of this chapter. Yet, the *Wednesbury* test is relevant as a shorthand (and not as an analogy) to understand what the ECtHR does in its case law. There are two important aspects of the test. First, the test turns the reasonableness review into an unreasonableness review. In principle, this has significant repercussions for the applicants. It is a higher standard because the Court has to decide that the steps taken by the state are such that no other state would have taken. Second, it indicates that the decision-making process of the Court moves beyond the boundaries of legal analysis and sits more comfortably with a moral, policy or plain factual appraisal.

The standard itself has been refined both by the courts and the literature. The best way to explain what a court may consider to be an unreasonable decision taken by an authority is as follows: unreasonableness decisions are demonstrably wrong decisions.[92] Decisions in the case of ECtHR jurisprudence may be substituted for measures, acts (normative or factual) and omissions by the respondent states. The explanation offers a qualification that is absent from the original dictum in *Wednesbury*. The ECtHR, for example, may only characterise the respondent state's conduct as unreasonable if the Court itself can clearly demonstrate that it is unreasonable. It is not enough for the Court to *consider* that the conduct was unreasonable; it must *show* that the conduct was unreasonable. Another way to state essentially the same idea of unreasonableness is that the Court does not determine whether the state got it right with the measures it adopted. Rather, in its reasoning the Court discards the choices that cannot be 'plausibly justified' in terms of public reason.[93]

Examining the case law from the point of unreasonableness review reveals the following. First, it seems that the Court is merely trying to see if something patently, and demonstrably, unreasonable is part of the legal framework or the acts and omissions at an operational level. This is the gist of the application of the standard of unreasonableness. In *Ribcheva*, for example, the Court straightforwardly applied the unreasonableness standard, as it held that it must examine 'whether any mistakes in the planning and control of the operation show that the authorities acted unreasonably'.[94] Things are seldom as clear as this statement is in the jurisprudence of the Court. In *Hämäläinen*, it found no violation, since the legal framework that allowed for a marriage to be converted to a registered partnership between a couple where the husband underwent gender reassignment was not

[91] Daly (n 90) 242 claims that: 'The case law is (almost) resolutely opaque. Mysterious references by reviewing courts to unreasonableness, multiple factors, judgment, and balancing are commonplace.'

[92] A Perry, '*Wednesbury* Unreasonableness' (2023) 82(3) *Common Law Review* 483, 486.

[93] M Kumm, 'Alexy's Theory of Constitutional Rights and the Problem of Judicial Review' in M Klatt (ed), *Institutionalized Reason: The Jurisprudence of Robert Alexy* (Oxford University Press, 2012).

[94] *Ribcheva* (n 19) para 175.

disproportionate – in other words, that it was not unreasonable.[95] What follows from this reasoning by the Court in *Hämäläinen* is essentially that having required anything more from the state would have been absurd. The use of the phrase 'not disproportionate' by the Court possibly indicates the equivalent of 'not unreasonable'. The alternative offered by Finland was a genuine option.[96] In *Albekov*, the respondent state said that it had marked a minefield,[97] and in the same breath said that the army did not know exactly where the minefield was.[98] The Court did not need to apply any legal standards here. The mere reading of the state's position was sufficient to hold that it was absurd because it was blatantly contradictory; therefore, it was easy to demonstrate that it was wrong.[99] *Makaratzis v Greece* was a case involving the applicant speeding through a police checkpoint in Athens and subsequently were shot at by the police.[100] The Court found that it was patently unreasonable for the state to rely on the legal framework regulating the use of firearms by the police since it dated back to the Second World War.[101] The age of the legislation and its inadequate wording were clear indications of unreasonableness. Moreover, the Court took into account the action of a terrorist group in Greece and the general climate of fear this generated. Given that the applicant was actually driving full speed in the centre of Athens, the Court accepted that to restrain the police to resort to the use of their weapons would be to impose an unrealistic burden on the state.[102] The ECtHR found the chaotic response of the police to be caused by an insufficient legal framework and therefore held Greece responsible for a violation of Article 2.[103]

The same approach to reasonableness appears in *Choreftakis*. The ECtHR answered in the negative as to whether the acts or omissions of the state formed a direct and strong causal link with the death of the applicants' son.[104] It also examined whether the legislation in place should be criticised as insufficient to protect the right to life. The Court held that the legislation must be patently insufficient so as to find a violation of the Convention and decided that this was not the case.[105] It looked at the reasoning of the Council's decision and it did not consider the inability of the Council to rely on the inmate's past disciplinary record as decisive on its own: the national judge in this Council could use further criteria to establish her

[95] *Hämäläinen* (n 68) para 87. The distinction between proportionality and reasonableness is a matter of contestation in the literature; see T Endicott, 'Why Proportionality is Not a General Ground of Judicial Review' (2020) 1 *Keele Law Review* 1. However, the ECtHR seems to be using both terms interchangeably; see Gerards (n 84) for a more nuanced approach.

[96] *Hämäläinen* (n 68).

[97] *Albekov* (n 53) para 76.

[98] ibid para 77.

[99] ibid para 88.

[100] *Makaratzis* (n 16) paras 11–12.

[101] ibid paras 62–63.

[102] ibid paras 65–66.

[103] ibid paras 70–72.

[104] *Choreftakis* (n 59) para 59.

[105] ibid.

decision.[106] Nonetheless, the ECtHR acknowledged that it would have been better if the law allowed the Council to take the disciplinary record of the inmate into account.[107] At every step, the Court leaned clearly towards an unreasonableness standard: the legislation must be patently insufficient. The disciplinary record was not decisive on its own, even though it would be better if the Council could rely on it.

While *Choreftakis* is useful in showing the typical reasoning of the Court when it comes to the application of the standard of unreasonableness, it is also useful to see how the Court handles cases with a similar factual background. *Mastromatteo* was a case where the applicants' son was killed by inmates that had been conditionally released. The Court held that the fact that the inmate's accomplice had used his leave to abscond in practice was not decisive.[108] The authorities, according to the Court, could not have foreseen that the two inmates would conspire to commit a fresh crime.[109] On the contrary, in *Maiorano*, the Court found for the applicants. It held that the state had plenty of information on the nature of the inmate's crimes in the past, his behaviour during the leaves of absence and his activities during his conditional release.[110] It found that the state did not exercise due diligence when appraising the conduct of the inmate.[111] Based on the evidence before the Court, the position of the state was not tenable.

The ECtHR employs, in most cases, a similar line of reasoning. The criteria used by the Court are informed by the understanding that the state cannot be omnipresent. The Court as usual mentions the difficulties in modern-day policing (when relevant), and takes consideration of the availability of resources and the state's choice of priorities.[112] Moreover, the Court inserts a constant reminder to the effect that it cannot substitute for the views of the state.[113] This context provides the Court with a wide array of considerations that are there, for the most part, to ensure that it does not encroach upon the freedom of the state to adopt the policies and take the decision as it sees fit under the circumstances. The unreasonableness standard is set against that background.

In the setting of the trilogy of released inmates (*Mastromatteo*, *Maiorano* and *Choreftakis*), it was not unreasonable for the authorities in *Mastromatteo* and *Choreftakis* to allow the release of the inmates. In *Mastromatteo*, it was not unreasonable to think that the fact that the abscondment of the inmate's accomplice meant that the inmate would conspire with him to commit a crime again. In *Choreftakis*, it was not unreasonable for the authorities (according to the legislation in place) to take into account the inmate's recent disciplinary record as opposed

[106] ibid paras 57–58.
[107] ibid.
[108] *Mastromatteo* (n 58) para 76.
[109] ibid.
[110] *Maiorano and Others v Italy* [GC] App No 28634/06, 15 December 2009, paras 119, 121.
[111] ibid 121.
[112] *Mastromatteo* (n 58) para 68; *Choreftakis* (n 59) para 46; *Maiorano* (n 110) para 105.
[113] *Makaratzis v Greece* (n 16); *Choreftakis* para 56.

to the older record. According to the law, the authorities could only access the inmate's disciplinary record from the two years immediately before the review according to the law. Yet in *Maiorano*, the knowledge of information possessed by the authorities on the conduct of the inmate combined with the surveillance of his movements was such that it would have been unreasonable to hold that the state acted diligently.

A secondary yet important takeaway point here, besides the application of the unreasonableness standard, is that if the conduct of the state is found not to be unreasonable, this does not mean that it was correct. In other words, the Court does not pass judgment on the correctness of the conduct of the state. This conclusion is also theoretically sound. The point of the unreasonableness test goes beyond the question of whether a decision or a course of conduct is wrong or not, or even whether it is rational or not.[114] The ECtHR in *Mastromatteo* and *Choreftakis* may or may have not believed that in either case the authorities took a wrong decision; what mattered was that they took a decision that was not unreasonable and it was difficult to show that it was. Even though in *Choreftakis* the dissent showed an alternative and possibly more convincing reasoning, the judgment of the majority simply balanced the reasons for and against the decision of the Prison Council differently.

The second element of unreasonableness is that it evades strict legal reasoning. The factual side of an unreasonableness review has been duly highlighted in the literature. In English tort law, for example, it has been maintained that reasonableness criteria 'allow the law to pass the buck … to standards of justification that are not themselves set by the law, and which therefore are only as good as the standards of justification used by the person or people to whom the buck is passed'.[115] In international law, it has been argued, correctly, that the term is employed whenever the law needs to leave a level of discretion to the decision-maker.[116] The decision-maker will then have to go outside the strict confines of the law.[117] It is not contested that that unreasonableness is a legal standard in the sense that it is dictated by law and that its application has concrete legal consequences, such as the obligation to provide just satisfaction if the ECtHR finds a violation based on the application of the standard.[118]

Even if the law instructs judges to balance certain considerations, if those considerations lie outside the law itself, the outcome is effectively the same as

[114] Perry (n 92) 487–88.

[115] Gardner (n 31) 279. This is in reference to the standard of reasonable man. In ECHR law, this does not apply as such, but it is essentially permeated by the same principles. Both in torts and in the jurisprudence of the ECtHR, the issue is the same: a deviation from strictly legal principles.

[116] J Salmon, 'Le Fait dans L'application de Droit International' (1982) 175 *Recueil des Cours de l'Académie de Droit International* 261, 351.

[117] ibid 306.

[118] As Corten states, 'the notion of 'reasonable' is considered as a regular positive law notion, not as a notion drawing from halfway categories between law and not-law, such as 'soft-law'; O Corten, 'The Notion of Reasonable in International Law: Legal Discourse, Reason, and Contradictions' (1999) 48(3) *International & Comparative Law Quarterly* 613, 621.

if no law had existed at all in the first place.[119] Therefore, the application of the standard, one way or the other, rests upon the considerations available to the judges. These may be factual or moral, but they are to be found outside legal doctrine. There is also the case where the Court distinguishes among the rights included in the ECHR as to their relative weight: the considerations do not apply to all rights equally. Since this is not inscribed explicitly in the text of the ECHR, it has to do more with moral, political and societal approaches than anything else.[120]

The issue of facts is sometimes complicated. It is not always easy to ascertain the nuanced differences between application of the law to the facts as being a question of law or a question of fact.[121] However, in the case of the ECtHR, it is clear that the application of the unreasonableness standard does not answer a legal question; rather, it answers a complex question that arises under the circumstances that the law prescribes. The question is complex because a violation of a positive obligation is complex by nature. The state adopts a conduct either normative (ie, adoption of measures and a domestic legal framework) or operational (ie, actions or operational decisions towards preventing harm in particular circumstances) that may have an impact on countless sets of circumstances. In one such set, the rights of one or more individuals are affected. The ECtHR enters a discussion wherein it must assess – but not substitute for – the conduct of the state. In doing so, the Court explicitly surrounds the unreasonableness test with considerations that can hardly be treated as questions of law. These range from the difficulties in policing, to the predictability of human nature, to considerations of the priorities and resources each state adopts. These are not legal issues. What is important is that the task in distinguishing between legal and extra-legal reasoning is simplified here. It is the Court itself that provides the criteria against which the unreasonableness of the state's conduct is measured.

The picture that emerges is as follows. The Court in fact applies an unreasonableness standard, trying to see whether the state has adopted a conduct (normative or otherwise) that is demonstrably unreasonable. This standard is a higher one than a reasonableness standard. In the application of the standard, the Court takes into account several considerations. These include the weight and the content of the right in question. They primarily include considerations that are geared towards giving deference to the state. The availability of resources, the hierarchy of priorities, the difficulties in policing and the unpredictability of human behaviour are

[119] Gardner (n 31) 281.

[120] The legal differentiation dictated by *jus cogens* norms and non-derogable rights of course applies. The discussion on whether this differentiation is based on subjective value judgments of the drafters of human rights instruments, or the judges that apply them and legal writers is open; see, for example, the arguments in A Bianchi, 'Human Rights and the Magic of *Jus Cogens*' (2008) 19(3) *European Journal of International Law* 491. Things can be simpler of course and the differentiation in human rights may be just obvious. As Meron (n 67) 4 suggests, 'some human rights are obviously more important than other human rights'.

[121] T Endicott, 'Questions of Law' (1998) 114 *LQR* 292, 297–98.

all considerations that give the state considerable leeway. This is coupled with the standard dictum of the Court that it is not meant to substitute its views for those of the state. In general, it seems that the Court applies the unreasonableness standard in the context of positive obligations in a show of prudence and restraint.[122] And it does so exactly because it does not want to restrain the state authorities excessively.[123] Given the open and context-dependent nature of positive obligations, this approach is not unreasonable. This is so despite cases where the Court might have been too reluctant in its analysis (such as *Choreftakis*).[124] But this is the gist of any review based on standards such as reasonableness, or unreasonableness in this case. Reasonableness 'is used in order to legitimize an assertion which is, by definition, subject to challenge'.[125]

V. Concluding Remarks

There are a few conclusions to be drawn here. First, the unreasonableness standard (as proposed in this chapter) is applicable in two, not always distinct, instances by the Court: first, when it discusses the scope of responsibility limb of the causal test; and, second, when it criticises the measures the state has adopted to protect and fulfil the rights of the applicant. The Court does not differentiate in its use of the standard in either case. It is also often unclear which of the two operations is underway in the reasoning of the Court.

The framework of the standard of unreasonableness is set by the ECtHR in broad terms. It takes into account the nature of the right that has been violated. It considers, for instance, whether the resources and priorities of the state are such that they justify the measures taken. It is the same process that the Court follows when it looks into an indeterminate host of other extraneous circumstances (knowledge, resources and the like) in order to reach its decision.

Within this broad framework, the ECtHR applies a standard of unreasonableness. The concept of unreasonableness is borrowed from the judicial review precedent of *Wednesbury* in UK administrative law. In essence, the ECtHR proceeds to a review of legislation, administrative measures and decisions, as well as of regulatory frameworks to determine their link to the harm complained. This review is, in a very narrow sense, akin to the administrative law-type judicial review, thus allowing for the loan from administrative law. Examining case law through the lens of unreasonableness review shows the Court trying to determine if something is patently, and demonstrably, unreasonable. Examples include finding authorities acted unreasonably in operational planning, or that legislation dating back to the

[122] Sicilianos (n 4) 129.
[123] ibid.
[124] See the Dissenting Opinion in *Choreftakis* (n 59).
[125] Corten (n 118) 618.

Second World War was patently unreasonable for regulating police firearm use. The application of this standard means that the Court raises the bar for the applicants because it looks for measures that no reasonable state may take and shows restraint on behalf of the ECtHR in finding violations of the ECHR.

The actual balancing the Court performs among the multitude of considerations it takes into account shows the limits of the legal analysis expected by courts. The ECtHR does not substitute its views for those of the public authority that has taken the measures that the applicant claims lie at the core of the violation of her rights. However, the Court does look into alternative measures or, at the very least, points out the flaws of these measures that lead to a violation. To do so, it follows a moral or a policy or a factual analysis, but not a strictly legal one. Not only does the ECtHR follows a line of reasoning that often escapes legal boundaries, but it may be that it must actually do so. In other words, the Court should look beyond the law to reach a decision on the reasonableness of the measures in question. The factors it considers may be related to policy (in cases where the state has favoured a particular policy choice over another) or they could be value or morality-based (in cases where the state prioritises one choice over another on these grounds). The Court also clearly distinguishes among cases, taking into account the subject matter before it. For example, it treats cases where the activity in question is inherently dangerous or risky differently from cases where the activity does not entail any particular risk.

The application of the unreasonableness standard draws the limits between law and non-law. This opens the door to considerations regarding the role of the Court (such as consistency, transparency and the like) that go beyond the scope of the chapter and are certainly fertile ground for further research.

9

Correlativity in Human Rights Law

JOHAN VORLAND WIBYE

I. Introduction

According to the correlativity thesis, there cannot, as a matter of conceptual necessity, be a legal right without an attendant duty, or a duty without an attendant right. The right is *defined* in terms of its correlate duty, for the two are merely placements within the same legal relation.[1] Within an applied context such as human rights law, the necessary link between rights and correlative duties can be argued from first principles. Human rights are made meaningful through their impact and effect on legal outcomes. The legal order is a system for regulating human activity, and so impact must be measured in terms of conduct.[2] Conduct, in turn, is guided by duties.[3] To sever the link between rights and duties, then, is to jettison a crucial part of the concept of a right.[4]

The correlativity thesis is firmly established within legal theory.[5] Yet while the notion of correlativity appears to be accepted amongst human rights scholars,[6] its

[1] M Kramer, 'Rights without Trimmings' in M Kramer, N Simmonds and H Steiner (eds), *A Debate over Rights* (Clarendon Press, 1998) 26.

[2] WN Hohfeld, *Fundamental Legal Conceptions as Applied in Judicial Reasoning* (Lawbook Exchange, 1964) 75.

[3] H Steiner, *An Essay on Rights* (Blackwell, 1994) 55; TM Scanlon, *The Difficulty of Tolerance: Essays in Political Philosophy* (Cambridge University Press, 2003) 151.

[4] O O'Neill, 'The Dark Side of Human Rights' (2005) 81 *International Affairs* 427, 450; J Tasioulas, 'On the Foundations of Human Rights' in R Cruft, SM Liao and M Renzo (eds), *Philosophical Foundations of Human Rights* (Oxford University Press, 2015) 47.

[5] See, eg, H Kelsen, 'Law and Logic' in *Essays in Legal and Moral Philosophy* (Springer, 1973) 221; P Schlag, 'How to Do Things with Hohfeld' (2015) 78 *Law & Contemporary Problems* 185, 200; Kramer, Simmonds and Steiner (n 1) 26; HM Hurd and MS Moore, 'The Hohfeldian Analysis of Rights' (2018) 63 *American Journal of Jurisprudence* 295, 300; K Barker, 'Private Law, Analytical Philosophy and the Modern Value of Wesley Newcomb Hohfeld: A Centennial Appraisal' (2018) 38 *Oxford Journal of Legal Studies* 585, 589; A Halpin, 'Choosing Axioms of Correlativity' (2019) 64 *American Journal of Jurisprudence* 225, 228.

[6] See, eg, R Alexy, *A Theory of Constitutional Rights* (Oxford University Press, 2009) 296; S Fredman, *Human Rights Transformed: Positive Rights and Positive Duties* (Oxford University Press, 2008) 88; 281; MC Nussbaum, *Frontiers of Justice: Disability, Nationality, Species Membership* (Belknap Press, 2006) 281; A Mowbray, *The Development of Positive Obligations under the European Convention on Human Rights by the European Court of Human Rights* (Hart Publishing, 2004) 224; L Lavrysen, 'The Scope of Rights and the Scope of Obligations' in J Gerards and E Brems (eds), *Shaping Rights in the Echr* (Cambridge University Press, 2013) 173.

necessary implications are not. The stakes can be set out constructively in terms of added clarity, or negatively in terms of avoiding miscommunication and fallacies. The argument for added clarity is the easiest to make. An awareness of the necessary interplay between rights and duties can lead to greater analytical precision and legal doctrinal certainty, for instance, when searching for concrete duties in the operative parts of European Court of Human Rights (ECtHR) judgments and their formulation of execution measures.[7] Analytical rigour can also be used as a tool to reveal hidden policy judgments and normative claims within legal arguments. More generally, correlativity provides clarity to right holders by highlighting what they can expect from others.[8]

The negative argument concerns barriers to the effective communication of legal findings. On a surface level, scholars generally agree that the legal content of a human right can be spelled out by identifying the many duties of abstention, protection and fulfilment that need to be discharged in order to fulfil the right.[9] Go deeper, however, and cracks start to appear.[10] In particular, correlativity implies that any statement about the content of a right is interchangeable with a statement about its correlative duty.[11] The statement that states have a positive duty to protect protesters under Article 10 of the European Convention on Human Rights (ECHR), for instance, expresses the same legal content as the statement that protesters have a claim-right to state protection. Yet once this conceptual move is translated into practice, and the language of rights starts to be used interchangeably with the language of duties, various factors can cause resistance. The potential result is a disconnect between reasoning about rights and reasoning about duties.

The causes of resistance to correlativity are rarely spelled out, and thus rarely examined. As a result, the thesis occupies an awkward middle ground, where it enjoys notional support, but where its necessary implications are neither consistently employed nor reflected in legal reasoning. The state of human rights law therefore echoes Halpin's observation about the correlativity thesis more generally:

> [T]here remains a widespread though unarticulated consensus that the basic idea of correlativity is stable. Yet the idea is left hanging in metaphorical space rather than being treated with analytical rigor.[12]

[7] V Stoyanova, 'Correlativity between Human Rights and Positive Obligations' (2024) *European Convention on Human Rights Law Review* 1, 25.

[8] PZ Eleutheriades, *Legal Rights* (Oxford University Press, 2008) 118.

[9] See, eg, Hurd and Moore (n 5) 329; R Alexy, 'On Constitutional Rights to Protection' (2009) 3 *Legisprudence* 1, 296; E Brems and J Gerards, *Shaping Rights in the Echr: The Role of the European Court of Human Rights in Determining the Scope of Human Rights* (Cambridge University Press, 2013) 173; Mowbray (n 6) 224.

[10] Shue, for instance, acknowledges the correlativity of 'particular' rights and duties, without specifying whether these particular rights and duties can account for the full content of human rights: H Shue, *Basic Rights: Subsistence, Affluence, and US Foreign Policy* (Princeton University Press, 1996) 155.

[11] S Besson, 'Human Rights in Relation' in S Smet and E Brems (eds), *When Human Rights Clash at the European Court of Human Rights: Conflict or Harmony?* (Oxford University Press, 2017) 28.

[12] Halpin (n 5) 229.

To use Halpin's terms, a token acceptance of correlativity does not necessarily translate into rigorous application within human rights law. This chapter argues that human rights scholars have neither fully realised the explanatory power of correlativity nor accepted the conceptual constraints that correlativity imposes. It seeks to highlight the possible causes of this predicament and examine ways in which to bridge the gap between theory and practice.

Section II charts the main features of correlativity. Rather than retreading theoretical debates, it attempts to convey the nature and implications of correlativity using imagery and metaphors. This approach is motivated by the suspicion that resistance to correlativity is not chiefly rooted in theoretical disagreements, but rather in intuitions. Section III sets out the value of correlativity for legal doctrinal scholarship. Section IV examines the first potential source of friction: that the state choice of fulfilment avenues renders duties indeterminate, and thus exempt from correlativity. I argue that this objection conflates different levels of rights specification. Whereas human rights exhibit apparent indeterminacy at high levels of abstraction, correlativity re-emerges at the level of granular, individualised rights. Section V examines the second potential objection, namely that the correlativity thesis is unhelpful for normative reasoning about rights, meaning arguments about the justification of human rights, their relative value and their attainability. My response is to accept the charge while ring-fencing the implications. While the correlativity thesis is normatively inert, the only way to implement *outcomes* of normative reasoning is by positing and enforcing legal rights, and these must have attendant duties. The third potential hurdle, addressed in section VI, is that human rights are aggregate bundles of legal positions that cannot be disassembled without loss and that their components are somehow analytically inseparable. It is true that states must fulfil a diverse and broad range of duties in order to ensure that human rights are made real and effective. However, normative interdependence does not imply analytical inseparability. On the contrary, it is only by distinguishing the individual duties within human rights that they can be effectively recognised, litigated and enforced.

Two common themes emerge from this examination, which both have wider ramifications. The first is that we need to be clear about the level of specification at which rights analysis takes place. The second is that we should endeavour to keep normative arguments and legal analysis separate. The correlativity thesis is not an easy notion to digest and apply, and doubts about its coherence and usefulness will likely persist. However, its explanatory benefits – and its lasting resilience to attempts at undermining it – make continued endorsement and application worthwhile.

II. Conceptualising Correlativity

Sentences that describe jural correlatives express the same legal content. To point out that individuals have a claim not to be subjected to degrading treatment in state custody pursuant to Article 3 ECHR is the same as claiming that states have a duty not to subject individuals in custody to inhuman treatment pursuant to Article 3 ECHR. The equivalence stems from the fact that the 'claim' and 'duty' in these two statements denote the same bipartite legal relationship between individuals and states. If we posit the existence of a duty to abstain from degrading treatment, there is no need to tack on a description of the companion claim. The claim and the duty are mutually implied. The upshot for legal doctrinal scholars, meaning scholars using established legal methodology and sources to interpret the scope and content of human rights law, is that any exhaustive analysis of the content of human rights doubles as a complete analysis of correlated duties, and vice versa.

The mutual implication of rights and duties is a key feature of what has become the *lingua franca* when engaging with legal rights – the Hohfeldian system.[13] Within this system, the mutual implication of claims and duties is held up not as a contingent property of legal relations, but as a conceptual necessity.[14] It is a feature of the way in which all rights and duties are *defined*.[15] As Barker puts it:

> [The] 'rights' that A might have are sometimes collectively referred to as 'legal advantages', and their correlatives as legal 'disadvantages', each disadvantage being simply the flip-side of the advantage to which it is correlated and being necessarily semantically entailed by it.[16]

Here, Barker follows the established approach of treating a legal 'right' as some form of legal advantage, and 'duty' as some form of legal disadvantage or burden.[17] In simple terms, '[r]ights are something that we may well want to have; duties are irksome'.[18] What the Hohfeldian system offers is a means of naming the *forms* of legal advantages that human rights can grant, and sorting them within the analytically distinct categories of claims, liberties, powers or immunities.[19]

[13] SM Wise, 'Rattling the Cage Defended' (2001) 43 *Boston College Law Review* 623, 669.

[14] Hohfeld (n 2) 39. An overview of the system and its practical application is provided in Barker (n 5). For a brief summary of the system and its conceptual implications, see M Brinkmann and JV Wibye, 'Towards Non-essentialism: Tracking Rival Views of Legitimacy as a Right to Rule' (2023) 43 *Oxford Journal of Legal Studies* 497, 499.

[15] Halpin (n 5) 228.

[16] Barker (n 5) 589.

[17] See, eg, Hohfeld (n 2) 36; CH Wellman, 'On Conflicts between Rights' (1995) 14 *Law and Philosophy* 271, 277; Kramer, Simmonds and Steiner (n 1) 96; J Bentham, *An Introduction to the Principles of Morals and Legislation* (Clarendon Press, 1907) 235; N MacCormick, 'Rights in Legislation' in PMS Hacker and J Raz (ed), *Law, Morality and Society: Essays in Honour of HLA Hart* (Clarendon Press, 1977) 202; L Wenar, 'The Nature of Rights' (2005) 33 *Philosophy & Public Affairs* 223, 224. In his chapter, David McGrogan argues convincingly that states may derive certain political advantages from the positivisation of rights (see ch 2). However, political and legal advantage need not coincide. Even if a state may secure consent and stability through rights fulfilment, the specific actions and expenditures required for such rights fulfilment can still be considered disadvantageous.

[18] JL Mackie, 'Can There Be a Right-Based Moral Theory?' (1978) 3 *Midwest Studies in Philosophy* 350, 352.

[19] A *claim* requires for its fulfilment the (in)action of a duty bearer. A *liberty* grants freedom for the right holder to act without violation of a duty. A *power* is the ability to enact changes to

Being afforded a human right is such a legally advantageous position; aggregate human rights are bundles of such legal advantages.[20] The entailed duty, or bundle of duties, imposes a corresponding disadvantage on the state.[21] As such, human rights are best thought of as fully relational.[22] Positing the existence of human rights is to call attention to a legal relationship between persons as right holders and states as duty bearers. This is fairly intuitive. If we grant that human rights law is made meaningful by guiding state conduct, correlativity is assumed. It is also conceptually necessary. According to the correlativity thesis, it is not possible to be entitled to such an advantage without it being an advantage towards someone, just as it is not possible to be constrained without someone doing the constraining.[23] Any human right implies duty in the same way that stating 'A is taller than B' implies that 'B is shorter than A'.[24]

It must be acknowledged that these somewhat abstract points on correlativity can be challenging to digest and incorporate in legal doctrinal analysis. To aid in this process, and to mediate between theorists and practitioners, we may employ some comparisons and metaphors. One approach is to focus on the cost side of rights. Whenever a legal right is granted, a corresponding disadvantage, or burden, is created. A negative human right, meaning a right requiring for its fulfilment an abstention, involves an opportunity cost.[25] Upholding a criminal suspect's right against threats of bodily harm, for instance, is to deprive interrogators of a potential means of gathering information. The burdens of positive rights are more straightforwardly measurable in terms of the costs of protective and fulfilment actions. Deploying barricades or riot police to protect peaceful protestors requires administrative efforts and funding.[26] So does enabling access to voting stations by constructing access ramps or providing voter transportation.[27] The correlativity thesis, then, can be envisaged as the legal version of double-entry bookkeeping. For every legal right added to the ledger, a

legal positions. An *immunity* grants protection from attempts at such changes in legal positions. The correlative disadvantages are, respectively, *duties* (in the narrow sense), *no-rights*, *liabilities* and *disabilities*; see Hohfeld (n 2) 36. In keeping with common nomenclature, this chapter uses the term 'duty' to refer both to the specific correlate of legal claims and to the correlate of rights in general. Amongst legal doctrinalists, 'duties' are commonly referred to as 'obligations'. The two terms are treated as synonymous.

[20] Wenar (n 17) 224.

[21] V Stoyanova, *Positive Obligations under the European Convention on Human Rights: Within and Beyond Boundaries* (Oxford University Press, 2023) 7.

[22] Besson (n 11) 25.

[23] C Wellman, *A Theory of Rights* (Rowman & Allanheld, 1985) 22. See also Hohfeld (n 2) 75; H Kelsen, *Reine Rechtslehre*, 2nd edn (Deuticke, 1960) 33.

[24] Liberties are correlated with no-claims, powers with liabilities, and immunities with disabilities. By 'identity', I do not contend that claims share identity with duties, but that they are both part of the same legal relation; see Halpin (n 5) 231.

[25] On the distinction between positive and negative human rights, see, eg, Stoyanova (n 21); JV Wibye, 'Beyond Acts and Omissions: Distinguishing Positive and Negative Duties at the European Court of Human Rights' (2022) 23 *Human Rights Review* 479, 483.

[26] *Plattform 'Ärzte Für Das Leben' v Austria* App No 10126/92, 21 June 1988.

[27] *Molka v Poland* App No 56550/00, 11 April 2006.

corresponding legal duty must be entered in, and the two columns must always match.[28]

Further imagery can be used to illustrate the complexity of human rights. The term 'human right' is somewhat ambiguous. On the one hand, it can refer to an aggregate and evolving bundle of right-duty relations, such as when the term is used to refer to the content of entire ECHR provisions. On the other hand, a 'human right' can refer to any one of the many lesser rights and duties *within* aggregate bundles.[29] Correlativity can be used to reconcile the two usages of the term by imagining an aggregate human right as a collection of threads – relations – between a state and individual right holders.[30] Each thread governs an action or an omission, be it deploying police barricades or refraining from threats of bodily harm. Crucially, it is in the nature of a thread that it must have two ends – for human rights, individuals occupy one end and states the other. While the legal relationship appears different from the perspective of the two parties, the thread – the legal relation – is the same. Note that in practice, this web of threads can be exceedingly complex. The right to security in Article 5 ECHR, for instance, contains a multitude of state duties of action and omission, including so-called framework duties to ensure procedural guarantees, create and maintain administrative institutions, exercise legislative powers and so on. It would not be fair to register this complexity as a point against correlativity. The complexity of human rights is a factual and legal reality; correlativity merely captures it.

Lastly, correlativity can be illustrated by dwelling on a particular property of legal relations: their normative asymmetry. The right holder's advantage is the duty bearer's burden. Thus, correlativity can be portrayed by using the simple metaphor of a slope. In a claim-duty relation, the right holder stands at the top of the slope and the duty bearer at its base. For the former, the relation looks like a decline, while for the latter, it looks like an incline, but the slope – the legal relation – is the same.[31] Likewise, the holders of Hohfeldian liberties, powers and immunities occupy the advantageous position in similarly slanted relationships. While the *perspectives* of right holders and duty bearers are different, they are both participants in the same legal relationship. Once we internalise this understanding of correlativity, positing the existence of a human right without companion duties becomes as incoherent as pointing to the top of a slope without acknowledging that the slope must also have a base.

[28] P Schlag, 'Hohfeldian Analysis, Liberalism and Adjudication (Some Tensions)' in S Balganesh, T Sichelman and H Smith (eds), *Wesley Hohfeld a Century Later: Edited Works, Select Personal Papers, and Original Commentaries* (Cambridge University Press, 2022) 9.

[29] Wibye (n 25) 491; JV Wibye, 'Reviving the Distinction between Positive and Negative Human Rights' (2022) 35 *Ratio Juris* 363, 369; C Fabre, 'Constitutionalising Social Rights' (1998) 6 *Journal of Political Philosophy* 263, 274; L Wenar, 'The Nature of Human Rights' in *Real World Justice* (Springer, 2005) 234.

[30] This is a variation on the theme of presenting rights and duties as two sides of a coin or (perhaps less informatively) as mirror images; see A Ross, *Om Ret Og Retfærdighed* (Nyt Nordisk Forlag, 1953) 191; EJ Weinrib, *The Idea of Private Law* (Oxford University Press, 2012) 144.

[31] Kramer, Simmonds and Steiner (n 1) 26.

III. The Stakes for Legal Doctrinal Scholarship

What are the practical implications of correlativity? Or, rather, what benefits does grappling with correlativity bring to the legal analysis of human rights law?

Analytical rigour can, as ever, provide greater precision. There is also an argument to be made that legal doctrinalists stand to benefit by aligning themselves with what has become the established approach to rights analysis amongst theorists. Yet analytical rigour also imposes costs. The notion of correlativity can be challenging to apply, in part by bringing the inner complexity of human rights to the fore. As it stands, the argument supporting the active use of correlativity within human rights scholarship can be extended beyond general promises of added clarity.

A key insight from correlativity is that statements about rights have the same content and meaning as statements about their corresponding duties. This is universal. Every legal situation that is 'describable with reference to rights can be redescribed with reference to duties',[32] and vice versa.

This content matching means that legal doctrinal analysis can, and should, shift freely between the language of rights and duties. This flexibility provides access to the respective benefits of the two. The language of *rights* has an inherent rhetorical weight. To designate something as a right is to signal a degree of normative import. This normative ballast is helpful when engaged with the exercise of balancing rights or when interpreting human rights in light of the values, aims and interests that underpin them. The language of duties, meanwhile, is more normatively insulated. This is helpful for conceptual analysis or value-neutral exposition of law. Arguably, choosing the language of duties can be an effective measure against the risk of blurring the lines between the legal analysis of human rights and their underlying human interests.[33] As the language of duties is less often used on an aggregate level, it may also be better suited to granular analysis. When engaging with a question about environmental measures, for instance, it is easier to tie the particular measures to their applicable duties than to the scope of the aggregate human right that is in play.

Besides providing flexibility, internalising correlativity can be a means of strengthening communication between scholars. The alternative, where scholars examining duties resist findings about the content of legal rights, is unnecessarily restrictive. A disconnect between rights and (allegedly indeterminate) duties can also impact adjacent debates about justiciability[34] or the normative justification

[32] ibid 27. If we accept Hohfeld's claim of having offered an exhaustive account, the language of rights or duties can be used to alternatively describe any and all legal relations; see Hohfeld (n 2) 64.

[33] Besson (n 11) 28; Tasioulas (n 4) 48.

[34] See, eg, G Dancy and CJ Fariss, 'Rescuing Human Rights Law from International Legalism and its Critics' (2017) 39 *Human Rights Quarterly* 1, 8; E Brems and L Lavrysen, '"Don't Use a Sledgehammer to Crack a Nut": Less Restrictive Means in the Case Law of the European Court of Human Rights' (2015) 15 *Human Rights Law Review* 139, 634.

of rights.[35] Note that such resistance or decoupling is rarely explicit. Resistance is likely to have more subtle roots and effects. Consider, for instance, Shue's *Basic Rights: Subsistence, Affluence, and US Foreign Policy*, where we find a claim that there are useful distinctions to be made between positive and negative duties, but that these distinctions are not applicable to rights because 'there are no one-to-one pairings between kinds of duties and kinds of rights'.[36] This is not an argument against correlativity, but rather against the disassembly of human rights, which is examined in section VI below. Shue acknowledges the correlativity of 'particular' rights and duties; his concern is with the usefulness of carving up human rights into their constituent components.[37] It may be tempting to interpret this highly influential text as a rejection of correlativity, making it less likely for the reader to accept the interchangeable use of the language of rights and duties.

For legal theorists, the greatest party trick of correlativity is spotting unexplained leaps in reasoning. As noted by Hurd and Moore, Hohfeldian analysis generally and the correlativity thesis more specifically have regularly been used as tools to unmask 'hidden policy judgments' and identify gaps in legal reasoning that require 'substantive argument (rather than value-neutral logical implication) to cross'.[38] The key underlying idea is that correlativity is not just a conceptual necessity, but the *only*[39] conceptually necessary implication between legal positions. A legal right implies the existence of a corresponding duty and nothing else. The upshot is that any further links between legal positions must be argued on non-analytical grounds. The most relevant and common error in the interpretation of law is to assume that a legal liberty to act must include protective claims against interference with attempts to exercise that liberty.[40] A liberty, however, can never imply the existence of a claim. Analytically, the presence of any such further claims must be established on independent doctrinal or moral grounds. Note also the distinction between analytical and normative reasoning at work here. While it is certainly beneficial to bolster the liberty to engage in political assembly under Article 11 ECHR with protective claims against interference from the state or third parties, such protective claims are not analytically entailed by the liberty. The grounds for combining the liberty with protective claims must, in this case, be found in an interpretation of Article 11 in conjunction with Article 1 and the case law of the ECtHR.

[35] J Tasioulas, 'Saving Human Rights from Human Rights Law' (2019) 52 *Vanderbilt Journal of Transnational Law* 1167, 1181; L Zucca, 'Law, Dilemmas and Happy Endings' in S Smet and E Brems (eds), *When Human Rights Clash at the European Court of Human Rights: Conflict or Harmony?* (Oxford University Press, 2017) 109.

[36] Shue (n 10) 52.

[37] ibid 155; Wibye (n 25) 367.

[38] Hurd and Moore (n 9) 307. For other examples of Hohfeldian 'unmasking', see Barker (n 5) 596.

[39] Note, however, that there is necessary *negative* relationship of mutual exclusivity between certain legal positions: the presence of rights or duties can be used to rule out their jural opposites. See, eg, Kramer, Simmonds and Steiner (n 1) 8.

[40] A Halpin, 'Correlativity and Its Logic: Asymmetry Not Equality in the Law' (2019) 32 *Canadian Journal of Law & Jurisprudence* 83, 96.

Unexplained leaps between moral reasoning and legal doctrinal reasoning are, as we will see in section VI below, a common risk factor. When formulating a legal argument, a judgment or an academic text, portraying normatively motivated conclusions as analytically necessary can lend them an air of unassailability. Maintaining correlativity as the only conceptually necessary link between legal positions allows us to cut through such arguments and demand further support. This point ties in with the final argument in favour of a more rigorous approach to correlativity: the notion of mutual implication between rights and duties supports a great deal of weight in moral philosophy. A weakening of the link between rights and duties also weakens the link between legal doctrinal scholarship and the many justificatory accounts that may be relevant for human rights and that rely on correlativity.[41]

Having set out the case for correlativity, the following is an examination of conceptual hurdles. It is limited to a legal human rights setting, which leads to a methodological challenge: objections to correlativity are hardly ever explicit. The few that are explicit can be either dismissed or set aside. One objection is that states, as nebulous groupings of persons and institutions, cannot be duty bearers. Such a view does not match observed human rights practice. It also leads to some notable incongruences. If we accept that states are capable of holding claims and powers to legislate, then the logical implication is that they can also bear duties.[42] Other explicit objections to correlativity are tied to debates within moral theory and do not translate into applied legal settings.[43] Instead of such direct objections, sources of possible resistance to correlativity have to be gleaned from implicit assumptions and premises. Some caveats are therefore necessary. The goal is not an exhaustive account of objections to the content or usefulness of the correlativity thesis. Nor is the goal to make bold claims about the convictions that human rights scholars have (or, perhaps more likely, do not have) about correlativity. The goal is only to provide an account of how correlativity generally features in legal doctrinal analysis of human rights law, and to highlight the most obvious and avoidable pitfalls.

IV. First Objection: Means-Selecting Discretion Renders Duties Indeterminate, thus Precluding Correlativity

A. Means-Selecting Discretion and Indeterminate Duties

The presence of state discretion is most visible in the context of positive state duties to enact protective or fulfilment measures. In the context of the ECHR, states have

[41] Halpin (n 5) 83.

[42] Barker (n 5) 599.

[43] See, eg, claims about one-directional moral duties in G Sreenivasan, 'Duties and Their Direction' (2010) 120 *Ethics* 465, 467; J Thomson, *The Realm of Rights* (Harvard University Press, 1990) 62.

a number of avenues for ensuring that positive duties are fulfilled, and it is not for courts or outside observers to dictate which exact measures should be taken.[44] The existence of multiple, independently sufficient paths to ensuring that states have taken sufficient action means that positive duties, unlike negative duties, provide means-selecting discretion.[45] For instance, the duty to supply urban areas with potable water can be fulfilled by preventing water loss during transport, *or* by a pricing mechanism to adjust demand, *or* by improving water security with additional reservoirs, *or* by purchasing agreements, *or* by desalination and so forth. Once sufficient potable water is made available, for instance by desalination, there is no further duty to pursue any of the alternative means.

The presence of means-selecting discretion lends itself to a possible objection to correlativity. A sceptic may argue that the availability of multiple, independently sufficient fulfilment alternatives makes it impossible for an observer to tie an aggregate human right to specific duties. The problem facing observers is the same as that of courts: added counterfactuals. Upon establishing that a state has not kept up with infrastructure maintenance, for instance, we cannot straightforwardly conclude that the duty to provide water has been breached. One must then evaluate whether the duty framed has been fulfilled through other means.[46] This, so the argument goes, makes the content of positive duties indeterminate, severing correlativity.

The response to this objection can be derived from the manner in which it is framed. Duties incumbent on states can be thought of in terms of ends, such as the duty to provide security, or in terms of means, such as deploying barricades to protect a particular crowd of protestors. As soon as states start to make legislative and administrative choices about how an end is to be achieved, they run into concrete compliance challenges. Such challenges can be identified and litigated by right holders as duties incumbent on states, and so the necessary correlativity between the human right and its companion duties re-emerges at the operative stage. How could anyone ever argue that a positive rights violation has occurred if there were no duties at the time of the state (in)action? In this sense, correlativity is an inherent feature of adjudication.[47] Without the necessary link, complainants could not argue for the performance of particular acts or omissions *as a matter of right*.[48] The very system of human rights adjudication and enforcement requires that correlativity holds at all times, even if means-selecting discretion impacts the visibility of particular duties.

[44] See, eg, *Pretty v United Kingdom* App No 2346/02, 26 July 2002, para 15; *Cevrioglu v Turkey* App No 69546/12, 4 January 2017, para 55; *Airey v Ireland* App No 6289/73, 9 October 1979, para 26; *Eremia v Republic of Moldova* App No 3564/11, 28 August 2013, para 50.

[45] M Klatt, 'Positive Obligations under the European Convention on Human Rights' (2011) 71 *Heidelberg Journal of International Law* 691, 694; Alexy (n 9) 16. Means-selecting discretion can be distinguished from, and does not imply, ends-selecting discretion or balancing discretion.

[46] Klatt (n 45) 695.

[47] I owe this perspective to a conversation with Andrew Halpin.

[48] Fabre (n 29) 274.

To be clear, pointing out that correlativity 're-emerges' should not be taken to mean that correlativity is ever severed. Legal relations do not disappear, even if they go unnoticed for a time. Their persistence becomes clear if and when they are contested, a situation that reveals how the applicable duties are, and always were, subject to a one-to-one pairing with the lesser rights that make up an aggregate human right. For comparison, a private contract which allows multiple means of duty fulfilment is never devoid of legal duties, or of the definitionally required correlative rights. Rather, the nature of the contractual relationship allows the duty bearer a choice amongst duty-fulfilling actions. Just as a contractual promisee can claim contractual breach if the multiple fulfilment paths have not been followed to the point of duty fulfilment, an individual right holder can claim a human rights violation if none of the multiple paths to positive duty fulfilment has been followed.

The objection to correlativity based on state discretion is thus revealed as a problem of visibility rather than absence, and a problem that requires awareness of the relevant *level of specification*. The correlativity thesis only points out 'one-to-one correlations between rights and duties of the same degree of specificity'.[49] We should not expect to be able to pinpoint all eventual duties of action or omission when observing a human right at a high level of abstraction. Correlativity only comes to the fore within the circumstances of a particular case.

B. Means-Selecting Discretion Post-adjudication

A similar objection can be formulated at a different stage, namely when interpreting and executing judgments. As Stoyanova has highlighted, scholars may query not just whether correlativity is reflected at the level of aggregate human rights, but also whether the judgments of the ECtHR can be reconciled with the thesis. More specifically, the correlativity thesis would seem to make certain requirements of the operative parts of a judgment, meaning the concluding stage (as opposed to the deliberation stage containing the reasoning of the court).[50] If correlativity holds, these operative parts should be able to provide a basis for state execution by describing the concrete measures that are necessary to rectify a finding of a breach. However, Stoyanova's analysis concludes that such correlativity seems absent:

> If the conclusion that there had been a violation were to be framed in a specific way, the Court would concretely indicate the measures that should have been undertaken so that the state could have complied with its primary positive obligation … However, even at the conclusion stage (ie. the operative part of the judgment), the requirements

[49] LK Donohue, 'Correlation and Constitutional Rights' in M McBride and V Kurki (eds), *Without Trimmings: The Legal, Moral, and Political Philosophy of Matthew Kramer* (Oxford University Press, 2020) 8.

[50] Stoyanova (n 7) 5.

> of particularity, completeness, and consistency that characterise deontic logic and Hohfeld's model are not reflected in the ECtHR's practice.[51]

The apparent upshot of this finding is that even if correlativity were to hold in the abstract, it is severed at the stage of adjudication. To use legal doctrinal terminology, correlativity may apply to primary obligations – those inherent in treaty law – without applying to secondary obligations – those stemming from adjudication determining the consequences (ie, the remedies) if a rights violation has been found. However, this more targeted objection rests on the same conceptual premises as the general objection and can be addressed in the same manner. The key is to acknowledge that means-selecting discretion can occur at several points in time, including when states choose their appropriate execution measures.[52] As Stoyanova notes, this recurring discretion is evident both in the institutional design of the ECHR and the realities of state compliance:

> The declaratory nature of the judgments implies that states have discretion as to how to 'abide by the final judgment' and to perform the 'execution'. In other words, states have a choice as to the concrete secondary execution measures.[53]

The situation post-judgment can thus be likened to the starting point of duty-fulfilment pursuant to the Convention. In fact, the Court in *Papamichalopoulos and Others v Greece* has directly equated these two instances of state discretion:

> [D]iscretion as to the manner of execution of a judgment reflects the freedom of choice attaching to the primary obligation of the Contracting States.[54]

The Court is clearly aware of its institutional limits. Just as legal reasoning regarding positive duties must acknowledge the existence of multiple, independently sufficient fulfilment paths, the operative parts of a judgment must be similarly open-ended. The upshot is that once a breach has been found, the process of exercising means-selecting discretion starts over. These two instances of discretion are conceptually identical, even if the second exercise of discretion is more factually circumscribed. This is not to say that scholars should refrain from pointing out tenuous links between rights and attendant duties, or from demanding a higher level of detail in the operative parts of court judgments. Rather, the point is that there is no novel objection against correlativity here. It is the same objection, framed within a new context. In theory, the objection could be repeated every time means-selecting discretion is triggered. If a state takes insufficient execution measures after a court judgment, the failure can once again be contested, triggering the same process. It is worth noting how the reality of (recurring) adjudication once again shows how correlativity is built into

[51] ibid 27.

[52] *Ilgar Mammadov v Azerbaijan* [GC] App No 15172/13, 29 May 2019, para 148; *Verein Gegen Tierfabriken v Switzerland* [GC] App No 32772/02, 30 June 2009, para 88.

[53] Stoyanova (n 7) 9.

[54] *Papamichalopoulos and Others v Greece* App No 14556/89, 31 October 1995, para 34.

the system. The ability to litigate and enforce execution measures *as a matter of right* means that correlativity must persist throughout.

C. The Usefulness of Indeterminate Duties

Can the objection about indeterminate duties be framed in more open terms? A detractor could, after surveying the practice and discourse of law, conclude that while correlativity may be a universal constant in the abstract, the thesis is not a helpful tool. To insist on identifying correlative rights to any duties, or vice versa, would, so the objection goes, make the process of delineating the proper scope of human rights inflexible. If, as, for instance, Stoyanova has argued, not even the operative parts of court judgments express the content of positive state duties with sufficient detail, then it may seem overly formalistic to insist on pairing all duties with correlative rights.

This approach reads more as a methodological injunction than as an objection, but it is worth pointing out some possible problems. For one thing, it is unclear why the inability to identify particular duties at all times should preclude the usefulness of correlativity. The correlativity thesis works when it matters, that being when determining the scope of particular (and perhaps contested) duties. Furthermore, the lack of detail in the operative parts of ECtHR judgments may be pragmatically motivated. A finding of breach is sufficient to address the case before the court without going into detail about how the breach is to be rectified. By not dictating execution measures, the court averts criticisms of judicial activism and maintains subsidiarity. Lastly, the court seems perfectly able to engage with granular duties when the situation calls for it. To give an example, the Article 8 ECHR right to respect for private and family life contains, amongst many other components, a duty for states to ensure that employers respect the privacy of employee communications. Such protection can be achieved in multiple ways, including statutory protection against the monitoring of communication channels. Once this legislative avenue is chosen, the content of the composite right can be chiselled down to identify legal relations governing single actions. In the case of *Bărbulescu*, this went so far as the court deliberating on the duty of national courts to assess whether employees had sufficient warning that they were being monitored, the reasons for monitoring, and to determine whether employees were given a chance to explain their private communications.[55] It is difficult to see how the components of the right-duty relation could have been spelled out further, or why the reasoning of the court in *Bărbulescu* is so imprecise as to hinder analysis in terms of correlativity.

[55] *Bărbulescu v Romania* [GC] App No 61496/08, 5 September 2017, para 131.

V. Second Objection: Correlativity is Unhelpful for Normative Reasoning

The first objection was that some human rights offer means-selecting discretion and lack determinate duties. The second objection is related, but targeted specifically at the perceived rigidity of the correlativity thesis. As with a methodological injunction to avoid correlativity for the sake of clear argument, one could argue that the human rights law is infused with values and interests, and that an insistence on the need to tie any right to its correlate is at best non-helpful and at worst a hindrance to normative reasoning about rights. For instance, one could argue that strict correlativity obscures the trade-offs between the rights of one person against the state and the rights of third parties.[56] The charge here would be that insistence on a bilateral analysis of the right to freedom of assembly under Article 11(1) ECHR, for example, somehow obscures the rights of third parties such as counter-protesters whose actions may interfere with the freedom of assembly, but who themselves have protection under Article 11(1) ECHR. Such challenges must be met by delineating the rights of protesters and those of counter-protesters, and seeking a balance between state protection and interference through a normative and political calculus.[57]

Overall, however, the basis for the charge is correct. The correlativity thesis, just like the Hohfeldian system of rights in which it features, is normatively inert. It offers no guidance for legislative and interpretational choices, and is not tethered to any underlying theory of rights or value.[58] Its function is not to tell us *what* to think of rights, only *how* to think about them.[59] In the context of human rights law, correlativity is a means of portraying the *outcomes* of normative reasoning. Or, as Eleftheriadis puts it, 'correlativity concerns singular deliberative conclusions, not deliberative reasons'.[60]

[56] These trade-offs are discussed by McGrogan in ch 2 in this volume. For a related discussion on correlativity and categorial duties, see A Zylberman, 'Human Rights, Categorical Duties: A Dilemma for Instrumentalism' (2016) 28 *Utilitas* 368, 369. On the two-party limitation of correlativity and interaction with third parties, see, eg, Kelsen (n 5) 221; KN Llewellyn, *The Bramble Bush: On Our Law and its Study* (Oceana Publications 1960) 85; JW Singer, 'The Legal Rights Debate in Analytical Jurisprudence from Bentham to Hohfeld' (1982) 6 *Wisconsin Law Review* 975, 988.

[57] It is this balancing which informs the ECtHR finding that protesters must be able to assemble without fear of being subjected to interference in the form of physical violence from counter-protesters, and that states therefore have a duty of active protection; see *Plattform 'Ärzte Für Das Leben' v Austria* App No 10126/92, 21 June 1988, para 38.

[58] Schlag (n 28) 442. As Hohfeld (n 2) 26 puts it, its purpose is only to 'aid in the understanding and in the solution of practical, everyday problems of the law'.

[59] Schlag (n 5) 189 See also Barker (n 5) 586. In particular, the thesis tells us nothing about justificational priority; see J Feinberg, 'The Nature and Value of Rights' (1970) 4 *Journal of Value Inquiry* 243, 250; J Waldron, *The Right to Private Property* (Clarendon Press, 1988) 69; Halpin (n 5) 229. Those who would seek to use the thesis to determine what comes first, and whether it is the right or duty side of the equation that is carrying the most normative weight, will come out disappointed.

[60] Eleutheriades (n 8) 119.

Before concluding that normative agnosticism makes correlativity more of a hindrance than an asset, it is worth reflecting on what practitioners and scholars want from the interaction of, on the one hand, normative and moral reasoning about rights and, on the other hand, legal doctrinal analysis of human rights law. Designing and implementing a body of law is a two-stage process. Once certain normative determinations have been made, the only way to implement those determinations is through the formulation of legal rights and duties. At this applied, doctrinal stage, analytical concepts like correlativity re-emerge as useful tools. Adding conceptual stringency at the applied, granular level does not preclude normative reasoning; it supplements it.

This same approach can be used to turn the objection on its head by arguing that normative reasoning about rights is actually facilitated by embracing correlativity. As noted, correlativity provides clarity by highlighting exactly what duty bearers must do as a matter of right, and helps to identify the competing rights and duties that must be entered into a normative calculus.[61] Thus, correlativity has been a fixture not just of legal doctrinal analysis but also of moral philosophy. In the words of Halpin, 'the actual state of any normative system, moral or legal, can best be captured by [its] finer-grained analysis'.[62] Adherence to the thesis can also avert confusion during interpretation and application. The absence of normative baggage means that correlativity can be employed universally and regardless of context.[63] Its agnosticism also helps with the ability to distinguish valid legal findings arguments from unjustified leaps in reasoning.[64] Human interests, while relevant, cannot straightforwardly determine the scope of human rights.[65]

Just as normative considerations can slip imperceptibly into legal reasoning, they can also colour our attitudes to the correlativity thesis. We are seeking an objection to correlativity at the stage of legal doctrinal analysis, meaning at the stage of using established legal methodology to unpack the content of human rights law. This requires us to establish exceptions to correlativity at the level of specified, fully unpacked rights and duties. Can we, in the judgments of the ECtHR, identify a single formulation of a specified, fully interpreted and contextualised right that is not tied to a companion state duty? No examples seem to be forthcoming.

[61] ibid 118; Fabre (n 29) 275; Wibye (n 25) 369.

[62] Halpin (n 5) 225.

[63] GJ Postema, *Legal Philosophy in the Twentieth Century: The Common Law World* (Springer, 2011) 105; A Halpin, 'The Value of Hohfeldian Neutrality When Theorising about Legal Rights' in M McBride (ed), *New Essays on the Nature of Rights* (Hart Publishing, 2017) 15.

[64] Kramer, Simmonds and Steiner (n 1) 22; J Harris, *Legal Philosophies*, 2nd edn (Butterworths, 1997) 93; Eleutheriades (n 8) 105.

[65] The same distinction should be kept in mind when reading scholarly contributions. For instance, when Raz describes law as a system of practical reasoning, consisting of rules, some of which justify some of the others, he is referring to the *justification* of rights – the grounds for holding someone to have a duty. See J Raz, 'Legal Rights' in *Ethics in the Public Domain* (Clarendon Press, 1984) 259 At this level, as Raz points out, Hohfeldian analysis and correlativity has nothing to offer. Correlativity may still have something to offer in non-justificatory settings, chief amongst them being doctrinal interpretation by judges or in commentary.

And even if they were, how would the necessary remedies for a rights violation be framed? Remedies must take the form of state action, or a cessation of state action, and such injunctions are duties.

VI. Third Objection: Human Rights cannot be Disassembled without Loss

Human rights are composites.[66] The Article 11 ECHR right to freedom of assembly, for instance, is a diverse and dynamic bundle of relations. It contains, at a minimum, a state duty not to intervene in assemblies, a duty to provide protection against third-party interference, and various framework duties to legislate and provide infrastructure ensuring that individuals have the required means to congregate.[67] It follows that an aggregate human right cannot be treated as uniformly having the property of being 'absolute', 'basic', positive or negative.[68] Such labels must refer to components *within* the bundle that makes up the aggregate. A possible objection to correlativity takes this inner complexity within human rights and introduces a further premise: that the diverse bundle making up a human right cannot be disassembled without loss. If the premise holds, then human rights cannot coherently be separated into individual components that are each subject to right-duty pairings.[69]

To respond, it is first necessary to clarify the nature of the charge. What does it mean to assert that human rights cannot be disassembled without loss? Intuitively, the objection suggests that human rights are more than the sum of their parts and that scholars lose sight of something crucial by breaking them apart. The *normative* argument for such a stance is fairly straightforward. Take liberties which are vulnerable to third-party disruption, such as the aforementioned right to freedom of assembly. Such rights allow the right holder to participate in a political demonstration without fear of duty violation, but this liberty would seem hollow without further additions and protections. To make the right real and effective, states must combine respect for the freedom of assembly with other duties, including the duty to provide protection against violent counter-protestors, and to ensure the availability of media and communication channels. The same holds true for ostensible positive rights. As Shue argues, the right to subsistence would be diluted without guarantees against the seizure of assets and property. He likens the idea of providing a right to subsistence without effective safeguards to furnishing someone with

[66] Wenar (n 17) 234.

[67] Wibye (n 25) 373.

[68] E Ashford, 'The Alleged Dichotomy between Positive and Negative Duties of Justice' in C Beitz and R Goodin (eds), *Global Basic Rights* ((Oxford University Press, 2009) 94; M Wesson, 'Disagreement and the Constitutionalisation of Social Rights' (2012) 12 *Human Rights Law Review* 221, 225.

[69] This is the likely basis for Shue's claim, cited above, that there are no useful distinctions to be made between positive and negative rights: Shue (n 10) 52.

a meal ticket, but providing no food[70] – hence Shue's claim that the division of human rights into analytical categories breeds confusion.[71] Overall, subsequent scholars have tended to treat attempts at dividing aggregate human rights into analytical subcategories with a degree of scepticism.[72]

Note, however, that these are *substantive* arguments for interdependence. They rely on normative considerations to argue that human rights *should* contain multiple components. As plausible as they are, they miss the mark as rejoinders to correlativity. In order to serve as an objection to correlativity, an argument must be offered on a *conceptual* level.[73] Put differently, it is one thing to argue that real and effective human rights should, normatively, be made up of multiple components, and another to argue that distinguishing those components leads to incoherence. Shue, for instance, while offering a convincing account of why certain basic rights require a multitude of components to be meaningful, never provides any conceptual reason why normative interdependence translates into analytical inseparability.[74] Instead, the line between normative and analytical reasoning seems blurred, with expressions that it is 'analytically necessary' for the enjoyment of the substance of a right to be protected against typical threats, or when he refers to the 'inseparable mixture of positive and negative elements' within rights.[75] It is true that human rights are composites, but to be a composite is to *contain* simpler rights, and these simpler rights can be subject to one-to-one pairings with simpler duties, even if the whole complex right cannot.[76] In other words, disassembly of a complex human right reveals many lesser rights.[77]

The worry here is that such scepticism of correlativity is to once again allow normative reasoning to influence analytical and legal determinations. The perception of a human right losing some of its meaning on a substantive and normative level should preclude making distinctions within human rights for the purposes of analysing specific cases and judgments.

Even if a conceptual argument against disassembly were to be established, it would have to be reconciled with the realities of adjudication and case law. The ECtHR provides a wealth of examples of how precisely the content of human rights can be delineated, and how flexibly these rights can be applied in particular factual circumstances. One example is *Pavlov*,[78] where the Court performed an evaluation of the technical approaches to safeguarding locals

[70] ibid 69.
[71] ibid 36.
[72] See, eg, Fredman (n 6) 69; L Lavrysen, *Human Rights in a Positive State* (Intersentia, 2016) 305.
[73] For some (failed) attempts, see Barker (n 5) 599.
[74] M Payne, 'Henry Shue on Basic Rights' (2008) 9 *Essays in Philosophy* 220, 223; PA Woodward, 'Shue on Basic Rights' (2002) 28 *Social Theory and Practice* 637, 663.
[75] Shue (n 10) 32, 192.
[76] Wibye (n 25) 367.
[77] Fabre (n 29) 274; T Pogge, 'Shue on Rights and Duties' in Beitz and Goodin (n 68) 128.
[78] *Pavlov and Others v Russia* App No 31612/09, 11 January 2023.

from environmental hazards that was unprecedented in its level of detail.[79] The degree of specification was likewise high in *Bărbulescu*, where the Court went into detail about the lines of inquiry national courts must pursue when evaluating safeguards for personal information. Or there is the majority opinion in *X and Others v Bulgaria*, which found that the authorities had failed to keep the legal representatives of the applicants adequately informed of the progress of the investigation into alleged child abuse.[80] When the practice and adjudication of duties reaches this level of detail, the burden of proof must be on detractors of correlativity to explain why something has been lost by disassembling the human right in question and interpreting the extent of one of its components. One possibility would be to argue that the legal duties framed by the ECtHR are still insufficiently detailed and that they can be specified further. That may be true. In *Bărbulescu*, for instance, we could ask: which omission by the national courts was crucial to the conclusion in the judgment? Did the finding of violation require a combination of state omissions? Yet rather than serving as an argument against the correlativity thesis, this line of inquiry seems to strengthen the case for correlativity as an analytical tool. Each question about further specification of state duties can be reframed in terms of the rights of the applicant – hence why the inseparability objection fails to resonate with the practice and adjudication of human rights. Since this practice takes place at the operational stage, it requires the identification, interpretation and, perhaps, balancing of discrete duties within human rights.

A last alternative, as with other objections, is to cast the objection to correlativity in more careful, methodological terms. What if resistance to correlativity is based on the notion that human rights are best treated *as if* they are inseparable bundles? It is an open question whether such an approach is actually worthwhile. Any benefits seem to accrue only at the stage of normative reasoning, or when observing human rights at an aggregate level. For the practitioner or scholar engaged with unpacking their exact legal content, an injunction to feign inseparability does not seem overly helpful. Instead, the approach carries with it the risk described by Shue in his afterword of the revised edition of *Basic Rights* of 'drifting unhelpfully saying merely that no right can be safely enjoyed unless numberless people perform innumerable duties'.[81] Going further, there is an argument to be made that treating human rights as monolithic entities can be actively detrimental to analysis and enforcement. Fabre, for instance, argues that by treating human rights as joint bundles, as opposed to neatly delineated right-duty relations, we take away 'the possibility of talking of the more specific rights in which these general rights can be broken down'.[82] It is only by accepting the disassembly of aggregate

[79] OW Pedersen, 'Case of *Pavlov and Others v. Russia*. App. No. 31612/09' (2023) 117 *American Journal of International Law* 689.
[80] *X and Others v Bulgaria* App No 22457/16, 2 February 2021, para 208.
[81] Shue (n 10) 157.
[82] Fabre (n 29) 275.

human rights into many lesser rights that right holders are able to demand the fulfilment of distinct duties.[83]

VII. Conclusion

Embracing the correlativity thesis – the claim that for every right there must be a companion duty, and vice versa – can strengthen legal doctrinal analysis, help to unmask leaps in reasoning, allow rights and duties to be analysed and discussed interchangeably, facilitate demands of duty fulfilment as a matter of right, and mediate between legal doctrinal scholarship and theorists. This chapter has identified three possible reasons to resist correlativity, none of which is persuasive. First, the apparent indeterminacy of duties in positive rights cases vanishes at the point of litigation and enforcement. Second, the value agnosticism of the correlativity thesis only applies to normative reasoning about rights, and does not preclude the use of correlativity to pick apart the legal outcomes of such normative reasoning. Third, while there is a strong case to be made that human rights must contain a multitude of interdependent duties in order to be real and effective, this starting point does not preclude the subsequent disaggregation of such duties, or the coupling of such duties with lesser rights.

It is possible, given the unconvincing nature of the conceptual case against correlativity in human rights law, that any resistance is rooted more in intuitive misgivings than in conceptual arguments. The correlativity thesis combines analytical abstraction with sweeping claims about the nature of legal relationships. Regardless of cause, the thesis continues to hang within Halpin's metaphorical space rather than being a consistent feature of legal doctrinal analysis. A change would be welcome. The explanatory benefits of correlativity are considerable, and adoption does not require practitioners or scholars to grapple with complex theory. All that is needed is to be willing to disaggregate human rights into lesser rights and duties, and to have confidence that the ties linking the two categories hold firm.

[83] Wibye (n 25) 369.

INDEX

Introductory Note

References such as '178–79' indicate (not necessarily continuous) discussion of a topic across a range of pages. Wherever possible in the case of topics with many references, these have either been divided into sub-topics or only the most significant discussions of the topic are listed. Because the entire work is about 'positive obligations' and 'human rights law', the use of these terms (and certain others which occur constantly throughout the book) as entry points has been minimised. Information will be found under the corresponding detailed topics.

www.ingramcontent.com/pod-product-compliance
Ingram Content Group UK Ltd.
Pitfield, Milton Keynes, MK11 3LW, UK
UKHW020816290926
15470UKWH00003B/1202

9 781509 991457